PSYCHOLOGICAL
STRATEGY
IN
CONTRACT
BRIDGE

THE TECHNIQUES OF
DECEPTION AND
HARASSMENT IN
BIDDING AND PLAY

OTHER BOOKS BY FRED L. KARPIN

The Point-Count System of Bidding in Contract Bridge
Contract Bridge: The Play of the Cards

PSYCHOLOGICAL STRATEGY IN CONTRACT BRIDGE

THE TECHNIQUES OF DECEPTION AND HARASSMENT IN BIDDING AND PLAY

by FRED L. KARPIN

HARPER & ROW, PUBLISHERS

New York and Evanston

CONTENTS

v

FOREWORD

THE FORMATIVE YEARS
AND THE FUTURE

Contract bridge was invented in 1925 by Harold S. Vanderbilt, world-renowned yatchsman. At this writing, although the game is but thirty-five years old, contract bridge has become the world's leading card game. Yet, the game is but an infant compared to pinochle, which was first played in the United States around the turn of the twentieth century, and to poker, which was introduced into the United States in 1837 in virtually the identical form in which it is now played. As an intellectual pastime, contract bridge is already considered by many to be superior to chess, the latter being hundreds and hundreds of years old. In common, both contract bridge and chess surpass all other known "mental" games in subtlety and skill. Those who play contract bridge will attest to the fact that it is the most intelligent and skillful card game that man has devised.

The primary reason for the widespread interest in contract bridge is the fact that the game combines the elements of "skill" and "luck" in the most palatable proportion: it has been estimated by various authorities that "skill" comprises about 65 percent while "luck" is about 35 percent. In order for a game to rise to the plane of universal popularity, it must possess these two essential ingredients. But, should a game have too much luck attached to it (as dice, for example), the stimulation and incentive to the player's skill are not sufficient to sustain his interest. On the other hand, should a game require too much thought and skill—as chess—the poorer player will turn to something else which will give him a better chance to excel. It is unquestionably the harmonious combination of skill and luck which has served to hold the interest of contract bridge's millions of disciples, although, in the main, they cannot be classified as good, or skilled, players. A story which typifies the oft-described fanaticism of bridge addicts is told of the commuter who, on his daily trips to the city from his suburban home, used to play bridge with his cronies. Last year, at the age of seventy, he retired from business, but he could not retire from the "habit" of bridge. Every morning now he still takes the 8:10 train, rides into the city with his friends as he formerly did, has his hour of bridge, and on reaching the city, takes another train back home—and awaits the morrow.

Since the birth of contract bridge, numerous "systems" of bidding have been devised, each having specialized innovations and divergent techniques, and each claiming that it was more "scientific" than its predecessors had been. Each new system was designed with the end in mind of reducing the vagaries of chance to a minimum. In short, it was the hope of the "system-makers" that skill would become more predominant, at the expense of luck, resulting in the creation of "better" players.

Some of the earliest systems were the Vanderbilt Club System, the Two Club System, the Reeveu System, the One-Two-Three System, the Official System, the Culbertson Approach-Forcing System, the One-over-One System—and probably dozens of others. With the passage of time scores of additional *new* systems, derived from the impact of revised experiences at the bridge tables, were created to captivate the minds of contract bridge devotees: the Goren System, the Roth-Stone System, the Stayman System, the Bulldog System, the Kaplan-Sheinwold System; and, of late, the Italian System, the proponents of which have compiled an amazing record of successes in international competition. All the above systems were created by Americans except the Italian System. This does not include the many systems of foreign origin which were developed in England, France, Austria, Sweden, etc.

Systemically speaking, it is my opinion that we haven't even scratched the surface with respect to unearthing, or manufacturing, systems of effective bridge bidding. Systems will perish as experience negates their assumed validity; and new systems, incorporating the sound tenets and principles of the superseded ones, will arise to take their place. The latter, too, eventually will pass away, leaving behind the accumulated guiding and workable principles as a heritage to the future generations of systems. To even faintly suggest that any contemporary or not-too-distant future system is the last and final word on "scientific" bridge bidding is to court ridicule by ignoring history. As has been amply demonstrated in the thirty-five years since the birth of contract bridge, no system incapable of daily modification, alteration, and growth is worthy of acceptance and survival, and inevitably it either withers away or is discarded as technologically unfit. The game of contract—and the systems which strive for optimum efficiency—will change as its players, fortified by experience, improve their technique and allow greater scope to their imagination.

In conclusion, we are still millenniums away from someone uttering the final word on contract bridge, if it ever will be uttered. It is my fervent hope that it never will be said. Should the time ever come when the game will cease to grow and be reinforced by additional knowledge, we will be forced to say "adieu," as we reluctantly search for a new game to conquer and master.

This work is, to a certain extent, a reference book, recording as it does the evolution of "psychological" bidding from the birth of contract bridge to the present day. I wish to make acknowledgment, and at the same time express my deepest gratitude, to Alphonse ("Sonny") Moyse, Jr., editor and publisher of *The Bridge World,* for permission to republish actual deals which depict this historical evolution, deals which were selected from the monthly issues of *The Bridge World* from the first issue of October, 1929, to the present. Without Mr. Moyse's permission to reprint these deals, this book would have become an impossible one to write, since *The Bridge World* has been our nation's sole recorder of the historical growth and development of contract bridge.

I also wish to express my indebtedness to the following individuals, each of whom was gracious enough to grant me special permission to reprint portions of works written by them:

S. Garton Churchill and Albert B. Ferguson, for permission to reprint verbatim five deals from their classic work, *Contract Bidding Tactics at Match Point Play.*

Terence Reese, of England, one of the world's finest players, and author of *Master Play* and *Reese on Play,* for permission to reprint in its entirety the addendum to Chapter 16, "Rare Deception." This addendum was reprinted verbatim from the April, 1957, issue of *The Bridge World.*

To the following individuals, the creators of the modern systems of bidding, I am most grateful not only for permission to reprint various deals which illustrate how their systems function, but especially for their advice and practical assistance in editing my interpretation of the basic tenets of their systems for inclusion into this book:

Alvin Roth and Tobias Stone, the originators of the Roth-Stone System.

Samuel Stayman, the author of the Stayman System.

Edgar Kaplan and Alfred Sheinwold, co-authors of the Kaplan-Sheinwold System.

William Hanna, Douglas Steen, and Sidney Lazard, creators of the Bulldog System.

Also, my appreciation to the following publishers for permission to quote from books published by them:

Simon and Schuster, for quotations from *Money Contract,* by P. Hal Sims.

Vanguard Press, for quotations from *Psychic Bidding,* by Dorothy Rice Sims.

McGraw-Hill, for quotations from the book, *Championship Bridge,* by Dunne and Ostrow.

And last, but not least, to the various bridge players whose names are mentioned in this book, I owe a debt of gratitude. Although they had nothing to do with the actual writing of this book, many of the deals which confronted them in combat have been assimilated into this work as illustrations of their highly imaginative psychological techniques of bidding and play. As a consequence of their real-life contributions, I was spared the time and effort of "creating" deals to describe the diverse psychological bidding and playing situations inherent in the game of bridge. My appreciation and thanks are hereby recorded.

August, 1960   FRED L. KARPIN

PART I

THE BIDDING

CHAPTER 1

THE NECESSITY FOR DECEPTIVE AND OBSTRUCTIONIST BIDDING TACTICS

In virtually every system of bidding that has been originated since contract bridge was invented, *all* the emphasis and stress has been directed toward the attainment of as perfect a constructive partnership bidding as is possible; that is, the attention of authorities, writers, and system makers in general has been concentrated *exclusively* on devising a bidding system that would safely and accurately enable its users to reach the high tempting contracts of game or slam when the cards held by a partnership offered a high probability of such contracts being fulfilled. How to determine correctly the precise partnership joint assets, how to find the proper trump suit, which suit to bid first, the requirements for an opening one no-trump bid, etc.—these were always deemed to be the *sole* important issues.

I certainly am not minimizing or underrating the importance of constructive bidding when one has the good fortune to hold a tremendous or a fine hand. However, since the law of averages has made it abundantly clear (in theory and in practice) that the good hands will be held by one's opponents about half the time,[1] it is rather surprising that so little attention has been focused on the

---

[1] Speaking facetiously, an authority once made the observation that, in traveling throughout the United States and questioning bridge players as to whether they were good-card holders or bad-card holders, the startling statistics revealed that 95 percent stated that they were bad-card holders!

important matter of devising methods of *interfering* with the normally smooth, constructive bidding of the aforementioned good holding by my opponents (or yours, as the case may be).

I would not like the reader to infer that I am casting stones on the authorities of the past and present. As the world of bridge players knows, it is difficult enough to bid hands correctly when the partnership has good tickets; and any assistance that experienced expert players and writers can render to those less learned players must be viewed as a firm step in the right direction. Nor am I pleading for the authorities to come out with a system that would permit the poor-card holders to steal the bid from the opponents when the latter has the overwhelming preponderance of good cards (although I must admit that the thought of this enticing delusion is most delightful). What I am reproving specifically is that so little attention has been devoted to the expertly proven techniques of disrupting the smoothly functioning bidding methods of the opponents, which techniques, when judiciously applied, can cause them to overbid, to underbid, or to misbid many of their big hands. Certainly the matter of interfering with the opponents' communication should be a major issue in any bidding system. Certainly the subject of misleading the adversaries when they have big hands is legitimate strategy and is just as intrinsic an element in proper contract bridge bidding as is, for example, the espousal of the Blackwood Slam Convention, cue bidding, ace showing, or other legitimate "constructive" bidding techniques that the good-card holder has at his disposal. Yet, through the years, virtually all the attention has been paid to the problems of those who *have;* the have-nots have become the forgotten generations.

During the 1950's, many measures were introduced for the benefit of the have-nots: the weak opening two bid, the weak jump overcall, the weak opening one no-trump bid, the weak jump response, the "disciplined" psychic opening, and others. As yet, these measures have not been adopted by the have-nots on a universal level, but they have become an integral component of many of our current systems of bidding.[2] It is certainly a welcome trend; and indications seem to be that, at long last, the have-nots can compete on more

---

[2] These new bids, and the systems into which they have been incorporated as component parts, are discussed in Chapters 7 and 8.

equitable terms with the haves for the right to survive. And there is tremendous satisfaction when the opponents are interfered with to such an extent that they get to an unmakable slam; or they fail to get to an easy game; or the "interferers" suffer a relatively small penalty in lieu of permitting the opponents to make a vulnerable game or slam. Surely, the have-nots should have at their disposal all available effective weapons for psychological and guerilla tactics. It is mandatory for their self-defense.

In addition, the authorities have withheld from the good-card holders the various strategic and deceptive tactics which are fundamental and essential weapons in the experts' military arsenal. It is acknowledged that no expert tries to play an absolutely sound "book" game against other experts. He must try to push the opponents into making mistakes. The devices he uses are many and varied. He may make completely fake cue bids, he may make psychic bids, he may bid weak suits to inhibit the opponents from leading that suit, he may deliberately underbid on certain types of hands in order to get "pushed" to the right contract, he may deliberately overbid in situations where it seems indicated that the opponents are likely to sacrifice, he may suppress a strong suit during the bidding, etc. While quite often the expert falls on his face because of his shenanigans, more often he accomplishes the intended purpose of his chicanery: he creates an incorrect impression in the mind of the adversary he is attempting to deceive.

And so, if you will pause to think about it for a moment, psychological strategy in bidding, obstructionist tactics in bidding, deceptive tactics in bidding, "psychic" bidding[3]—call it what you will —has a definite and important niche in proper bridge bidding. Now that bridge is coming of age, these hitherto expert "secrets" should no longer be concealed from those who have put their heart and soul (and time and money) into trying to become better bridge players. Our young nonexpert players are now old enough to understand deception, camouflage, and harassment of the enemy, as the experts practice them; and upon being permitted to observe expert usage, they can exercise selectivity and avail themselves of the opportunity to employ some of the experts' stratagems when the circumstances seem ideal. And, as one becomes more proficient in the art of psycho-

[3] "Psychic" bidding is the theme of Chapter 3.

logical strategy, he will learn that a preponderance of good cards does not necessarily guarantee victory. Conversely, he will also learn that when he holds bad cards, by timely deployment he can frequently make booms out of busts.

The primary reason behind my plea for more deception, for more interference with the "good-card" holders, and for more information on these subjects, is based on necessity; one cannot remain a stereotyped "book" player and expect to get the maximum mileage out of either his good or his bad cards. Making a game or slam by having misled or tricked the opponents counts exactly as much as a game made by brute force; and, defensively speaking, deceiving the good-card holders, and preventing them from locating their proper game or slam contract, actually puts the same profits into your pocket—if not more—that you would have made if they had arrived at some game or slam contract that you defeated by highly skillful defensive play.

But there is also an important secondary reason for my plea for exposing the deception "secrets" of the experts and making them common property for all to understand and to utilize if so desired. Deception and harassment, properly applied, will introduce urgently needed color and zest into the game. As the reader knows, bridge would become a dull and aggravating routine if all bidding were to proceed along preordained mathematical lines, with no deviation from precise valuation and rules for opening bids, raises, and over-calls ("Partner, you need 13 points for an opening bid; 26 points to make a game; 33 points to make a small slam. One no-trump, partner, shows 16–18 points, etc."). Under such circumstances, whichever pair has the big hands dealt to it calmly bludgeons the unfortunate opponents by virtue of the luck of the deal. The victims can neither fight back nor run away. They are trapped by their lack of knowledge of defensive and counterattacking tactics.

Most assuredly, skill and versatility when the odds are against you should be encouraged and made a virtue—in cards as in life. These qualities are much rarer and finer than mere mathematical calculations (which, however, should not be deprecated—they, too, have a seat of honor at the bridge table). And skill and versatility are also far more stimulating, mentally, than cold mathematics— both to those who employ them and to those who have to contend with them. There can be no doubt that the application of deceptive and harassing tactics will add life, zest, and hope to the game, in addition to giving the poor-card holder a chance. If deception were outlawed, the game of bridge would not be worth playing; one might as well sit down to play poker with all bluffing forbidden.

Someone might raise the point that if all bridge players were to learn and utilize the experts' deceptive strategy and tactics, their proficiency would rise tremendously, and luck would be superseded by skill. That is, the 65 percent skill and 35 percent luck proportion (referred to in my Foreword) would become heavily unbalanced in favor of skill; and the unadaptable bridge player, unable to cope with deceptive advances, would give up the game. This is utter nonsense! First, it is highly questionable—according to the experts—whether the average yield on deception is much more than 50 percent efficiency. Secondly, deception can be—and is—a two-edged sword, and its indiscriminate users often get caught in their own traps. Thirdly, if the less-skilled bridge players were to adopt all of the experts' deceptive and obstructionist tactics, they would probably become less skilled, for they would tend to substitute deception for proper technique, thereby becoming "fancy" when straightforward bidding would accomplish their objective. In my opinion, by *studying* the experts' approach to deception, and applying some of their stratagems when conditions seem favorable, the world of nonexpert bridge players will simply derive much more enjoyment out of the game of bridge than they have previously experienced. The palatable proportion of 65 percent skill and 35 percent luck will remain undisturbed.

Most assuredly, an elective course in deceptive, harassing, and obstructionist tactics would have no adverse affect on the Rock of Gibraltar game of bridge.

CHAPTER 2

THE RISE AND DECLINE OF STANDARD AMERICAN BIDDING

In the preceding chapter, I criticized the system makers for neglecting to bring out into the open the various known deceptive techniques which are available both to those who are attempting to establish and maintain partnership communication (the good-card holders), and those who are attempting—or should be attempting—to jam up or destroy the enemies' line of communication (the bad-card holders). You may feel that I have been unduly critical—and perhaps you are right. After all, contract bridge is a young game. In its days of immaturity, our first duty was to establish a foundation for the constructive bidding of good hands, to teach the players how to handle their big guns and how to wend their way with accuracy and assurance to the proper final contract without too much "obnoxious" interference. It was, in those days, fundamentally a matter of giving them their basic training before sending them out on the field of battle, of teaching them the basic strategy of the game before indoctrinating them with tactical maneuvers—in other words, training them to handle themselves and their weapons before teaching them how to destroy the opponents' weapons.

And certainly, from the viewpoint of good salesmanship, it was the natural and normal thing for the system makers to stress exclusively the proper methods of bidding games and slams, to illustrate how a particular system was the best—for, by using it, it was such a simple matter to arrive at a makable game or slam and show tremendous profits as a result. What could be more appealing to the neophyte and to the bridge player who was usually a loser? Everyone loves to bid game or slam and make it. As a consequence, the system makers addressed their advertising to those who wanted to know more about what to do with good cards and offered them a self-perpetuating panacea.

During the late 1920's and early 1930's, the dozens of warring systems which had been created fought with each other to obtain public favor. The defective systems fell by the wayside. By the early 1930's, Ely Culbertson had become the supreme authority, for the Culbertson approach-forcing system had dealt a deathblow to all the others.[1] Then peaceful days followed. Culbertson sold millions of books to bridge players who were avidly desirous of making the most out of their good cards. And so the Culbertson System or, lately, the Goren System was presented to the public as the epitome of bridge living, the finished product of the turbulent 1920's and early 1930's. It incorporated many of the sound principles of the deceased systems, thereby bringing into the fold many of the disciples of the superseded systems. By 1940, just about every beginner, average player, and expert employed the bidding framework of the triumphant Culbertson-to-Goren-to-the-masses system. American bidding had become standardized.

In their book, *How to Play Winning Bridge*,[2] Edgar Kaplan and Alfred Sheinwold dramatically put their finger on the reason for the stagnation and resultant ineffectiveness of standard American bidding and, at the same time, sound the call to arms:

By the 1940's, Standard American bidding was magnificently successful on every level, even the very highest. American teams consistently defeated European teams using different methods; our bidding was admired and imitated on five continents; the U.S. was king of the bridge world. For us

[1] In December, 1931, the "battle of the systems" found Ely Culbertson pitted against the twelve leading authorities in a systemic war. The twelve authorities had each renounced his own system and had agreed on one system in order to wage a final onslaught against Culbertson, the public favorite. They were vanquished and silently slipped away into the night—or climbed aboard the band wagon.

[2] Fleet Publishing Corporation, New York, 1958.

the system wars were over; we had reached a warm, high, sunny plateau and left the battle far below.

Well, now it's late in the 1950's and we're still on the same plateau. But the sun has started to set and it's getting a bit chilly up there. In successive years we have lost world championship matches to the English, to the French, and to the Italian,[3] and our prestige has never been lower. (In fact, it has been publicly suggested abroad that the European champion should not meet the U.S. champion for the World Title, but that the U.S. should enter its team in the European Championship.) Standard American bidding has lost most of its popularity abroad, and even here at home there is widespread dissatisfaction in the ranks. Many new systems and scores of new conventional gadgets have found favor. In a typical American tournament today, you would be hard put to find three pairs using identical bidding methods out of hundreds competing. The long Pax-Romana is ending; the walls are crumbling. The rest of the world has moved ahead. . . .

The British, French, and Italians who defeated us bid more effectively than we did because *they never forgot that they had opponents at the table* [My emphasis. FLK.] Standard American bidding tends to ignore the enemy. "Bid your own cards and let them worry about theirs" was a reasonable credo twenty years ago, but it won't work today.

If you open with one club on:

♠ K x x
♥ Q x
♦ A x x
♣ K J x x x

and partner responds with one diamond or two clubs holding:

♠ x x
♥ x x
♦ K Q x x x
♣ Q x x x

you will reach a fine contract—assuming the opponents stay out of the auction. You will bid and make two clubs. But why should they stay out of the auction when you have made it so easy for them to come in, using up almost none of their bidding room? Almost surely, they are cold for four hearts![4]

[3] Three times in a row to the Italians.
[4] In the Kaplan-Sheinwold System, the bidding would go: 1 NT (weak), 3 D (weak), pass by opener.

Keeping the opponents out of their best contract is fully as important as getting to your own top spot; and no bidding system that forgets this can compete effectively with a style that does not. If the opponents continually jam up your auction while you leave theirs strictly alone, you are going to lose. [My emphasis. FLK.]

Well, we like to win. The bidding system we advocate is designed for two-way action: to harass the enemy on losing hands; and to reach a maximum contract with accuracy and comfort on winning hands. . . .

There it is, then: the modern approach of those who feel that bidding techniques of the 1930's and 1940's have become antiquated and require a complete overhauling.

CHAPTER 3

THE ORIGIN OF DECEPTIVE BIDDING

I. TECHNICAL SKILL VERSUS DECEPTIVE TACTICS

A most valid reason for the system makers not emphasizing or teaching deceptive tactics in bidding during the first fifteen years of contract bridge's development was that, from a pedagogic viewpoint, deception couldn't be taught and applied until technical ability had been mastered—that is, until the student had mastered what was "right" and what was "wrong" in everyday, normal predicaments. After all, the most important weapon in the arsenal of the good bridge player *is* his technical skill in both bidding and play, his ability to handle each of the many diverse and routine situations that confront him in his day-to-day skirmishes at the bridge table. This knowledge and skill, accumulated through the years via book learning and experience, readily enable him to identify and diagnose each frequently recurring situation and, in most cases, to dispose of it in winning fashion. I do not mean that he handles these situations mechanically, but rather that from his arsenal he can instinctively select the weapon that will get the job done with the same facility as it has done in the past. Naturally, without the attribute of thinking he would become a doomed man; for no hand, no matter how simple to bid or play, can be handled in winning fashion without the thinking process becoming the first line of defense (or offense, as the case might be).

Technical ability should serve as the foundation and framework, but it should not be considered as the finished edifice. Although there can be no doubt that the primary reason that the experts and near-experts are such consistent winners is because they possess great technical skill, the fact remains that the possession and application of all the relevant technical knowledge is not sufficient in itself to make one a winning bridge player. Even if one (and his partner) becomes thoroughly familiar with all the principles of sound bidding and play, and with all of the involved situations which require special treatment, one cannot become a really good bridge player until he has learned *how to deceive and how to interfere with the enemy*. After all, there will arise numerous situations where technical skill will not be enough, where all seems lost, and where control of your destiny seems not to belong to you. Frequently, in these temporarily unhappy circumstances, the effective application of deceptive tactics, pre-emption, or chicanery can alter your apparent predestination.

According to Webster, *deception* is defined as the "art of misleading." As applied at the bridge table, deception might be described as the attempt to get your adversary to think as you want him to think, to get him to believe that some unreality is actually a fact—in brief, to lead him on, and then have him discover belatedly that what he thought was reality was nothing more than a mirage.

It is perhaps unfortunate that the word *deception*, as applied to real life, is associated exclusively with the social connotation of "fraud" and "deceit" and is considered "not nice." And, of course, the deceiver is frowned on by society. But, in bridge, deception is considered to be a wonderful personality trait to possess; and its owners are looked upon as the wise, the good, and the honest.

As has been stated, numerous situations arise at the bridge table in which a player does not possess the physical weapons needed to counterattack, and the only hope he has is to indulge in deceptive and/or sniping tactics in order to misdirect his opponents into bidding and playing incorrectly.[1] Surely, when viewed in this realistic light, deception becomes an honest weapon—and, frankly, an indispensable one.

[1] Deceptive tactics in the *play* of the cards is the subject of Part II of this text.

So we reach this conclusion: the possession and application of technical skill is not sufficient in itself to make one a good bridge player. Until he has learned how to outwit and outmaneuver and to harass his opponents, his arsenal of weapons is not modern, is not up-to-date—and he is fighting a losing cause.

II. THE PRE-WORLD WAR II ICONOCLASTS (1926–35)

While the system makers were introducing their systems and vying with each other for the right of their systems to become ingrained in the bridge public's mind, there were coexisting those rebellious spirits—writers, experts, and plebeians—who refused to become conformists and who foresaw the practical necessity for deceptive, pre-emptive, and harassing tactics.

Of the articulate, unquestionably the most famous, in the decade following the invention of contract bridge, was the late Dorothy Rice Sims, the originator and apostle of psychological bidding, or *psychics,* as it was called. The word *psychic,* by the way, has stayed with us through the years; and even today it still has the same meaning it had when Mrs. Sims coined the term: generally speaking, it means "bidding what you don't have, or bluffing, in order to create the illusion of strength, or to conceal a weakness." As I use the term *psychic* bid throughout this text, it is synonymous with *deceptive bid, camouflage, chicanery,* and *deceptive tactics.* A psychic bid, then, is in effect a major segment of the broad concept of psychological strategy in bidding.[2]

In her writings, Dorothy Sims displays an amazing understanding of the need for deception, especially when one considers that the game was only about six or seven years old at the time she wrote. The following passages from her works are submitted in evidence:[3]

[2] A crude definition of *psychic bidding,* coined in 1933, was: "bidding a suit which the adversaries thought they possessed until you bid it." Such a definition, of course, does not cover the various types of psychic bids that have been developed since then, but it does convey a good idea of what psychic bids are.

[3] Quotations 1–4, inclusive, are taken from *Money Contract* by P. Hal Sims (Simon and Schuster, New York, 1932); quotations 5–8, inclusive, are taken from *Psychic Bidding* by Dorothy Rice Sims (Vanguard Press, New York, 1932).

1. Psychic bids may be divided into four major groups:
   A. Defensive psychics, where there is a deliberate intention to take a penalty, the extent of which is approximately known.
   B. Psychics made to camouflage a serious weakness in a big hand.
   C. Psychics made to steer the declaration into the right hand.
   D. Psychics made with the object of arriving at the proper declaration.
2. No psychic should ever be made without a definite end in view.
3. Remember that you have a partner, and that however magnificently you may have planned your campaign, the laws of the game unfortunately grant him equal rights to back into the bidding, even at the most inopportune moments.
4. It is very seldom that psychic bidding should be employed with a big hand . . . but there are exceptions to this rule.
5. Psychics are dangerous in unskilled hands, for the more high-powered the machine, the greater danger it is to the unintelligent user. . . .
6. It is essential that there be a positive reason for every strategic bid. Aces and kings have their definite valuations, but when they have deserted us, situations may sometimes be molded to create pseudo values to head off the imminent attack. . . .
7. Some years ago, at the Independent Exhibition in Paris, a group of artists tied a paint brush to a mule's tail, backed him up to a canvas, and "a winter sunset" was conceived. Nature took its course, and this painting was proclaimed the masterpiece of the year. Similarly, the psychic bid in unskilled hands is as aimless as the brush at the end of the tail. A stab in the dark—the wheels of chance spin around, and the player anxiously watches the little ball to discover whether he is genius or a fool. . . .

And, in conclusion, on the Dorothy Rice Sims of 1932:

8. People say: "But this [deception] is not bridge." But if bridge is to be nothing but the dull mechanics of the point count [*sic!*] wouldn't it be better to rename the game of contract? Let us have strategy, let us have camouflage, let us flank with an imaginary army and have the thrill of leading a lost cause to victory. Would the count hounds raise their heads long enough from their cards to plot, to save a hopeless game even if they could, or would they rather go down safely with the system?

Actually, Mrs. Sims had a reasonably large number of followers. They, too, realized that psychological strategy was just as important to success as was technical proficiency. As a matter of fact, there was a brief period when a tidal wave of blind enthusiasm for psychic bids seemed to be sweeping over the country's bridge tables, and it appeared as though a malignant growth was being forced on an apparently healthy organism by the extremists. But the brief, intense mania for psychic, or bluff, bidding—which got to the point of becoming a sport of fabricating bids out of thin air—went into hibernation quickly, as the system makers began to engage in mortal conflict for the right to dictate by what system the good-card holders should exist.

It is interesting to note what Mrs. Sims had to say about contemporary bridge bidding some twenty-four years later. In an article in *The Bridge World*[4] she was quite bitter about the prevailing state of affairs and mourned the passing of the good old days. The following are excerpts from her article, entitled "Push-Button Bridge":

In the old days contract bridge was a game. A delightful stimulating game. You pitted your wits against the cards, and tried by strategy and psychology to make aces out of spaces; to make booms from busts. Those were the days of freedom for enterprise. Win or lose, you got action for your money. Then, suddenly, it was discovered that there was money in contract bridge. Big money.

Contract bridge has been subsidized. It is now Big Business. Big Business needs conformity. Books are being written, articles syndicated, all advocating one or another point-count system guaranteed to take all the thought out of thinking. . . .

Individuality is out. Reasoning is out. There is a formula for every situation. The moles living in darkness have lost their eyes. Push-button bridge players are shedding their brains. Why lug them around? . . .

Before the conversion [to point count] days, concealing your holdings from the opponents was a recognized art. It was called blind bidding. With certain unbalanced holdings, after you or your partner opened, the other evaluated the combination of hands and jumped to the final contract. With no sign post to guide them, the defenders were often put on the spot.

Unfortunately, despite often-excellent results, blind bidding does not meet standardized requirements. A monkey "might get into trouble." Push-button bridge is geared to take the strain off the monkey. . . .

Of course, I realize that push-button bridge is designed to turn out as

[4] *The Bridge World*, May, 1956.

quickly as possible a flow of new students and perennial alumni to fill the demand for a supply of new hands to clutch new cards and new books. But so many novices are flowing out from the assembly lines that push-button bridge has taken over. The multiple count has now become the official language of bridge.

What the future holds, no one knows. This article is merely a picture of the card world today. Let us hope there will soon be a tomorrow—or at least a yesterday. . . .

Mrs. Sims was not alone, in the early days of bridge, in her appeal for the inclusion and application of deceptive tactics on a greater and more far-reaching scale. Her husband, P. Hal Sims,[5] was acknowledged to be the prime bridge strategist and tactician of that era, and he was a firm believer and practitioner in the art of deception or psychological strategy. Some brief excerpts from one of his works[6] will serve to introduce him into the record:

Intelligently used, psychological bids are a necessary and valuable development of Contract, and they serve in addition as a corrective test of the bidding methods of every partnership against which they are employed. Only the best systems are able to cope with them.

The system I advocate is calculated to secure the best results on the big hands, both to conceal and protect doubtful holdings, and to interfere successfully with the opponents on the poor hands.

Contract bridge will cease to be the mechanical bidding exercise which most textbooks assume to be its highest destiny. Psychics will grow in favor. *Defensive openings bids and overcalls will be used flexibly in the hope of smashing the enemy offensive on big hands. Good players will jockey for "position" on certain types of hands, scrapping the shopworn habit of always mentioning "biddable" suits on certain types of holdings.* [My emphasis. FLK]

On the subject of psychic bids, Mr. Sims used to narrate this episode. In a 1931 tournament, the bidding went:

SOUTH	WEST	NORTH	EAST
2 ♣	Pass	Pass	?

Mr. Sims (East) turned to South and asked, "Madam, what system do you use?"

---

[5] If a contract bridge "Hall of Fame" is ever established, P. Hal Sims will be elected on the first ballot, even if the voters consist of his enemies.

[6] *Money Contract,* by P. Hal Sims, Simon and Schuster, New York, 1932.

"The forcing," she replied. "My partner *must* keep my two bids open."

Mr. Sims almost stumbled getting out of his way to pass.

But when the hand was over, and the declarer, struggling with a minimum hand, barely managed to make two clubs, she turned to Sims, who would normally have bid and made a game on this hand. Seeing the look of anguish on his face, she queried softly: "You bid psychics too, don't you, Mr. Sims?"

Another top authority of the old days, Willard Karn,[7] was also a staunch believer in the extension of deceptive tactics to contract bridge bidding. In his *Karn's Bridge Service*[8] a looseleaf publication which was supplemented every three months by additional material on "the experts' daring and brilliant innovation of today [that] becomes the convention of the average bridge player of tomorrow," Mr. Karn devoted quite a bit of space to the endorsement of "psychology and psychics." He noted that:

Psychic bids are made in the hope of creating a psychological barrier for your adversaries, that is, of putting an obstruction in the way of their reaching the correct final contract. The paramount question with regard to psychics is—do they pay? Are the results worth the risk entailed in departing from normal bridge? Indiscriminate psychic bidding is certainly an injudicious and downright dangerous practice, but on the other hand, a *few* bluff bids if perfectly timed and made with a partner who will not blindly *jump* the bidding, often prove of great value. This is particularly true if the system, as recommended in this book, is followed, namely that of keeping the bidding at the lowest possible level by making natural assists, overcalls, and takeouts. This system is, of course, the ideal one for psychics, which is one of the reasons almost all experts prefer it. . . .

Mr. Karn then goes on to classify psychics into three distinct types, and he illustrates them by many examples from actual competition.

No discussion of any aspect of bridge in the 1930's would be complete without presenting the attitude of Ely Culbertson, bridgedom's commander in chief during the 1930's. From December 7, 1931, when he went into the Systemic War and vanquished his

---

[7] Willard Karn was deemed to be one of the nation's finest players. He was with P. Hal Sims on the team known as "The Four Horsemen."

[8] *Karn's Bridge Service*, Long and Smith, Inc., 1933.

challengers in a head-to-head battle, it was advertised that 95 percent of all players play "according to Culbertson." Judging from the number of books Mr. Culbertson sold, the 95 percent does not appear to be an exaggerated figure.

Mr. Culbertson, although a keen strategist and psychologist at the bridge table (and in orienting the minds of million of players), was categorically opposed to deceptive bidding for the masses. His reason was a simple and logical one: as constituted authority, the approach and techniques of his system were designed to create and maintain partnership harmony and partnership confidence; and any deceptive bidding, which unquestionably is a unilateral, individualistic action, quite naturally tended to destroy the precision of bidding which his system was trying to create. In his voluminous writings, Mr. Culbertson devoted much space to the primary importance of the partnership functioning as a unit, the "personal equation," as he called it. And he was fully aware that deceptive bidding obtained a beneficial result just a little over half the time in the hands of highly skilled players. To attempt to foist deceptive tactics on unskilled students—even if he personally employed them at the bridge table[9]—would certainly have been bad psychology, and bad business. Mr. Culbertson was a realist—and he recognized that to introduce revolutionary tactics could result only in destroying the empire he had spent years to build.

An expert once approached Mr. Culbertson and inquired why he was so opposed to deceptive bidding, pointing out that the percentage of success figured to be great since the deceiver had two opponents whom he could trick, as opposed to just one partner. Mr. Culbertson's answer was, "Mathematically, you are right. Two to one is good odds. But, unfortunately, the opponents may not believe my bid; *my partner will believe my bid.* If he doesn't, regardless of the result on any one hand, our partnership, at that moment, has begun to disintegrate."

A few direct quotes from Ely Culbertson's writings will attest to his above-described position on deception:[10]

---

[9] In the Culbertson-Lenz match in the winter of 1931–32, Mr. Culbertson, as dealer, bid 1 ♠ on: ♠ 9 7 6 3 2, ♥ 7 6 4, ♦ Q 6, ♣ 8 6 3.
[10] *The New Gold Book of Bidding and Play,* by Ely Culbertson, The John Winston Company, Philadelphia, 1949.

A psychic bid calculated to assure the opponents that the sure tricks and solid suits staring them in the face are not there at all—are simply mirages—has not a very good chance of succeeding. Even the weakest players trust their own eyesight. . . .

The only rational reason for psychic bids of all descriptions is to lead the opponents to think that their Kings and Queens are apt to be trapped by superior honors or that their suits will not break.

Thus, we have viewed the position of some of the leading authorities of the Miocene Era of Contract Bridge. There can be observed therein an undercurrent of opposition to the orthodoxy of the system makers, as embodied in Ely Culbertson, the master system maker.

Let us now turn our attention to actual deals played in the period under discussion, wherein deceptive bidding tactics were used. If, in the deals to be presented, the deceptive bidding seems to be rather crude and obvious, well—*it was!* But then, it is now a few generations later, and we have grown much more sophisticated. We have had much more experience to guide us in recognizing the enemies' deceptive tactics and antics. Our forefathers were not as "advanced" as we are, but presumably they were just as intelligent—and the fact is that they were duped by the deceptive tactics employed against them.

CHAPTER 4

PRIMITIVE DECEPTION IN
CHAMPIONSHIP PLAY (1926-35)

A word of advice is in order before proceeding to the actual deals contained in this chapter. The advice relates to your approach while examining the deceptive and harassing bidding tactics of years gone by.

In reading through this chapter, try to focus your attention on the *motives*, the *raison d'être*, that gave birth to each of the deceptive or harassing or obstructionist bids, as opposed to attempting to memorize each of them with a view toward employing them the next time out. In adopting this approach, you will learn how to utilize your imagination so that it can rise to the fore via its own momentum when the circumstances for its practical employment arise.

Each deal in this chapter, and all the description, analysis, and running remarks appended thereto, are taken verbatim, in their entirely, from the source in which they appeared in the literature of the 1930's. I believe these deals will speak for themselves in depicting how our "primitive" forefathers employed deceptive and harassing bidding tactics and the reasoning that motivated them. Where I have a clarifying comment to interject, or in summary at the end of each deal, my words will be bracketed.

If my summary comments seem to be too brief at times, and you thereby conclude that I have left unsaid many points which should have been brought out into the open and clarified, let me answer that if a reader were unfamiliar with the "standard bidding" of the early 1930's a more detailed explanation would be meaningless.

Hence the presentation of facts, to the virtual exclusion of editorial comment. Except where I have indicated, every deal in this chapter is reported in the words of the original authors.

1.

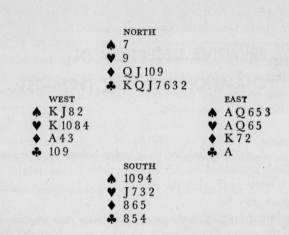

```
                        NORTH
                    ♠ 7
                    ♥ 9
                    ♦ Q J 10 9
                    ♣ K Q J 7 6 3 2
      WEST                               EAST
   ♠ K J 8 2                          ♠ A Q 6 5 3
   ♥ K 10 8 4                         ♥ A Q 6 5
   ♦ A 4 3                            ♦ K 7 2
   ♣ 10 9                             ♣ A
                        SOUTH
                    ♠ 10 9 4
                    ♥ J 7 3 2
                    ♦ 8 6 5
                    ♣ 8 5 4
```

This hand was played in a recent [pre-1934. FLK] team-of-four contest. At one table, two members of the team sat in the North and South positions. At a second table, the remainder of the team occupied the East and West chairs, playing the identical hand. The results were astonishing. At the table where part of the team was playing North and South, the bidding was:

SOUTH	WEST	NORTH	EAST
Pass	Pass	2 NT (1)	Double (2)
Pass	Pass (3)	3 ♣ (4)	3 ♠ (5)
Pass	4 ♠ (6)	Pass	Pass (7)
Pass			

(1) This is a psychic bid of the highest order, made by Dorothy Sims, intended to deny adversaries the opportunity of making an informative double and to prevent them from exchanging information adequately. If South holds a bust, East-West can probably make a slam. North has a safe out at any time in the club suit.

(2) Holding 4½ quick tricks, vulnerable, would you double a bid
     of two no-trump, or risk a three-spade bid? Imagine, for the
     sake of argument, that South's and West's hands were reversed.
     In this case, if you double the two no-trump bid, South would
     redouble and North-South could make three no-trump. [Except
     that North would run out to three clubs. FLK.] Or, if you bid
     three spades [still] assuming the interchange of South's and
     West's hands, South would double and the loss would be at
     least 3 tricks—900 points [the old scoring]. [Again, in this case,
     North would run to four clubs, unless he were clairvoyant.
     FLK] North's two no-trump bid creates just this problem for
     East to puzzle over, and all he can do is to make the best guess
     possible.

(3) West certainly does not wish to disturb East's penalty double of
     two no-trump.

(4) Mrs. Sims now extricates herself, as planned, by bidding three
     clubs.

(5) East knows that North's first bid was a psychic, and he therefore
     bids three spades.

(6) The assist to four spades seemed to West to be the limit of his
     strength.

(7) Further bidding on the part of East might be dangerous, al-
     though West afterward maintained that East should have bid
     five clubs, inviting a slam.

[Using our current standards of bidding as a guide, one would conclude that West simply didn't know the value of his cards. Surely,
East figured to have a tremendous hand in view of his immediate
double of two no-trump; and West's raise to four spades certainly
didn't describe the value of his hand (especially when one remem-
bers that East's double was a penalty double which West would have
passed with a bust). But, be that as it may, North's opening bid in
this instance rendered it virtually impossible for even a clairvoyant
partnership to arrive at the makable seven-heart contract. Seven
spades, as can be observed, is unmakable. FLK]

When the hand was replayed at the other table, where Mrs.
Sims' partners were sitting East and West, the bidding went as
follows:

SOUTH	WEST	NORTH	EAST
Pass	Pass	Pass	1 ♠
Pass	2 ♠	3 ♣	4 ♣
Pass	4 ♦	Pass	5 ♥
Pass	6 ♥	Pass	7 ♥
Pass	Pass	Pass	

This bidding, when compared to that at the other table, furnishes a striking illustration of the tremendous advantage of preventing, whenever possible, the adequate exchange of information by adversaries. The "swing" on this hand amounted to 1500 points [old scoring. FLK]. The seven-heart contract is easily made if South is played for 4 hearts (indicated by North's club bid). East's fourth heart must be used to ruff dummy's losing club.

2. In another team-of-four match, the following hand was played, with similar results. Ed Hymes sat in the North position, and his teammates, playing the same hands, sat at the East-West positions at another table.

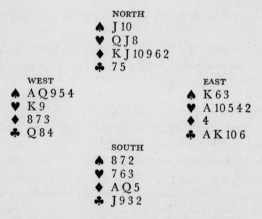

```
                      NORTH
                    ♠ J 10
                    ♥ Q J 8
                    ♦ K J 10 9 6 2
                    ♣ 7 5
        WEST                          EAST
      ♠ A Q 9 5 4                   ♠ K 6 3
      ♥ K 9                         ♥ A 10 5 4 2
      ♦ 8 7 3                       ♦ 4
      ♣ Q 8 4                       ♣ A K 10 6
                      SOUTH
                    ♠ 8 7 2
                    ♥ 7 6 3
                    ♦ A Q 5
                    ♣ J 9 3 2
```

At Mr. Hymes' table, the bidding was as follows:

SOUTH	WEST	NORTH	EAST
Pass	Pass	1 ♠ (1)	Double (2)
Pass	Pass (3)	2 ♠ (4)	Double (5)
Pass	Pass	3 ♦ (6)	3 ♥ (7)
Pass	Pass	Pass	

(1) A psychic bid, with diamonds as an "out" for the hand.
(2) Indicating to partner a strong hand.
(3) Creating a penalty double by passing partner's informative double.
(4) A further effort to confuse the adversaries.
(5) Another business double. (So? FLK)
(6) Bidding his real suit and willing to take a sacrifice.
(7) East was criticized for making this bid. What would you have done? If you do pass, what action would you expect West to take?

A game can be made in hearts, or a small slam in spades. Do you think you would have risen to the occasion by bidding spades in the West position?

[Frankly, I am uncertain as to whether East or West was the more guilty party. If East had bid three spades (instead of three hearts), the partnership would have arrived at a game contract in spades (East, of course, knew that West had a good spade suit, since this was indicated by West's original pass of one spade doubled). But, then, East's bidding had denoted a tremendous hand, and West was absolutely wrong in passing three hearts (in my opinion, West should have bid three spades over three hearts). To discuss who was at fault in failing to arrive at a slam is out of order—they didn't even reach game! And, further, the reason for the presentation of this deal is not to criticize the opponents who were duped, or who couldn't cope with a perplexing situation, but rather to point out that Mr. Hymes' psychic spade bids certainly confused the opponents, which was the intended effect. FLK]

At table 2, the more normal bidding was:

SOUTH	WEST	NORTH	EAST
Pass	Pass	1 ♦ (1)	Double
Pass	2 ♠ (2)	Pass	3 ♥ (3)
Pass	3 ♠ (4)	Pass	4 ♣ (5)
Pass	4 ♥	Pass	6 ♠
Pass	Pass	Pass	

(1) A psychic diamond bid. This bid rarely proves of any benefit, especially if made in the third hand psychic [*psychic* here means "light opening." FLK] seat, as it has been used so much that it

is completely ignored if the opponents have the values to justify a game or slam bid.

(2) A jump forcing response, requiring that the bidding be kept open until a game or slam contract is reached.

(3) There is no need to show spade support immediately, especially as West may have made the bid on a 4-card suit. West, having forced, must, in any event, bid again.

(4) Rebidding spades and indicating thereby a 5-card suit.

(5) Spades can be supported on the next round. It is important to show West the real strength of the hand, and as a four-club bid is less than game, West is still forced to respond.

3. A psychic of the offensive or constructive type is occasionally bid to cause adversaries to lead a suit by a process of elimination, instead of their leading from their strong suit, the latter having been bid against them. This kind of bid is also called lead-directing [lead-*inhibiting*, in contemporary terms. FLK], and is illustrated in the hand given below:

Both sides vulnerable.

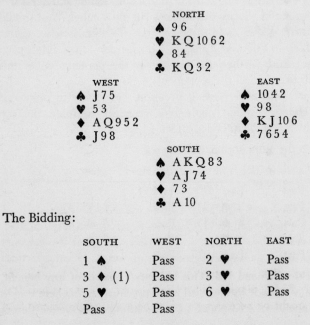

```
                        NORTH
                     ♠ 9 6
                     ♥ K Q 10 6 2
                     ♦ 8 4
                     ♣ K Q 3 2
        WEST                          EAST
     ♠ J 7 5                        ♠ 10 4 2
     ♥ 5 3                          ♥ 9 8
     ♦ A Q 9 5 2                    ♦ K J 10 6
     ♣ J 9 8                        ♣ 7 6 5 4
                        SOUTH
                     ♠ A K Q 8 3
                     ♥ A J 7 4
                     ♦ 7 3
                     ♣ A 10
```

The Bidding:

SOUTH	WEST	NORTH	EAST
1 ♠	Pass	2 ♥	Pass
3 ♦ (1)	Pass	3 ♥	Pass
5 ♥	Pass	6 ♥	Pass
Pass	Pass		

(1) South is planning a six-heart contract, and this bid is made for the purpose of preventing a diamond lead.

Mr. Richard Frey, South, made this brilliant and daring bid. He was fortunate enough to inspire East to make an original club lead. A grand slam was made, whereas if diamonds had been opened, even six hearts would have been defeated one trick.

[Let's say that West could have doubled South's three-diamond bid, in which case the story would have had a different ending. Undoubtedly, after the hand was over, West's partner told West the same thing. FLK]

4. East-West vulnerable.

```
                        NORTH
                      ♠ Q 4
                      ♥ K 2
                      ♦ Q 9 8 7 3 2
                      ♣ K 8 7
        WEST                          EAST
      ♠ A 10 9 6 5                  ♠ K 8 7 3
      ♥ 10 8 5                      ♥ J 9 6 4
      ♦ 6 4                         ♦ A 5
      ♣ 10 6 4                      ♣ Q J 3
                        SOUTH
                      ♠ J 2
                      ♥ A Q 7 3
                      ♦ K J 10
                      ♣ A 9 5 2
```

The Bidding:

SOUTH	WEST	NORTH	EAST
1 ♣ (1)	Pass	1 ♦	Pass
1 ♠ (2)	Pass	2 ♦	Pass
3 NT	Pass	Pass	Pass

(1) Bidding the lower-ranking of two 4-card biddable suits.
(2) A psychic bid, made for the purpose of preventing a spade lead. It can readily be seen that a spade lead will defeat the contract 2 tricks. Since game can be made at no other declaration than no-trump, the bid seems justifiable. [The end justifies the means? FLK] Should North hold spades and support the bid, it might be necessary to go as high as four no-trump, but

in that event the bid could probably be made. This aggressive type of psychic was bid by Mr. John Rau in a National Tournament.

[Nothing much to say. This type of psychic has persisted through the ages, down to the present day, and is employed on frequent occasions. Sometimes it works, sometimes it doesn't. I don't know what West's opening lead was, presumably a heart or a club; but whatever it was, it was pretty difficult for East to switch to spades rather than return partner's suit when East obtained the lead via the ace of diamonds. In retrospect, of course, it's easy. In a rubber bridge game, the switch to spades might have been found by East, since, in view of dummy's established diamonds, there was no other hope of defeating three no-trump except through the spade suit. But in a duplicate game—which this was—the overtrick might be worth more than the game itself; and East's primary concern (and duty) was to aid in establishing whichever suit partner had opened and to hold declarer to the minimum number of tricks. FLK]

5. Neither side vulnerable.

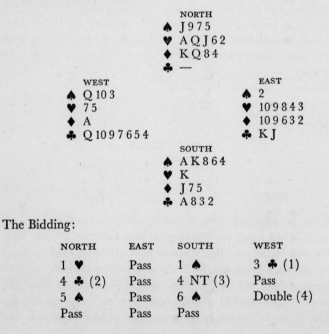

```
                        NORTH
                     ♠ J 9 7 5
                     ♥ A Q J 6 2
                     ♦ K Q 8 4
                     ♣ —
      WEST                              EAST
   ♠ Q 10 3                          ♠ 2
   ♥ 7 5                             ♥ 10 9 8 4 3
   ♦ A                              ♦ 10 9 6 3 2
   ♣ Q 10 9 7 6 5 4                  ♣ K J
                        SOUTH
                     ♠ A K 8 6 4
                     ♥ K
                     ♦ J 7 5
                     ♣ A 8 3 2
```

The Bidding:

NORTH	EAST	SOUTH	WEST
1 ♥	Pass	1 ♠	3 ♣ (1)
4 ♣ (2)	Pass	4 NT (3)	Pass
5 ♠	Pass	6 ♠	Double (4)
Pass	Pass	Pass	

(1) An aggressive psychic bid, made for the purpose of inducing North-South to a slam bid that can be doubled and probably defeated, if played at spades.

(2) Showing adequate support for the spade suit, no losers in clubs, game certain, and a slam possible.

(3) Showing control of the club suit in case it is advisable to play at no-trump instead of at spades.

(4) West is certain of the diamond ace and can reasonably expect to win the queen or ten of spades.

This excellent psychic was bid by Mr. Joseph Cain, of Indianapolis.

[First, the jump-shift overcall (three clubs by West) in those days showed a good hand, and was considered to be a semiforcing bid. West didn't have his announced values, hence the designation of his bid as psychic (in our modern days, the jump-shift overcall, in certain systems, is used to denote a bad hand, with the bid suit being of 6- or 7-card length). And secondly, as is quite frequently the case, as soon as North realized that West was psyching, he felt that the opposition was trying to rob him out of a slam. Goaded into action by West, North did just what West wanted him to do, although in all honesty, North would probably have arrived at a small slam in spades without West's intervention. The contract was an excellent one—but, as was stated, so was West's deceptive obstructionist bid. Let's call it a draw. FLK]

6. East-West vulnerable.

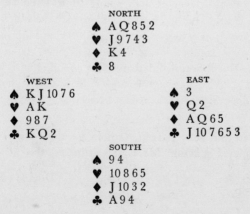

```
                          NORTH
                        ♠ A Q 8 5 2
                        ♥ J 9 7 4 3
                        ♦ K 4
                        ♣ 8
        WEST                            EAST
      ♠ K J 10 7 6                    ♠ 3
      ♥ A K                           ♥ Q 2
      ♦ 9 8 7                         ♦ A Q 6 5
      ♣ K Q 2                         ♣ J 10 7 6 5 3
                          SOUTH
                        ♠ 9 4
                        ♥ 10 8 6 5
                        ♦ J 10 3 2
                        ♣ A 9 4
```

NORTH	EAST	SOUTH	WEST
Pass	Pass	1 ♠ (1)	Double
2 ♥ (2)	3 ♣	3 NT (3)	Double
4 ♠ (4)	Pass	Pass	Double
Pass	Pass	5 ♥ (5)	Double
Pass	Pass	Pass	

(1) Fearing an adverse game in spades.

(2) A splendid bid, with spades as a haven if hearts are doubled.

(3) Taking away the opponents' bid, with a run out to hearts if three no-trump is doubled.

(4) This is what North was waiting for. He feels secure—for a moment.

(5) The psychic spade opening is exposed to everybody at the table. North passes, wisely, and the contract is defeated 2 tricks. [In the old scoring, down two, doubled, and not vulnerable, cost only 200 points. FLK] East-West can make three no-trump, which contract they would undoubtedly have arrived at had South passed originally and permitted West to open fourth hand.

[To bid as North-South did necessitates not only perfect partnership understanding, but also the realization and awareness of the fact that partner frequently makes psychic bids. Most assuredly, the majority of the nation's bridge players (both past and present), holding the North hand, would have jumped to four spades directly over West's double, even though South's third-hand opening might have been light. Whether East would then have bid five clubs or doubled instead, or whether North would eventually have bid five spades in some competitive sequence, will never be known. As it turned out, North-South did themselves proud. But I wonder why East didn't open his singleton spade? If he had, the contract would have gone down three at five hearts. FLK]

7. John Rau and Billy Barrett, famous for their psyching proclivities, are depicted in action. Mr. Rau is sitting South.

```
                          NORTH
                        ♠ 8 5 2
                        ♥ A K 9 6 3
                        ♦ A Q 4
                        ♣ 7 3
        WEST                              EAST
      ♠ K J 10 7 4 3                    ♠ A Q 9
      ♥ 7                               ♥ 4
      ♦ J 10 6 2                        ♦ K 9 8 7 5 3
      ♣ 9 4                             ♣ 8 5 2
                          SOUTH
                        ♠ 6
                        ♥ Q J 10 8 5 2
                        ♦ —
                        ♣ A K Q J 10 6
```

Both sides are vulnerable.

NORTH	EAST	SOUTH	WEST
1 ♥	Pass	1 ♠ (1)	Pass
2 ♥	Pass	6 ♣	Pass
6 ♠ (2)	Pass	7 ♣ (3)	Double
Pass	Pass	Redouble (4)	Pass
Pass	Pass		

(1) Intending to get to a heart slam, and trying to prevent the spade lead.

(2) How was North to know South was psyching?

(3) What choice did South now have?

(4) An excellent bid. Most bridge players would have bid seven hearts instead. [Most bridge players would not have made the one-spade response, and hence would not have found themselves in Mr. Rau's position. FLK] The reason for the grand slam bid in clubs was to put West on lead, for West, even if he held the spade ace, would probably not have led it after South had redoubled. [Had West held the spade ace, and not led it, I wonder what East would have said? FLK] West chose to open a diamond, and Mr. Rau scored his grand slam.

[Here was a partnership versed in psychic bidding, and look at the mess they got themselves into! The fact that they escaped, and received a citation for "gallantry above and beyond the call of duty," is of no import—they were lucky. (Personally, I would have had them court-martialed.) From this deal, the danger of psyching is quite apparent, for psyching, even in the hands of skilled wielders, can become a deadly boomerang. One bid of Mr. Rau's should be noted: his bid of seven *clubs* rather than seven hearts. The reason behind it was that if *clubs* were the contract, West would never lead away from his king of spades; whereas, if North were the declarer at the heart contract, and East happened to have the king of spades, East *might* lead away from it, deceptively. FLK]

8. Both sides vulnerable.

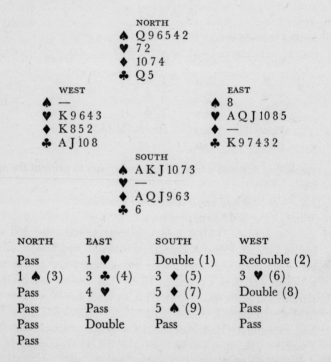

NORTH	EAST	SOUTH	WEST
Pass	1 ♥	Double (1)	Redouble (2)
1 ♠ (3)	3 ♣ (4)	3 ♦ (5)	3 ♥ (6)
Pass	4 ♥	5 ♦ (7)	Double (8)
Pass	Pass	5 ♠ (9)	Pass
Pass	Double	Pass	Pass
Pass			

(1) Creating the impression that he had a balanced hand, rather than the distributional one he actually held. The purpose was to prevent the opponents from sacrificing.

(2) Conveying to his partner the information that he held a fine hand.

(3) Although possessing a poor hand, North felt that he could afford to show his spade suit at so low a level.

(4) Possibly an overambitious bid, but West's redouble made it a certainty that East-West had a game in either hearts or clubs. Thus, the forcing bid of three clubs.

(5) The deception gains momentum. South knew that East's three-club bid was forcing, and that the bidding couldn't stop at this point. The acknowledgment of spade support could safely be held in abeyance until later on.

(6) An inadequate bid, considering that East had made the forcing jump rebid of three clubs. Possibly a leap to six hearts was West's proper action at this juncture; or, as a second choice, conceivably the cue bid of three spades, to denote the void in spades.

(7) With tongue-in-cheek, hoping for a double by the adversaries.

(8) Showing a winner in the adversely bid suit, and denying any interest in a slam.

(9) The deceptive pussy-footing triumphs! Who could visualize South's hand to be as it was? The doubled spade contract was fulfilled. East-West could have made a grand slam in either hearts or clubs.

[Without a doubt, South's bidding was magnificently deceptive, and his reward was well deserved. But West, in my opinion, should give up the game of bridge and utilize his talents in some other field. Not only did East open the bidding with one heart, but subsequently East jumped to three clubs, which our reporter tells us was a *forcing bid*. Surely at the moment that East made this forcing bid, West should have known—not merely suspected, but *known*—that East-West had at least a small slam in either hearts or clubs or both. I assume that the game was an honest one. Yet, what reason other than collaboration with the enemy can be advanced in support of West's Caspar Milquetoast bidding? Also, his pass of five spades was not what one would call a thing of beauty. As to East's double of South's five-spade bid, all one can say is that the partnership functioned in perfect disharmony. FLK]

9.

NORTH
♠ K 7 4 2
♥ 8 3
♦ Q 10 7
♣ 8 7 5 3

WEST
♠ A J 10 8 5 3
♥ A Q 10 9 4
♦ 6 3
♣ —

EAST
♠ Q 9 6
♥ K J 7
♦ A K J 8 4
♣ K J

SOUTH
♠ —
♥ 6 5 2
♦ 9 5 2
♣ A Q 10 9 6 4 2

East-West vulnerable.

EAST	SOUTH	WEST	NORTH
1 ♦	2 ♥ (1)	Double (2)	Pass
Pass	2 ♠ (3)	Double (4)	Pass
Pass	2 NT (5)	Double	Pass
Pass	Redouble (6)	Pass	3 ♣
Double	Pass	Pass	Pass

(1) With favorable vulnerability conditions, South initiates a series of psychic bids designed to give him a profitable escape at a three-club contract. He assumed that the opponents could make at least a game; and, even if he were doubled at three clubs, the loss figured to be less than the opponents could score at their game or slam.

(2) West knows that South has put in a psychic, yet he has no other choice but to double.

(3) South continues his deception.

(4) What else can West do?

(5) To the opponents, South seems to be searching for an escape.

(6) Obviously, this could not be interpreted as a desire to play the hand at two no-trump redoubled; and hence, must be interpreted by partner as a plea for rescue. North unhesitatingly bid three clubs, which was promptly doubled by East, an unwise decision. East-West could have made a small slam, and they

would undoubtedly have arrived there had they not been molested by South. The three-club contract was defeated 1 trick, for a loss of 100 points.

[I have a feeling that East-West were actually lucky, with their plus score of 100 points. Observing what North-South did to them in the bidding, I imagine that if East-West happened to arrive at a six-heart contract, North would have had the clairvoyance to open a spade, South ruffing, after which an equally clairvoyant South would have led either a heart or a diamond instead of a club. Eventually, North would then have obtained a spade trick, thereby defeating the slam. Obviously, plus 100 points is better than minus 100 points. Any other comment? FLK]

10.

```
                    NORTH
                  ♠ 6 4
                  ♥ 6 5 3
                  ♦ 5 4 2
                  ♣ 6 5 4 3 2
    WEST                          EAST
  ♠ A Q 8 3                     ♠ J 9 5 2
  ♥ A K Q 9 7 4                 ♥ 2
  ♦ —                           ♦ K Q 10 8 7 3
  ♣ A Q J                       ♣ 9 7
                    SOUTH
                  ♠ K 10 7
                  ♥ J 10 8
                  ♦ A J 9 6
                  ♣ K 10 8
```

Neither side vulnerable.

NORTH	EAST	SOUTH	WEST
1 NT (1)	2 ♥ (2)	Pass (3)	3 ♥ (4)
Pass	4 ♦ (5)	Pass	4 ♥ (6)
Pass	4 ♠ (7)	Pass	6 ♠ (8)
Pass	Pass	Double	Redouble
Pass	Pass	Pass	

(1) North's opening bid must be singled out for special recognition. Never before have I encountered an opening no-trump bid with

such worthless cards. [I, too. And I've lived 25 years longer. FLK]

(2) Trying to confuse the issue, with an escape to diamonds planned should the heart bid be doubled.

(3) South has the values to bid, but he simply has no convenient bid to make. Hence his pass, to await developments.

(4) Aware of the fact that East cannot have a legitimate overcall, but having no option but to raise.

(5) East has become the victim of his own subterfuge.

(6) Although cognizant of the fact that East has put in a psychic overcall in hearts, West feels that hearts, nevertheless, is the correct trump suit.

(7) Possibly going from the frying pan into the fire, but figuring the fire can be no worse and might be better.

(8) A most logical bid, as was his subsequent redouble.

[Thank goodness I have documented evidence on the authenticity of the bidding as it is given above! It certainly is more fantastic than any episode in *Alice in Wonderland*. And I really must extend my condolences to the unfortunate South player, who imagined he had a really good chance of beating the six-spade contract. I still don't believe the bidding, proof positive notwithstanding! FLK]

11.

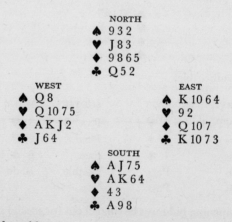

```
                        NORTH
                        ♠ 9 3 2
                        ♥ J 8 3
                        ♦ 9 8 6 5
                        ♣ Q 5 2
        WEST                            EAST
        ♠ Q 8                           ♠ K 10 6 4
        ♥ Q 10 7 5                      ♥ 9 2
        ♦ A K J 2                       ♦ Q 10 7
        ♣ J 6 4                         ♣ K 10 7 3
                        SOUTH
                        ♠ A J 7 5
                        ♥ A K 6 4
                        ♦ 4 3
                        ♣ A 9 8
```

East-West vulnerable.

NORTH	EAST	SOUTH	WEST
Pass	Pass	1 ♦ (1)	Double (2)
Pass	1 NT	Pass	2 NT
Pass	3 ♠	Pass	3 NT
Pass	Pass	Double	Pass
Pass	Pass		

(1) Sitting in the third-hand psychic seat [light-opening, FLK], with a powerful 4-quick-trick hand, South bids one diamond in preference to spades (or hearts):

    1. If partner has some strength, game in no-trump seems likely, especially if the diamond weakness is concealed.

    2. If partner takes out in hearts or spades, game seems sure, especially if the feared diamond suit is not opened.

    3. Opponents may hold strong diamonds and other strength sufficient to cause them to misread the type of psychic South has bid. (This is what occurred.)

(2) West knows that South is bluffing in diamonds, but fails to realize the danger of attempting to convey this information to partner. *West should pass, not double.* Weak informative doubles are all too often expensive, as in this case.

The rest of the bidding requires no comment. [This is the actual bidding of a tournament hand. East-West were defeated 2 tricks—under the old score, 600 points. FLK]

[Once again, the psychic pushed the opponents in over their heads. When East responded with one no-trump, showing (presumably) a stopper in the adversely-bid diamond suit, West, with 3 stoppers in that suit, was convinced that South had a bad hand. His raise to two no-trump was based not on his own strength, but on South's presumed weakness. Thus, West's two bad bids were costly. FLK]

12.

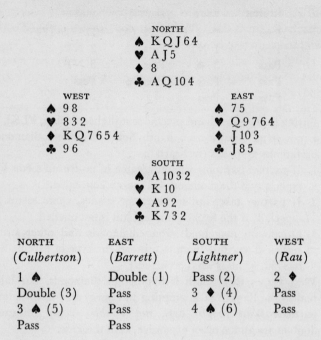

NORTH
♠ K Q J 6 4
♥ A J 5
♦ 8
♣ A Q 10 4

WEST
♠ 9 8
♥ 8 3 2
♦ K Q 7 6 5 4
♣ 9 6

EAST
♠ 7 5
♥ Q 9 7 6 4
♦ J 10 3
♣ J 8 5

SOUTH
♠ A 10 3 2
♥ K 10
♦ A 9 2
♣ K 7 3 2

NORTH (*Culbertson*)	EAST (*Barrett*)	SOUTH (*Lightner*)	WEST (*Rau*)
1 ♠	Double (1)	Pass (2)	2 ♦
Double (3)	Pass	3 ♦ (4)	Pass
3 ♠ (5)	Pass	4 ♠ (6)	Pass
Pass	Pass		

This hand and the one that follows were marked by psychic bids
more widely discussed than any other in the history of bridge. [Pre-
1935. FLK] In the above hand, Mr. Barrett and Mr. Rau represented the Columbia University team and Mr. Culbertson and Mr.
Lightner the Bridge World team. The hand was played at Asbury
Park in the summer of 1930, at which time psychic bidding had
just begun to assume the prominence it has since enjoyed as a
feature of contract. [This was written in 1934. FLK] The comment
on the bidding follows:

(1) A psychic double, intended to create the impression that East
held 3 or more quick tricks and that a game might be difficult to
make. This bid erected a psychological barrier in the adversaries' path, which was the effect the bidder hoped to achieve.
It did not prevent a game bid, but it forestalled a slam.

(2) South should have redoubled. [In the words of Gilbert and Sul-
livan, "of that there is no doubt, no possible doubt whatever."

FLK] In that event, he and his partner would surely have reached a small slam. Whether or not they would have reached a grand slam is questionable.

(3) This double indicates a hand much stronger than that shown by the original bid. [That is, much more than a minimum opening bid. FLK]

(4) This is a distinct indication on the part of South that he is prepared to play the hand at spades. It also indicates no losing diamonds [in contrast to the present-day concept of first-round control. FLK], which in this case is not true; but he must do something to overcome his failure to redouble.

(5) A rebid of spades to show that it is a suit of at least 5 cards and fairly strong. A bid of four clubs would probably have been more effective, but North is still under the influence of the first informative double and of his partner's failure to redouble.

(6) The only possible explanation of this bid is that South either thought his partner's hand was very weak, despite the opening bid and the redouble on the second round, or he was still under the impression that East had a strong hand. Had South bid five spades, North would certainly have bid six clubs, and the final declaration would have been either six spades or seven spades.

[Our correspondent has hit the nail squarely on the head: South's failure to redouble was the beginning of the end for North-South— and there was no recovery. But, again, the point involved in this psychic bid—as in all the others—is *not* how proper bidding could have, or might have, overcome the psychological barrier erected by the disrupters, but rather to demonstrate that the psychic can induce an erroneous train of thought in the minds of the potential victims. It should be noted that Ely Culbertson and Theodore Lightner were not simply two guys named Ely and Teddy. They were of the class consisting of the world's best. And, whatever the direct cause of their aberration, certainly it was induced by East's psychic double. FLK]

13. This hand was played in the famous Culbertson-Lenz match which took place in the fall of 1931:

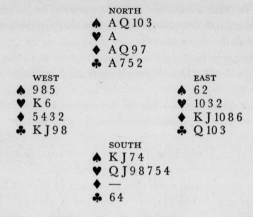

NORTH
♠ A Q 10 3
♥ A
♦ A Q 9 7
♣ A 7 5 2

WEST
♠ 9 8 5
♥ K 6
♦ 5 4 3 2
♣ K J 9 8

EAST
♠ 6 2
♥ 10 3 2
♦ K J 10 8 6
♣ Q 10 3

SOUTH
♠ K J 7 4
♥ Q J 9 8 7 5 4
♦ —
♣ 6 4

SOUTH (*Jacoby*)	WEST (*Culbertson*)	NORTH (*Lenz*)	EAST (*Lightner*)
1 ♥ (1)	Pass	3 NT (2)	Pass
4 ♥ (3)	Pass	4 NT (4)	Pass
5 ♥ (5)	Pass	6 NT (6)	Pass
Pass	Double (7)	Pass (8)	Pass
7 ♥ (9)	Double (10)	Pass	Pass
Pass			

(1) This is an original psychic bid, and, as partner has not yet passed, it is usually as dangerous a bid as it proved to be in this case.

(2) As Mr. Lenz was playing the Official System, his correct bid was two spades, a jump forcing bid, requiring that the bidding be kept open until game contract, at least, was reached. He did not know that Mr. Jacoby's bid was a psychic, but his holding caused him to suspect it.

(3) Having started, he feels justified in continuing, hoping to terminate the bidding at four hearts.

(4) Mr. Lenz seems determined to play no-trump in order to score 150 points for the 4 aces. His bid is also a slam invitation. [The "chameleon" four no-trump, no doubt. FLK]

(5) Still insisting that the hand be played at hearts.

(6) Again wishing the higher score for no-trump and the honor score.

(7) Mr. Culbertson makes a pretty penalty double, based on his holding of the heart king, his strength in clubs, and the further fact that the bidding indicates a serious misfit in opponents' hands.

(8) Satisfied to play the hand at six no-trump, doubled.

(9) Conscious that he has deceived his partner as to the quick trick content of his hand, he now bids seven hearts.

(10) The defeat of the contract is almost a certainty.

[At the time the Culbertson-Lenz match was played, this deal received publicity in virtually every newspaper in the country. The reviews pointed out how dangerous an implement the psychic bid is—and the deal served as an object lesson. The unfortunate part of the hand, of course, was that seven spades was makable, and the spade suit was never mentioned. I wonder what Mr. Lightner would have led against the doubled six no-trump contract?]

14. The following deal arose in the 1931 National Team-of-Four Championships. North was Commander Winfield Liggett, Jr.

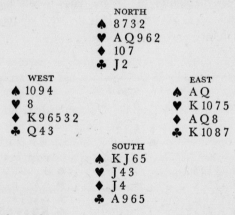

```
                        NORTH
                    ♠ 8 7 3 2
                    ♥ A Q 9 6 2
                    ♦ 10 7
                    ♣ J 2
        WEST                            EAST
    ♠ 10 9 4                        ♠ A Q
    ♥ 8                             ♥ K 10 7 5
    ♦ K 9 6 5 3 2                   ♦ A Q 8
    ♣ Q 4 3                         ♣ K 10 8 7
                        SOUTH
                    ♠ K J 6 5
                    ♥ J 4 3
                    ♦ J 4
                    ♣ A 9 6 5
```

East-West vulnerable.

NORTH	EAST	SOUTH	WEST
1 ♥	Double	Pass	2 ♦
Pass	2 NT	Pass	3 NT
Pass	Pass	Pass	

The opening one-heart bid was of a semipsychic nature, and it did not prevent the opponents from arriving at their proper contract of three no-trump. But the bid did mislead the East declarer, Oswald Jacoby, in the play of the hand. When, during the play, South was revealed as the possessor of the club ace, Mr. Jacoby was certain that North had the king of spades for his opening bid. So he finessed for the king of spades, and was held to just three no-trump.

When the deal was replayed, George Unger, of the Commander's team, had no opening bid to contend with. He attacked the clubs, and never touched the spade suit, thereby developing two club tricks, and making four no-trump. The extra trick won a match point for Commander Liggett's team, and it was by this one match point that the Commander's team won this championship event.

[This is the first deal where the psychic bid has been introduced in terms of the effect that it has on the play of the opponents. This most important aspect of psychic bidding will be presented in greater detail in subsequent sections of this text. In my opinion, as of the present day, psychic bidding no longer tends to talk the opponents out of their best spot, but it still tends to—and will continue to—mislead them in their play. FLK]

15.

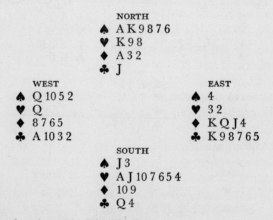

NORTH
♠ A K 9 8 7 6
♥ K 9 8
♦ A 3 2
♣ J

WEST
♠ Q 10 5 2
♥ Q
♦ 8 7 6 5
♣ A 10 3 2

EAST
♠ 4
♥ 3 2
♦ K Q J 4
♣ K 9 8 7 6 5

SOUTH
♠ J 3
♥ A J 10 7 6 5 4
♦ 10 9
♣ Q 4

North-South vulnerable. The bidding:

SOUTH	WEST	NORTH	EAST
(*J. Rau*)	(*S. Fry, Jr.*)	(*C. Lockridge*)	(*E. Hymes, Jr.*)
Pass	Pass	1 ♠	4 ♠ (1)
Pass	Pass	Pass	

(1) When North opened the bidding, East, Edward Hymes, Jr., had a premonition that the opposition could make a game. It was his intention to ultimately bid five clubs as a sacrifice, but he decided to muddle the issue by bidding four spades first. Of course, he expected to be doubled at this contract, after which he would retreat to five clubs.

To his surprise, he was permitted to play at four spades, incurring a 4-trick set, for a loss of 200 points. [He took six tricks? FLK] At a game contract in hearts, North-South could have scored 650 points.

The reason behind North's failure to double was that he knew East must have an escape suit, and North felt that his profit at four spades undoubled would be greater than he would make at East's escape suit. [He was right. East-West would have gone down only 1 trick at the doubled five-club contract. FLK]

[Each of the four gentlemen at the table, in addition to having a justly deserved reputation for technical ability, was equally well known for his psyching proclivities. I am sure that when Mr. Hymes bid four spades, Mr. Rau thought that Mr. Lockridge might have psyched the opening spade bid (despite the vulnerability). Mr. Fry, of course, simply sat and listened—and probably was not too astonished when Mr. Hymes was revealed as the possessor of a rather inadequate trump suit. And Mr. Lockridge knew that he could get a sure profit at East's four spade contract—how could he dream that North-South could make five hearts right on the nose? (Actually six hearts could be made via double-dummy play.) FLK]

16.

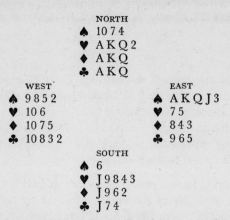

NORTH
♠ 10 7 4
♥ A K Q 2
♦ A K Q
♣ A K Q

WEST
♠ 9 8 5 2
♥ 10 6
♦ 10 7 5
♣ 10 8 3 2

EAST
♠ A K Q J 3
♥ 7 5
♦ 8 4 3
♣ 9 6 5

SOUTH
♠ 6
♥ J 9 8 4 3
♦ J 9 6 2
♣ J 7 4

North-South vulnerable. North and South were employing the Two Club System of bidding, in which the opening bid of two clubs was forcing.

NORTH	EAST	SOUTH	WEST
2 ♣	2 ♦	Double	Pass
Pass	2 ♥	Double	Pass
Pass	2 ♠	Pass	Pass
3 NT	Pass	Pass	Pass

East, having the spade suit as a retreat, indulged in a psychic diamond bid and then a psychic heart bid. North was evidently annoyed by East's obvious psychics, and his emotions conquered his judgment when he jumped to three no-trump. East, of course, took the first 5 tricks. North-South could have made a small slam in hearts.

[If one stops to think of it, North should have known that it was impossible to make three no-trump. South had doubled two diamonds with, at most the jack of diamonds; he had doubled two hearts with, at most, the jack of hearts; and South had passed *two spades,* which certainly denied possession of the jack of spades (or better). So South's "revealing" bidding—big joke—went for nought.

[Of course, North should have bid four hearts, on the sound assumption that South, for his double of two hearts, surely figured to have a minimum of J x x x of hearts. As to the slam being bid,

it would be pretty difficult for North to deduce that South had a
singleton spade. FLK]

17.

NORTH
♠ A 4 2
♥ 8 7 5
♦ 8 5 3
♣ 10 8 5 4

WEST
♠ Q J 10 9 8 7
♥ —
♦ A 4
♣ A Q J 6 2

EAST
♠ 5 3
♥ A K Q 4
♦ K Q 9 7 6 2
♣ K

SOUTH
♠ K 6
♥ J 10 9 6 3 2
♦ J 10
♣ 9 7 3

East-West vulnerable.

EAST	SOUTH (*Oswald Jacoby*)	WEST (*Ely Culbertson*)	NORTH
1 ♦	2 ♥ (1)	3 ♠ (2)	Pass
4 ♦	Pass	4 ♥	Pass
4 NT	Pass	5 ♣	Pass
5 NT	Pass	6 ♦ (3)	Pass
Pass	Pass		

(1) Since the jump overcall shows a good hand, Mr. Jacoby's bid
is a psychic.

(2) West (Ely Culbertson), undaunted by Mr. Jacoby's apparent
strong bid, also made a strength-showing jump bid.

(3) Mr. Jacoby's psychic overcall pushed the opponents into water
over their heads.

Had Mr. Jacoby opened any suit but spades, the six-diamond
contract would have been fulfilled. But he chose to make the
splendid [and deceptive, FLK] lead of the six of spades, and the
defenders quickly cashed the first 2 tricks.

[I am of the opinion that Culbertson (properly) assumed that
Jacoby did have some high-card strength in hearts; and that, hence,

Culbertson's partner figured to have some strength in spades. Surely Culbertson could never imagine that his partner held the A K Q x of hearts. However, the fact remains that if Jacoby had not made his jump overcall, East-West would probably not have arrived at the unmakable slam. And yet, if Jacoby had not led a spade, his psychic would have had a most unhappy ending for him—like the operation was successful, but the patient died. FLK]

18.

NORTH
♠ A 8 4
♥ 10 3
♦ Q J 7 2
♣ K Q 10 5

WEST
♠ K Q 10 7 2
♥ Q J 7 6
♦ A 9 3
♣ 6

EAST
♠ J 9 5 3
♥ A K 9
♦ K 8 5
♣ A 8 2

SOUTH
♠ 6
♥ 8 5 4 2
♦ 10 6 4
♣ J 9 7 4 3

East-West vulnerable.

WEST	NORTH	EAST	SOUTH
1 ♠	1 NT (1)	Double	Pass
Pass	2 NT (2)	Double	3 ♣
Pass	Pass	Double	Pass
Pass	Pass		

(1) The no-trump overcall is proper. [1930 style. FLK]
(2) Obviously, this did not denote a desire to play at two no-trump, since if North wanted that, he could have passed the doubled one no-trump contract. Hence, North was requesting South to name the trump suit. Fortunately, South picked clubs.

South was set 1 trick, a most profitable sacrifice, since the opponents could have made a small slam in spades.

[It has never ceased to amaze me that so many bridge players, holding 4 or more of partner's trumps, fail to realize that this detracts from their defensive possibilities. (Of course, I am no longer amazed that many players, holding 4 trumps, fail to raise partner.) What motivated East into believing that his profit would be greater at three clubs doubled than at his own contract of four spades, will always remain a mystery. As to this particular East-West pair getting to a slam—well, they didn't even get to a game, so the subject is definitely out of order. FLK]

19.

NORTH
♠ Q 6 3
♥ A Q
♦ A K Q 5 3
♣ J 9 4

WEST
♠ J 9 8 7
♥ 8 7
♦ 9 7
♣ K Q 6 5 2

EAST
♠ 5
♥ K 10 6 4
♦ J 6 4 2
♣ A 10 8 7

SOUTH
♠ A K 10 4 2
♥ J 9 5 3 2
♦ 10 8
♣ 3

North-South vulnerable.

NORTH	EAST	SOUTH	WEST
1 ♦	1 ♠ (1)	Double	Pass
Pass	2 ♣	2 ♥	2 ♠ (2)
Double	3 ♣	Pass	Pass
3 ♠ (3)	Pass	4 ♠	Pass
Pass	Pass		

(1) A pure bluff bid by East, who had a hunch that spades was the opponents' suit.

(2) West also bluffed, since it was apparent that East had psyched the spade suit. West figured that two spades would be doubled, and he could then escape to three clubs, which was East's suit.

(3) North recognized, too, that East-West were bluffing in spades, and conveyed that information to partner by bidding that suit, to denote support in it. The game contract at spades was fulfilled.

[It is refreshing to see some intelligent bidding. It makes one realize that all of the bridge players of that era were not naïve and gullible. My thanks are hereby recorded to the anonymous declarer for restoring my confidence in bridge mankind. It is hoped that he also played the hand brilliantly—our correspondent does not describe the play—for four spades is a rather difficult contract to fulfill against a club opening and repeated club leads. FLK]

20.

NORTH
♠ J 9 5
♥ J 7
♦ Q 5
♣ A J 9 8 5 2

WEST
♠ K 8 2
♥ Q
♦ A J 9 7 4 3
♣ 6 4 3

EAST
♠ 10 7 4
♥ A 10 9 8 6 4 3 2
♦ 10
♣ K

SOUTH
♠ A Q 6 3
♥ K 5
♦ K 8 6 2
♣ Q 10 7

Neither side vulnerable.

SOUTH	WEST	NORTH	EAST
1 NT	2 ♥ (1)	3 ♣	3 ♦ (2)
3 NT	Pass	Pass	Pass

(1) Beclouding the issue, with an escape to diamonds contemplated should the two-heart bid be doubled.

(2) East knew that West's overcall was a "fancy," and East's bid of three diamonds—which figured to be West's run-out suit—was intended to convey the impression to West that East had excellent support, for why otherwise was he bidding a suit that he couldn't possibly have? [And the echo answers: Why? FLK]

Against three no-trump, West opened his heart queen and the contract was set five tricks.

[For some reason or other, the East-West bidding reminds me of the story told by Carl Sandburg of the fellow who was watching two trains approaching each other on the same track, one coming from the East and the other coming from the West. When the inevitable collision occurred, the fellow remarked: "That's a helluva way to run a railroad!" Had West not bid hearts, East would have done so—and West would automatically have led the queen of hearts.

[Incidentally, if East captured the opening lead with the ace of hearts, and returned a heart, West showing out (stamping East with an original holding of 8 hearts), South should have taken the safety play of laying down the club ace, to keep East out of the lead if at all possible. South would then have made at least three no-trump—and East-West would have been sorry that they hadn't sacrificed at four hearts, which would have been down one. But, as Dorothy Sims remarked: "The wheel of chance spins around, and the player anxiously watches to discover whether he is a genius or a fool!" FLK]

21. In the play-off for the Vanderbilt Cub Championships last year [1932. FLK], the Four Horsemen played a match against the Cavendish Club team headed by Howard Schenken. North and South were vulnerable, and we[1] were not, and this hand was dealt:

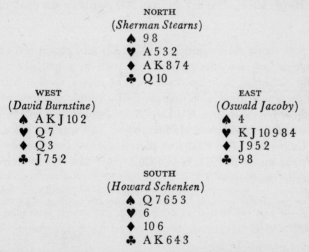

NORTH
(*Sherman Stearns*)
♠ 9 8
♥ A 5 3 2
♦ A K 8 7 4
♣ Q 10

WEST
(*David Burnstine*)
♠ A K J 10 2
♥ Q 7
♦ Q 3
♣ J 7 5 2

EAST
(*Oswald Jacoby*)
♠ 4
♥ K J 10 9 8 4
♦ J 9 5 2
♣ 9 8

SOUTH
(*Howard Schenken*)
♠ Q 7 6 5 3
♥ 6
♦ 10 6
♣ A K 6 4 3

---

[1] This deal is taken from the Four Horsemen's *One Over One* (Blue Ribbon Books, Inc., 1932). The author of this book, and narrator of this hand, is David Burnstine (now David Bruce), one of the members of the Four Horsemen. The others were P. Hal Sims, Willard Karn, and Oswald Jacoby. *One Over One* presents their bidding system, which has served as the foundation of today's one-over-one bidding.

Stearns dealt and bid one diamond, Jacoby overcalled with two hearts. Schenken bid two spades. I passed. Jacoby's two-heart bid was in the nature of a psychic; he bid two instead of one in order to make it difficult for the opponents. The point I want to emphasize, however, is my pass.[2] The second round of bidding after that pass went: Stearns, two no-trump; Jacoby, pass; Schenken, three no-trump; Burnstine, double. I had hoped that our opponents would interpret my pass as a sign of weakness and bid more than they could make. This they did with their three no-trump, and were set 1000 points.

[When this board was replayed at the other table, Walter Malowan and John Mattheys held the cards that Jacoby and Burnstine had held, while P. Hal Sims and Willard Karn played the cards that Stearns and Schenken had held. At that table the bidding went: North, one diamond; East, one heart; South, one spade; West, double. This double warned Sims and Karn of their danger and they stopped at three clubs, which was set 100 points. Thus the Four Horsemen made a net profit of 900 points on the deal. FLK]

[It was stated earlier in this text that Ely Culbertson was opposed to psychic bids for "the masses," although in actual play he personally employed them on occasion. The following deal features a hand on which Mr. Culbertson psyched a couple of times, with the hoped-for happy ending. His East-West opponents, it will be noted, were rather weak in their bidding, which fact was not unknown to Mr. Culbertson. The deal was played against two gamblers in a high-stake match in 1927, before Culbertson had started on his path of empire building. FLK]

[2] The pass should certainly be classified under the heading of psychological strategy—a pass can be just as deceptive, or deliberately misleading, as an aggressive psychic bid.

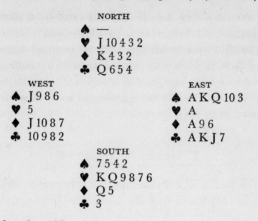

NORTH
- ♠ —
- ♥ J 10 4 3 2
- ♦ K 4 3 2
- ♣ Q 6 5 4

WEST
- ♠ J 9 8 6
- ♥ 5
- ♦ J 10 8 7
- ♣ 10 9 8 2

EAST
- ♠ A K Q 10 3
- ♥ A
- ♦ A 9 6
- ♣ A K J 7

SOUTH
- ♠ 7 5 4 2
- ♥ K Q 9 8 7 6
- ♦ Q 5
- ♣ 3

North-South vulnerable.

The bidding:

EAST	SOUTH (*Mrs. Ely Culbertson*)	WEST	NORTH (*Ely Culbertson*)
1 ♠	2 ♥	2 ♠	3 ♣
3 ♠	Pass	Pass	4 ♣
Double	Pass	Pass	4 ♥
Double	Pass	Pass	Pass

[As is obvious, four hearts was made with ease. As is equally obvious, the opponents were not psyched out of anything. They had stopped at three spades on their own power. I guess East didn't like his hand. FLK]

[The five deals that follow are taken verbatim from the classic book by S. Garton Churchill and Albert B. Ferguson, *Contract Bidding Tactics at Match Point Play* (1936). I have added no comments, for none are necessary. Churchill's analysis of the situations that are presented are quite sound and self-explanatory, in addition to being most witty and humorous. Mr. Churchill has always been accepted as one of the nation's finest players and analysts; and even in these early days he was a revolutionary who refused to accept the tenets of a varying group of authorities who ruled the bridge world for the preceding decade. He was (and is) a person of independent intellectual resources who challenged boldly many accepted rules that arose with the birth of contract bridge. He was among the first to introduce certain apparently radical principles which have now been accepted as sound, as, for example, the weak no-trump. The five psychic deals presented were all played by either Mr. Churchill or by his adherents.]

1. Masters Individual, 1934

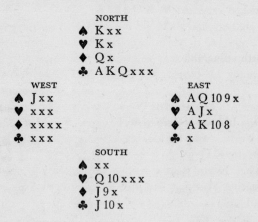

NORTH
♠ K x x
♥ K x
♦ Q x
♣ A K Q x x x

WEST
♠ J x x
♥ x x x
♦ x x x x
♣ x x x

EAST
♠ A Q 10 9 x
♥ A J x
♦ A K 10 8
♣ x

SOUTH
♠ x x
♥ Q 10 x x x
♦ J 9 x
♣ J 10 x

North-South vulnerable.

WEST (*S. Garton Churchill*)	NORTH (*David Burnstine*)	EAST	SOUTH
1 ♠ (1)	2 ♣	2 ♦ (2)	Pass
Pass	? (3)		

(1) There are a few hands that are so desperate that an intimidating bid is almost compulsory. The 4-3-3-3 with only a jack or two is the type. With an intelligent partner, the opening psyche should do no harm and may do some good. The opponents may be intimidated into bidding too little, annoyed into bidding too much, or they may get into the wrong suit, or may misguess

the hand in the play. What is more important, the bid operates as a tip-off to partner. He may hold such a big hand that it will be impossible for him to stay out of game, at least if you never have an opportunity to make a free pass of his opening bid. If he knows that your hand is so terrible as to justify an opening psyche, he'll have the warning he needs.

In first or second position, one of the higher ranking suits affords the best psyche. Third position, where the tip-off feature is not so important, the four-card minor should be bid, in the hope that the reading of the psyche may come before the bidding has progressed very far.

(2) The chances are about 99 out of 100 that West has made a dealer psyche, if North can insert a vulnerable overcall. East should make a bid that will enable him to confirm his opinion, and thank his partner for letting him know that the hand is dead. Three spades is not bad, though two diamonds is better. Neither will be passed if West should happen to have a normal opening like ♠ K J x x x ♥ K Q x x ♦ x x ♣ A x. Conceivably North could be making the overcall on an 8- or 9-card suit to the K Q J.

(3) Whether North should reopen the bidding is very close. He knows that West has lied, but he's not so sure his own partner is not blank.

In this particular case, Burnstine didn't have that problem. Over his two-club bid, East bid six spades! This is, of course, an inexcusable bid. If West should have a normal opening, the hand should produce seven spades or seven no-trump, but West with a minny could not possibly bid it.

Note: This hand was played by every East and West team at four spades, except ourselves, of course. The two-diamond bid would have given us a top in the Masters', as three spades would have. Two spades was maximum, but no East player would have been justified in stopping at that contract without the tip-off psyche. All East needs for game is ♠ J x x x, ♥ K x x, ♦ 9 x x, ♣ x x x, and it is submitted that no West player should ever put in a free bid with that.

2. National Team of Four, Summer of 1933, Asbury Park

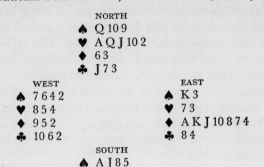

NORTH
- ♠ Q 10 9
- ♥ A Q J 10 2
- ♦ 6 3
- ♣ J 7 3

WEST
- ♠ 7 6 4 2
- ♥ 8 5 4
- ♦ 9 5 2
- ♣ 10 6 2

EAST
- ♠ K 3
- ♥ 7 3
- ♦ A K J 10 8 7 4
- ♣ 8 4

SOUTH
- ♠ A J 8 5
- ♥ K 9 6
- ♦ Q
- ♣ A K Q 9 5

North-South vulnerable.

SOUTH (*W. Malowan*)	WEST (*S. G. Churchill*)	NORTH (*J. Mattheys*)	EAST (*G. Kennedy*)
1 ♣	Pass (1)	1 ♥	2 ♦ (2)
2 ♥ (3)	Pass	3 ♥ (4)	3 ♠ (5)
Double (6)	Pass	Pass	3 NT (7)
Double (8)	Pass	Pass	4 ♥ (9)
Double (10)	Pass	Pass	4 ♠ (11)
Double (12)	Pass	Pass	4 NT (13)
Double (14)	Pass	Pass	5 ♣ (15)
Pass (16)	Pass	Pass (17)	

(1) Should be opened, but scarcely strong enough to overcall.

(2) Immediate psyche probably justified rather than the normal two-diamond bid.

(3) One of the few instances on record where proper and adequate protection was given to what might have been a loose one-over-one response by North. The proper bid of two spades can't be made, because South doesn't know whether North holds a face card.

(4) Showing he has some values and protecting the minimum that South might hold.

(5) The time for desperate tactics has come.

(6) A mistake. Confirms North's suspicion that South holds a minimum. Only sound if he assumes East is a fool.

(7) "I'm a bigger fool than you thought."

(8) "I agree."

(9) "Have no losing hearts."

(10) "You have if you play the hand at hearts."

(11) "Would your reaction be any different now?"

(12) "Fundamentally the same, but more pronounced."

(13) "Certainly, there are other bids than 'double' in your vocabulary."

(14) "Not at the moment."

(15) "Then carry on."

(16) "I really think you go too far, but a double would seem to be superfluous. Maybe I can collect more from setting you here undoubled than I could (1) from bidding our game or (2) from doubling you at five diamonds. Obviously, there can be no slam for us."

(17) Weird ideas should be running through North's brain by this time, (1) that West holds all the outstanding hearts and (2) any honors that may be out in spades, (3) that two diamond tricks will be lost immediately, and (4) that the club suit may not be solid, and, if not, that West probably holds the missing honors. Game would seem to be problematical. It is submitted that the probability that a slam was being missed would not even occur to North on the bidding.

Result: Down eleven tricks undoubled. Even four hearts, making six, would have resulted in a plus score of 780 at that time.

3. Eastern Pair Championships, 1935

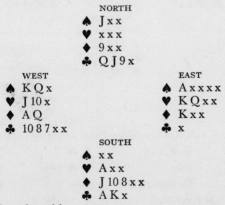

```
                    NORTH
                  ♠ J x x
                  ♥ x x x
                  ♦ 9 x x
                  ♣ Q J 9 x
    WEST                          EAST
  ♠ K Q x                       ♠ A x x x x
  ♥ J 10 x                      ♥ K Q x x
  ♦ A Q                         ♦ K x x
  ♣ 10 8 7 x x                  ♣ x
                    SOUTH
                  ♠ x x
                  ♥ A x x
                  ♦ J 10 8 x x
                  ♣ A K x
```

Neither side vulnerable.

SOUTH	WEST	NORTH	EAST
(*S. G. Churchill*)			
1 ♦	Double	1 ♠	Double
Pass	Pass	2 ♥	Double
2 ♠	Double	3 ♣	Pass
Pass	3 NT	Pass	Pass
Double	Pass	Pass	Redouble
Pass	Pass	Pass	

The club lead was made. Down one. Four spades will make with an overtrick. Churchill entitled this deal: "Jockeying the opponents into the wrong contract." And in his description of the deal, he made the statement: "Bad psychics are occasionally productive of fine results. The above variety not recommended."

4. National Team of Four, Fall of 1932

Re: Trapping the Psycher

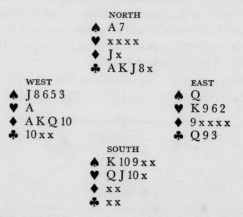

```
                    NORTH
                 ♠ A 7
                 ♥ x x x x
                 ♦ J x
                 ♣ A K J 8 x
       WEST                          EAST
    ♠ J 8 6 5 3                   ♠ Q
    ♥ A                           ♥ K 9 6 2
    ♦ A K Q 10                    ♦ 9 x x x x
    ♣ 10 x x                      ♣ Q 9 3
                    SOUTH
                 ♠ K 10 9 x x
                 ♥ Q J 10 x
                 ♦ x x
                 ♣ x x
```

East-West vulnerable.

SOUTH	WEST	NORTH	EAST
(*Nat Schwartz*)	(*S. G. Churchill*)	(*Mrs. Schwartz*)	(*Von Zedtwitz*)
1 ♠ (1)	2 ♦ (2)	3 ♣	3 ♦ (3)
Pass	Pass	3 ♠ (4)	Pass
Pass	Double (5)	Pass	Pass
Pass			

(1) Much too fine for a dealer psyche, as Nat well knew. It's the ineffective variety, anyway.

(2) Courts a heart bid and would normally be bad for that reason. No sure situation of own. Only justified by probability that dealer is trying to outwit him and the excellent chance afforded to trap the psycher. Solidity of diamonds should offer reasonable protection against an immediate double. Obviously a double would give the show away.

(3) The kind of faith that's appreciated by one's partner. Makes South's pass ambiguous.

(4) Shouldn't fall, despite the ambiguity. Opening bidder could scarcely refuse to find a three-spade or three-heart bid in answer to partner's free bid in the three zone.

(5) "Maybe I'm the 'sucker,' after all."

No. Down 700.

5. Masters' Pair Championship, Summer of 1934

Outpsyching the Psycher

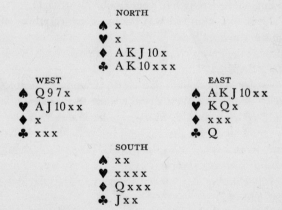

NORTH
♠ x
♥ x
♦ A K J 10 x
♣ A K 10 x x x

WEST
♠ Q 9 7 x
♥ A J 10 x x
♦ x
♣ x x x

EAST
♠ A K J 10 x x
♥ K Q x
♦ x x x
♣ Q

SOUTH
♠ x x
♥ x x x x
♦ Q x x x
♣ J x x

Both sides vulnerable.

EAST (B. J. Becker)	SOUTH (Mrs. P. H. Sims)	WEST (S. G. Churchill)	NORTH (Ed Hymes, Jr.)
1 ♠	Double (1)	3 ♣ (2)	3 ♦ (3)
3 ♠ (4)	Pass (5)	4 ♠ (6)	5 ♣ (7)
Pass (8)	Pass (9)	Double (10)	Pass
5 ♠ (11)	Pass	Pass	Pass (12)

(1) Too dangerous vulnerable, even with a fine partner like Eddie. May place him in an impossible position. Some excuse if partner has passed, and more reason to fear a slam.

(2) Bidding what is a likely "out" of the opponents, and endeavoring to cramp their style.

(3) Eddie in the role of "catcher" instead of "pitcher" for a change. Plays the part nobly. Reads both South's and West's bids as psychics, and doesn't bother to double. Gets in the diamond bid as cheaply as possible, so that his subsequent bidding will be clear.

(4) "Can't be certain yet what is going on, but I have a beautiful spade suit, and better than a bare opening."

(5) Even Dorothy has to give up. Her piece has been "spoke" and she's not so certain that it was in order.

(6) "Couldn't have done all this talking unless I could play spades."

(7) "My clubs are at least as long as my diamonds, and you know I have at least five of the latter. Don't be alarmed. I'm not bidding on the strength of your double."

(8) "Take it your club bid was phony. I am counting on you to take some action."

(9) "Maybe they won't double five clubs. Can go to diamonds if they do."

(10) If partner can't double five clubs, it is quite possible the bid can be made. But West doesn't want to take any action that would court a six bid. Moreover, he knows that partner has now read him for a psyche, and hopes to dissuade North and South from a sacrifice in the minors. Five spades should be bid with the average player.

(11) "O.K. we'll play it in spades. I have no particular defense, but great offense."

(12) At this point, Eddie asked to be excused and spent ten minutes on the piazza of the Convention Hall. Can you blame him? He returned with, "I am sorry. I can't get the answer. There just is no such bidding. I pass."

Note: It is obvious that six clubs is down only one trick. Without partner's double, Eddie would of course have defended at six clubs.

He probably should have done so anyway. The possibility existed, of course, that West had 4 clubs to the Q J and that he couldn't stand the punches in spades if he played the hand at diamonds. He no doubt read South for being long in hearts, the unmentioned suit. South might conceivably take a heart trick, also. The possibility that he would take 3 defensive tricks in his own hand was too remote to consider seriously, and I dare say he didn't.

And so we conclude this kaleidoscopic description and portrayal of deceptive bidding in the embryonic days of bridge. There is no doubt that the primitive techniques of deception, as practiced by our forefathers, were crude, according to our mature standards; and we are perhaps amazed that its intended victims were so gullible and naïve. Nevertheless, the facts speak for themselves, as the reader has observed.

With the passage of time, and the impact of experience, the vast majority of American players became less gullible, less naïve, and more sophisticated; they learned to recognize the feints and hoaxes that the would-be deceiver had attempted to thrust at them, and they learned how to parry his thrusts in many instances. But the deceiver didn't give up his deceptive tactics and go into hibernation: he invented new gadgets, new gimmicks, new and less crude deceptive and harassing techniques, to impose upon his adversaries—and his quest for victims persisted with the same determination and tenaciousness as in days gone by.

Let us now direct our attention to deceptive and harassing bidding in the period 1936–48, and observe how it became more refined and more subtle, and thereby more difficult for its victims to identify and counterattack successfully. But, before getting to this, let us cast a brief glance at the coronation of a new king.

CHAPTER 5

THE ASCENDANCY OF
CHARLES H. GOREN

As has been pointed out, the history of the 1930's is the history of Ely Culbertson and the Culbertson System of Bidding. Even before the winter of 1931–32, when Mr. Culbertson vanquished his twelve rivals in the "battle of the century," most people considered him to be the nation's leading system maker: his *Contract Bridge Blue Book* leaped to the best-seller lists in 1931, and within a few years sold more than a million copies. Although his bridge-playing exploits became obscured by his fame as a writer, teacher, and America's No. 1 authority, in the period 1928–31 he had won every tournament in sight; he had no further need of glory, no need to win additional tournaments in order to remain in the public eye and in public favor. He had reached the pinnacle of success. Royalties from his best-selling books were making him rich. So, in 1932, he quietly stopped playing competitive tournament bridge (except on rare occasions) to rest on his hard-earned laurels.[1] All his energies were then expended in writing and selling books, in establishing

[1] Actually, his last big splash in bridge's major leagues came in 1935, when his team won the National Open Team-of-Four Championship. As J. P. Dunne and A. A. Ostrow record in their book, *Championship Bridge*, ". . . The multifarious Culbertson enterprises were making Ely a millionaire. The competition was getting tougher and more numerous. Culbertson felt the time had come to withdraw from the public arenas. [After 1935] he played no more."

bridge schools, in bestowing "degrees" upon teachers who were spreading the gospel of the Culbertson System—in a word, in preserving, maintaining, and universalizing the Culbertson way of life. Orthodoxy had climbed to the zenith; and it remained perched there in supine comfort, idly scanning the lovely world below, little realizing that a threat to it was looming on the horizon and would all too soon make its appearance known and its presence felt.

In 1936, Charles H. Goren, already established as a highly successful tournament player, published his first book, *Winning Bridge Made Easy;* and, in 1937, he suddenly burst into bloom. He began to win more tournaments than anyone else and, as a natural consequence, he found himself with a reputation. Throughout the nation people were going into stores and demanding his books—and becoming Goren disciples.

Shortly after Goren's *Winning Bridge Made Easy* was published, and it became apparent that it was on its way to becoming a bestseller, Ely Culbertson, perceiving the threat to his domain, took steps to emerge from his self-imposed retirement at bridgedom's Mt. Olympus. Whether this was induced by the observation that Goren was making a bid to supplant him as Public Hero No. 1, or whether it was based on the observation that success depended not only on writing good bridge books, but also on being a winner in top-flight competition, is not certain. But, at any rate, Ely Culbertson, the Champion, issued a public challenge to all comers, possibly not realizing that Goren would risk his growing reputation against the acknowledged master. Goren accepted the challenge. After arrangements for the match had been agreed upon tentatively, Culbertson suddenly called the match off, the ostensible reason being an essential business trip to Europe. The match never did take place—and Culbertson never did return to play tournament bridge.

Throughout the 1936–45 decade, Goren continued to edge Culbertson out of the national and international picture, sometimes imperceptibly, sometimes quite obviously, as Goren continued to win tournament after tournament. By 1945, Goren's triumph had become quite evident: Columnist Goren was appearing in more syndicated bridge columns than was Columnist Culbertson; and Author Goren was selling more bridge books than was Author Culbertson. The old order was changing; the new was replacing the old within the orthodox hierarchy of the Kingdom of Bridge. Goren was arriving on the same pedestal from which Culbertson was toppling.

This does not mean that Culbertson was replaced, or exiled, in 1945, or that Goren was elected to a term of office in 1945. What I am attempting to depict is that, as of 1945, Goren had, in racetrack parlance, come zooming down the stretch in an attempt to overtake the leader, and although now running nose to nose with Culbertson, it was obvious that Goren was going to pull away with every subsequent stride and would emerge as the winner. Actually, it wasn't until about 1948 that Goren became acknowledged as the official winner, the No. 1 authority who had supplanted Culbertson; while Culbertson, although demoted to the No. 2 spot, still sold millions of books, and was viewed in the same light with respect to bridge as Jack Dempsey was to boxing, as Babe Ruth to baseball, and as Bobby Jones to golf. He was still an idol to the public, but an idol who, though admired reverently, was known to have passed his prime.

Basically, the Goren System is (and was) essentially identical to the Culbertston System.[2] Virtually all attention is focused on bidding one's good cards, with no attention being to harassing, obstructionist, interference bidding by the poor-card holders. Goren's classic work, *Contract Bridge Complete,* does not contain even one chapter on deceptive bidding or deceptive tactics (although it does contain a small section on standard deceptive *plays,* plus a half-page on "exposing the psychic," plus almost a page and a half on opening preemptive bids, plus about three pages on the weak jump overcall, which, in 1957, he adopted as a substitute for the strong jump overcall. In addition, he makes passing reference to the existence of the weak two-bid and the weak no-trump). But, be that as it may, Goren became a legend, and his system of bidding became recognized as the Standard American Bidding System.

During this period of 1936–45, the period of the ascendancy of the Goren System, the proponents of more deceptive and harassing

[2] It wasn't until 1949 that the 4-3-2-1 point-count was introduced as a quality substitute for Culbertson's honor tricks, and later incorporated into the Goren System as the foundation of present-day bridge bidding. Goren's adoption of the point-count came after his fame had already been established, and was, in essence, a refinement of what his point-count contemporaries had done before him.

bidding tactics paled into insignificance as the Culbertson-Goren struggle for the preservation of orthodoxy rose to the fore. While undoubtedly deceptive bidding tactics were not dispensed with, or outlawed, during this decade, the literature of the period, and subsequently written histories of the period, tended to ignore or make very little mention of the aspect of psychological strategy in bidding; and, in many instances, either to openly oppose any emphasis on it or to point out that its application was not conducive to winning bridge. The approach of the Goren way of life—as of the Culbertson way of life—was to stress and teach the application of proper scientific techniques for the good-card holders, the haves; and to let the bad-card holders, the have-nots, take a back seat and wait for better days when they, too, would become good-card holders.

The two paragraphs that follow, written in 1951, are typical of the attitude regarding deceptive bidding in the period 1936–48.[3] I use these quotations, rather than quotations made by some obscure authority during the period under discussion, because their author is a famous player, teacher, and authority, and one who has had his finger on the pulse of the nation's bridge players for a long time; and he has not only made diagnoses, but he has also been highly instrumental in prescribing the treatment and influencing future behavior patterns. The statements that follow reflect the position of Goren and other leading bridge authorities of the period under discussion; and this attitude has become a part of the permanent platform and philosophy of the converts to the Goren System of bidding.

Charles Goren, in all the years we have played together, has never made a psychic bid.[4] His record speaks for itself. Johnnie Crawford, in spite of a self-created reputation as a fancy bidder, is pretty much right down the middle. . . .

Watch Howard Schenken, George Rapee, B. J. Becker, Helen Sobel, or any of a long list of perennial and looming bridge stars, and you discover they seldom bid what they don't have. Thus, if you seek to approach the pearly path to bridge supremacy, you should restrict such activities to carefully selected and rare instances.

[3] From *Silodor Says,* by Sidney Silodor, Pageant Press, 1952.
[4] With other partners he has made psychic bids, as will be observed in Chapter 6. But again, he has never advocated them for his students.

Once again, let me state unequivocally that I am not advocating the promiscuous use of deceptive or harassing bidding tactics. I am merely trying to present the historical development—and historical neglect—of these tactics and, at the same time, urge that greater attention should be devoted to the study of these tactics, an approach which has been deliberately overlooked in the past by constituted authority. While fully recognizing that the mastery of technical proficiency is the primary ingredient of prosperous bridge living, it is nevertheless my firm conviction that deceptive, harassing, and preemptive bidding tactics should be viewed, and treated, as also being a basic ingredient of prosperous bridge living. Psychological strategy and obstructionist tactics are a necessity, not a luxury—and should be accepted as such.

It was mentioned at the close of the preceding chapter that the deceptive bidding tactics of the 1936–48 period had become somewhat less crude and more subtle. Let us now examine some specific illustrations and judge for ourselves whether deceptive tactics did, in reality, become more deceptive and, simultaneously, to note whether they have the potentiality of becoming a most vital weapon in the struggle for the survival of the fittest.

CHAPTER 6

DECEPTION AND HARASSMENT
IN ACTION (1936–48)

1. A beautifully deceptive bid that turned out to be costly.

Team-of-Four: 1937

```
                         NORTH
                      ♠ K 9 6 5
                      ♥ —
                      ♦ K 5 4
                      ♣ A K Q 7 3 2
      WEST                                    EAST
   ♠ 7 4 3                                 ♠ 8
   ♥ K Q 10 8 6 5 4                        ♥ A J 9 2
   ♦ Q J 7                                 ♦ 10 9 8 3
   ♣ —                                     ♣ 10 8 6 4
                         SOUTH
                      ♠ A Q J 10 2
                      ♥ 7 3
                      ♦ A 6 2
                      ♣ J 9 5
```

North-South vulnerable.

WEST	NORTH	EAST	SOUTH
(*Mrs. Ralph C. Young*)		(*Charles Goren*)	
Pass	1 ♣	Pass	1 ♠
4 ♥	5 ♥	6 ♣ (1)	Pass
Pass	Double	6 ♥	Pass
Pass	6 ♠	7 ♥ (2)	Pass
Pass	7 ♠ (3)	Pass	Pass
Pass			

(1) Mr. Goren was convinced that the opponents could make six
spades, and his bid of six clubs was to denote a void in clubs,
so that Mrs. Young would lead a club against the six spade
contract. Of course, when this bid would be doubled, he intended to revert to six hearts, as he did.

(2) Certain that the opponents would not dare go to seven spades
in the face of his earlier cue bid of clubs, since he figured to
trump the first round of clubs.

(3) Evidently deciding that Goren was psyching. He was right. The
grand slam was made with ease.

2. A psychic overcall which misled declarer in his play of the
hand.

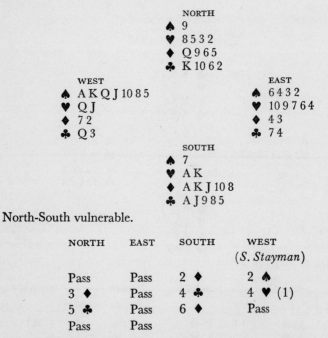

NORTH
♠ 9
♥ 8 5 3 2
♦ Q 9 6 5
♣ K 10 6 2

WEST
♠ A K Q J 10 8 5
♥ Q J
♦ 7 2
♣ Q 3

EAST
♠ 6 4 3 2
♥ 10 9 7 6 4
♦ 4 3
♣ 7 4

SOUTH
♠ 7
♥ A K
♦ A K J 10 8
♣ A J 9 8 5

North-South vulnerable.

NORTH	EAST	SOUTH	WEST
			(*S. Stayman*)
Pass	Pass	2 ♦	2 ♠
3 ♦	Pass	4 ♣	4 ♥ (1)
5 ♣	Pass	6 ♦	Pass
Pass	Pass		

(1) To get declarer to misguess the club queen—a safe psych.

A spade was led, then a shift to hearts. South could have checked
on the distribution by ruffing the third heart, but he trusted Sam.

When West showed up with two diamonds, and had bid spades and hearts, declarer decided to finesse East for the queen of clubs.

3. A psychological overbid.

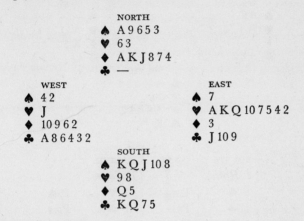

NORTH
♠ A 9 6 5 3
♥ 6 3
♦ A K J 8 7 4
♣ —

WEST
♠ 4 2
♥ J
♦ 10 9 6 2
♣ A 8 6 4 3 2

EAST
♠ 7
♥ A K Q 10 7 5 4 2
♦ 3
♣ J 10 9

SOUTH
♠ K Q J 10 8
♥ 9 8
♦ Q 5
♣ K Q 7 5

Neither side vulnerable.

NORTH (O. Jacoby)	EAST	SOUTH (Mrs. O. Jacoby)	WEST
1 ♦	4 ♥	4 ♠	Pass
7 ♠ (1)	Pass	Pass	Pass

(1) West chose to open the ace of clubs instead of a heart, and Mrs. Jacoby waltzed in with her grand-slam contract. From Jacoby's point of view, he assumed that the opposition would figure him for a void in hearts—for how, otherwise, could he bid a grand slam unless he controlled the heart suit? And he felt that if West had the ace of clubs, he would surely lead it. What would you have opened if you had been in the West seat?

4. A psychic response that kept the opponents out of a makable grand slam.

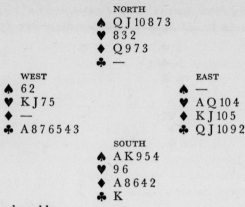

NORTH
♠ Q J 10 8 7 3
♥ 8 3 2
♦ Q 9 7 3
♣ —

WEST
♠ 6 2
♥ K J 7 5
♦ —
♣ A 8 7 6 5 4 3

EAST
♠ —
♥ A Q 10 4
♦ K J 10 5
♣ Q J 10 9 2

SOUTH
♠ A K 9 5 4
♥ 9 6
♦ A 8 6 4 2
♣ K

East-West vulnerable.

SOUTH (*A. Roth*)	WEST	NORTH (*T. Stone*)	EAST
1 ♠	Pass	2 ♥	Pass
2 ♠	Pass	3 ♠	Pass
4 ♠	Pass	Pass	Pass

The four spade contract was defeated one trick. East-West could
have made seven clubs (or seven hearts with West as declarer).

5. This deal became a *cause célèbre*. B. J. Becker, one of the
world's greatest players but one who never bids impulsively or rashly,
suddenly stepped out of character. But how could the opposition
have known this?

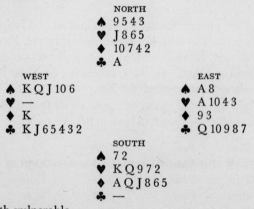

NORTH
♠ 9 5 4 3
♥ J 8 6 5
♦ 10 7 4 2
♣ A

WEST
♠ K Q J 10 6
♥ —
♦ K
♣ K J 6 5 4 3 2

EAST
♠ A 8
♥ A 10 4 3
♦ 9 3
♣ Q 10 9 8 7

SOUTH
♠ 7 2
♥ K Q 9 7 2
♦ A Q J 8 6 5
♣ —

North-South vulnerable.

SOUTH	WEST	NORTH	EAST
(*B. J. Becker*)	(*G. Rapee*)	(*Helen Sobel*)	(*S. Stayman*)
1 ♥	2 ♣	2 ♥	4 ♣
4 ♦	5 ♣	Pass	Pass
6 ♥	6 ♠	Double	7 ♣
Pass	Pass	Double	Pass
Pass	Pass		

East-West were 2460 points ahead with 14 boards left to play. Could they have afforded permitting Becker to play a vulnerable slam rather than take out cheap insurance in the form of a small set? In retrospect, the answer is *yes*.

6. Confusion reigned supreme.

NORTH
♠ 2
♥ 10 8 6 2
♦ 10 6 5 4 2
♣ K J 4

WEST
♠ K J 7
♥ A J 9 4 3
♦ 9 7
♣ 10 9 6

EAST
♠ Q 9 8 4 3
♥ K Q 7 5
♦ 8 3
♣ 8 2

SOUTH
♠ A 10 6 5
♥ —
♦ A K Q J
♣ A Q 7 5 3

North-South vulnerable.

WEST	NORTH	EAST	SOUTH
		(*H. Schenken*)	
Pass	Pass	1 ♠	Pass
2 ♥	Pass	2 ♠	Double
Pass	Pass	2 NT	Double
Pass	Pass	3 ♥	3 ♠
Pass	Pass	Pass	

As can be observed, North-South have a grand slam in diamonds, but Schenken really threw a monkey wrench into the works with his semi-psychics. South's ultimate spade bid gave the impression that he had a good spade suit, and North, thoroughly confused, passed to complete the fiasco. Three spades went down one.

7. An example of how talking across the table was utilized to great advantage is the theme of the deal that follows.

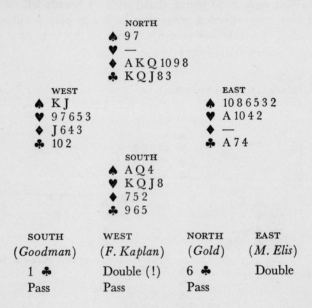

NORTH
♠ 9 7
♥ —
♦ A K Q 10 9 8
♣ K Q J 8 3

WEST
♠ K J
♥ 9 7 6 5 3
♦ J 6 4 3
♣ 10 2

EAST
♠ 10 8 6 5 3 2
♥ A 10 4 2
♦ —
♣ A 7 4

SOUTH
♠ A Q 4
♥ K Q J 8
♦ 7 5 2
♣ 9 6 5

SOUTH	WEST	NORTH	EAST
(*Goodman*)	(*F. Kaplan*)	(*Gold*)	(*M. Elis*)
1 ♣	Double (!)	6 ♣	Double
Pass	Pass	Pass	

The king of spades was led! Declarer took the trick and led a club to the jack. Elis won and returned a spade, and the sight of declarer's queen was too much. Elis said: "Now *that* was a lead! You could have opened a heart, diamond, or a club and have beaten the hand!"

Goodman trusted Elis' analysis (then, now, and forever). If a diamond could beat the hand, then Elis must be void. So Goodman took a diamond finesse after drawing trumps.

8. Psychics keep opponents out of a sure small slam and a respectable grand slam.

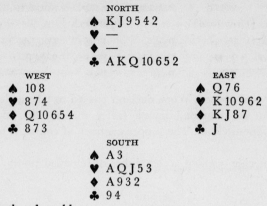

NORTH
- ♠ K J 9 5 4 2
- ♥ —
- ♦ —
- ♣ A K Q 10 6 5 2

WEST
- ♠ 10 8
- ♥ 8 7 4
- ♦ Q 10 6 5 4
- ♣ 8 7 3

EAST
- ♠ Q 7 6
- ♥ K 10 9 6 2
- ♦ K J 8 7
- ♣ J

SOUTH
- ♠ A 3
- ♥ A Q J 5 3
- ♦ A 9 3 2
- ♣ 9 4

North-South vulnerable.

SOUTH	WEST	NORTH	EAST
	(*H. Harkavy*)		(*J. H. Block*)
1 ♥	Double	2 ♣	2 ♦
Pass	Pass	3 ♦	Double
Redouble	3 ♠	Double	Pass
Pass	3 NT	Double	Pass
Pass	5 ♦	Pass	Pass
Double	Pass	Pass	Pass

Down 4—minus 700.

9. A psychic opening and a psychic response steered the opponents away from their proper contract.

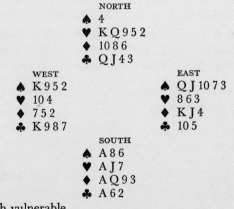

NORTH
- ♠ 4
- ♥ K Q 9 5 2
- ♦ 10 8 6
- ♣ Q J 4 3

WEST
- ♠ K 9 5 2
- ♥ 10 4
- ♦ 7 5 2
- ♣ K 9 8 7

EAST
- ♠ Q J 10 7 3
- ♥ 8 6 3
- ♦ K J 4
- ♣ 10 5

SOUTH
- ♠ A 8 6
- ♥ A J 7
- ♦ A Q 9 3
- ♣ A 6 2

North-South vulnerable.

WEST	NORTH	EAST	SOUTH
(*Crawford*)		(*Jacoby*)	
Pass	Pass	1 ♠	Double
2 ♥	Double	Pass	3 NT
Pass	Pass	Pass	

A spade was opened. When declarer elected to take a club finesse rather than the diamond finesse (after running the hearts), he suffered a one-trick set. The proper contract, of course, is hearts.

10. A psychic opening accomplishes its intended result.

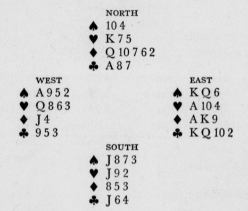

```
                    NORTH
                 ♠ 10 4
                 ♥ K 7 5
                 ♦ Q 10 7 6 2
                 ♣ A 8 7
    WEST                          EAST
 ♠ A 9 5 2                     ♠ K Q 6
 ♥ Q 8 6 3                     ♥ A 10 4
 ♦ J 4                         ♦ A K 9
 ♣ 9 5 3                       ♣ K Q 10 2
                    SOUTH
                 ♠ J 8 7 3
                 ♥ J 9 2
                 ♦ 8 5 3
                 ♣ J 6 4
```

East-West vulnerable.

SOUTH	WEST	NORTH	EAST
(*J. Crawford*)		(*P. Leventritt*)	
1 ♥	Pass	2 ♥	Double
Pass	2 ♠	Pass	3 ♠
Pass	Pass	Pass	

Three no-trump is an easy contract. The psychic opening kept the opponents out of a game.

11. Alas, poor North!

NORTH
- ♠ A K Q J 8
- ♥ Q 4 3
- ♦ Q 4
- ♣ 7 4 3

WEST
- ♠ 10 6 4
- ♥ 6 5
- ♦ K 10 9 6
- ♣ K Q J 5

EAST
- ♠ 7 3
- ♥ A J 2
- ♦ A J 8 7 3
- ♣ A 6 2

SOUTH
- ♠ 9 5 2
- ♥ K 10 9 8 7
- ♦ 5 2
- ♣ 10 9 8

Neither side vulnerable.

EAST	SOUTH	WEST	NORTH
1 ♠	Pass	2 ♦	Pass
2 NT	Pass	3 NT	Pass *
Pass	Pass		

* Police!

A heart lead was made.

12. On overcoming a few psychics.

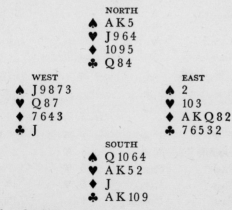

NORTH
- ♠ A K 5
- ♥ J 9 6 4
- ♦ 10 9 5
- ♣ Q 8 4

WEST
- ♠ J 9 8 7 3
- ♥ Q 8 7
- ♦ 7 6 4 3
- ♣ J

EAST
- ♠ 2
- ♥ 10 3
- ♦ A K Q 8 2
- ♣ 7 6 5 3 2

SOUTH
- ♠ Q 10 6 4
- ♥ A K 5 2
- ♦ J
- ♣ A K 10 9

North-South vulnerable.

EAST (D. Burnstine)	SOUTH (von Zedtwitz)	WEST (H. Schenken)	NORTH (H. S. Vanderbilt)
1 ♦	Double	2 NT	Double
3 ♠	Double	Pass	Pass
4 ♦	4 ♥	Pass	Pass
5 ♦	5 ♥	Pass	Pass
Pass			

In this high-class game, the psychic bids utilized by East-West failed to keep North-South from finding their proper contract. It is interesting to note that South rebid a four-card suit, with the expectation of finding support in partner's hand—and he did.

13. A super-light opening, plus a psychic response, got a top-flight pair to a bad slam contract, which, with luck, was made.

NORTH
♠ —
♥ A K 10 8 7 6 3 2
♦ Q 9
♣ Q 10 2

WEST
♠ A K Q 8 4 2
♥ 9
♦ J 10 4
♣ J 7 6

EAST
♠ 10 9 6 5
♥ —
♦ 8 6 5 3
♣ A K 9 8 4

SOUTH
♠ J 7 3
♥ Q J 5 4
♦ A K 7 2
♣ 5 3

North-South vulnerable.

SOUTH (J. Crawford)	WEST	NORTH (H. Schenken)	EAST
1 ♥	1 ♠	2 NT	3 ♥
Double	3 ♠	4 ♥	4 ♠
Pass	Pass	5 ♥	5 ♠
Pass	Pass	6 ♥	Pass
Pass	Double	Pass	Pass
Pass			

Schenken's two no-trump response was designed to prevent a sacrifice at spades, and to invite a spade opening. This deal arose in the National Open Pair Championships of 1944, and North-South received 45 out of 45 match points for fulfilling the doubled slam contract. It was made via a squeeze on East, after a spade opening. All of North's trumps were led, and East found it impossible to protect both the clubs and the diamonds.

14. A psychic response makes it rough for the opponents.

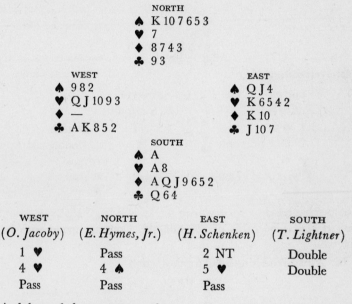

```
                        NORTH
                    ♠ K 10 7 6 5 3
                    ♥ 7
                    ♦ 8 7 4 3
                    ♣ 9 3
        WEST                            EAST
    ♠ 9 8 2                         ♠ Q J 4
    ♥ Q J 10 9 3                    ♥ K 6 5 4 2
    ♦ —                            ♦ K 10
    ♣ A K 8 5 2                     ♣ J 10 7
                        SOUTH
                    ♠ A
                    ♥ A 8
                    ♦ A Q J 9 6 5 2
                    ♣ Q 6 4
```

WEST (O. Jacoby)	NORTH (E. Hymes, Jr.)	EAST (H. Schenken)	SOUTH (T. Lightner)
1 ♥	Pass	2 NT	Double
4 ♥	4 ♠	5 ♥	Double
Pass	Pass	Pass	

A club was led—contract made.

At the other table:

WEST	NORTH	EAST	SOUTH
1 ♥	Pass	2 ♥	Double
3 ♥	3 ♠	Pass	3 NT
Pass	4 ♠	Pass	5 ♦
Pass	Pass	Pass	

A club was led—contract made.

15. A psychic rebid turns out nicely.

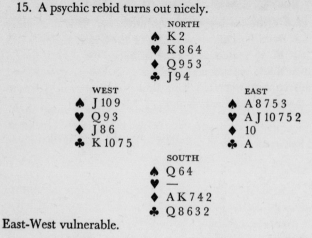

NORTH
♠ K 2
♥ K 8 6 4
♦ Q 9 5 3
♣ J 9 4

WEST
♠ J 10 9
♥ Q 9 3
♦ J 8 6
♣ K 10 7 5

EAST
♠ A 8 7 5 3
♥ A J 10 7 5 2
♦ 10
♣ A

SOUTH
♠ Q 6 4
♥ —
♦ A K 7 4 2
♣ Q 8 6 3 2

East-West vulnerable.

SOUTH (*F. Karpin*)	WEST	NORTH (*B. Kaufman*)	EAST
1 ♦	Pass	1 NT	Double
2 ♥	Pass	3 ♥	Double
4 ♣	Double	4 ♦	Pass
Pass	Double	Pass	Pass
Pass			

A psychic rebid by opener, with the knowledge that the opponents had at least nine cards of the suit bid. Contract made with bad defense.

16. A lead-inhibiting rebid for protection.

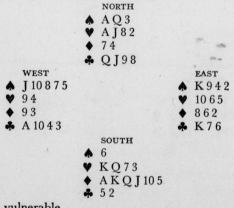

NORTH
♠ A Q 3
♥ A J 8 2
♦ 7 4
♣ Q J 9 8

WEST
♠ J 10 8 7 5
♥ 9 4
♦ 9 3
♣ A 10 4 3

EAST
♠ K 9 4 2
♥ 10 6 5
♦ 8 6 2
♣ K 7 6

SOUTH
♠ 6
♥ K Q 7 3
♦ A K Q J 10 5
♣ 5 2

Neither side vulnerable.

NORTH	EAST	SOUTH	WEST
(*J. Parish*)		(*F. Karpin*)	
1 ♣	Pass	1 ♦	Pass
1 ♥	Pass	3 ♣ (!)	Pass
3 NT	Pass	6 ♥	Pass
Pass	Pass		

Another psychic cue bid, with the intent of bidding a small slam. In this case, it worked. However, even without the false three-club bid (which I knew my partner couldn't pass), a club would not have been led.

17. On the next deal, East and West stopped at three no-trump when six no-trump was a fine contract. Whether they would have arrived at the small slam without the opposing psychic will never be known. But the fact is that the psychic threw them off balance, and they never recovered.

```
                      NORTH
                   ♠ J 8 2
                   ♥ 9 5 3
                   ♦ J 10 8 4 3
                   ♣ J 5
      WEST                          EAST
   ♠ K Q 6 5                     ♠ A 10 3
   ♥ K 10 7                      ♥ Q J 8 2
   ♦ A K 6 2                     ♦ Q
   ♣ K 10                        ♣ A 9 8 7 6
                      SOUTH
                   ♠ 9 7 4
                   ♥ A 6 4
                   ♦ 9 7 5
                   ♣ Q 4 3 2
```

NORTH	EAST	SOUTH	WEST
(*B. Lebhar*)		(*P. Leventritt*)	
Pass	Pass	1 ♥	Double
Pass	3 ♣	Pass	3 NT
Pass	Pass	Pass	

18. In the deal that follows, East and West tried to psych the opponents out of a slam, but succeeded in getting them into a slam that couldn't be made.

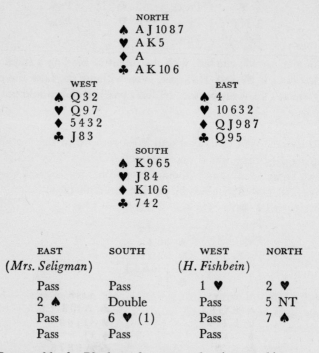

NORTH
♠ A J 10 8 7
♥ A K 5
♦ A
♣ A K 10 6

WEST
♠ Q 3 2
♥ Q 9 7
♦ 5 4 3 2
♣ J 8 3

EAST
♠ 4
♥ 10 6 3 2
♦ Q J 9 8 7
♣ Q 9 5

SOUTH
♠ K 9 6 5
♥ J 8 4
♦ K 10 6
♣ 7 4 2

EAST	SOUTH	WEST	NORTH
(*Mrs. Seligman*)		(*H. Fishbein*)	
Pass	Pass	1 ♥	2 ♥
2 ♠	Double	Pass	5 NT
Pass	6 ♥ (1)	Pass	7 ♠
Pass	Pass	Pass	

(1) Presumably the Blackwood response showing two kings.

North guessed the spade queen, but a club trick had to be lost. Had Fishbein possessed the queen of clubs instead of the eight or three (Q J x), the grand slam would have been made via a double finesse in clubs—and the story would have had a different ending.

19. The "exposing" of a psychic goads the good-card holders into unwarranted positive action.

```
                        NORTH
                     ♠ Q 7 6 2
                     ♥ A 6 5
                     ♦ K 5 4
                     ♣ J 6 3
        WEST                        EAST
     ♠ J 8 4                     ♠ 10 5 3
     ♥ Q J 2                     ♥ 10 9 7
     ♦ 10 9 8 6                  ♦ J 7 3 2
     ♣ K Q 8                     ♣ 10 9 5
                        SOUTH
                     ♠ A K 9
                     ♥ K 8 4 3
                     ♦ A Q
                     ♣ A 7 4 2
```

Neither side vulnerable.

EAST	SOUTH	WEST	NORTH
1 ♣	Double	Pass	1 ♠
Pass	2 NT	Pass	4 NT
Pass	5 ♣	Pass	5 ♥
Pass	6 ♥	Pass	6 NT
Pass	Pass	Pass	

South's jump to two no-trump was a slight overbid, while North's original response of one spade was a slight underbid. When North then jumped to four no-trump, he had made up for his underbid (and it was known that he didn't have a big hand, since he had failed to jump originally). South's failure to stop at four no-trump was undoubtedly due to the realization that East had psyched.

20. A psychic cue bid induces fear in psycher's mind about going to a slam with a losing doubleton.

Neither side vulnerable.

```
        WEST                        EAST
     ♠ A J 9 6 5 3               ♠ K Q 7 4
     ♥ A Q 5                     ♥ K 8 3 2
     ♦ Q 10                      ♦ K
     ♣ K 9                       ♣ A 5 3 2
```

WEST	NORTH	EAST	SOUTH
(*A. Casner*)		(*W. Seamon*)	
1 ♠	Pass	3 ♠	Pass
4 ♦	Double	5 ♣	Pass
5 ♠	Pass	Pass	Pass

A phony diamond bid to inhibit the lead of the suit—but there is always the question as to whether to make an honest or a psychic cue bid under such circumstances. West, having two losing diamonds, was now afraid to bid the slam.

21. Another lead-inhibiting bid backfires.

Team-of-Four in Europe.

NORTH
♠ A K 10
♥ 6 4
♦ K Q 8 5
♣ Q 9 5 4

WEST
♠ 5 2
♥ K Q 10 9 8 7 5 2
♦ —
♣ A K 3

EAST
♠ Q 9 8 4
♥ A J 3
♦ A 7 6 3
♣ 8 2

SOUTH
♠ J 7 6 3
♥ —
♦ J 10 9 4 2
♣ J 10 7 6

North-South vulnerable.

SOUTH	WEST	NORTH	EAST
Pass	1 ♥	Double	Redouble
1 ♠	2 ♠	Pass	3 ♥
Pass	6 ♥	Pass	Pass
Pass			

After a long huddle, the ace of spades and king of spades were cashed. Another psychic bid that didn't work.

22. Truth *is* stranger than fiction.

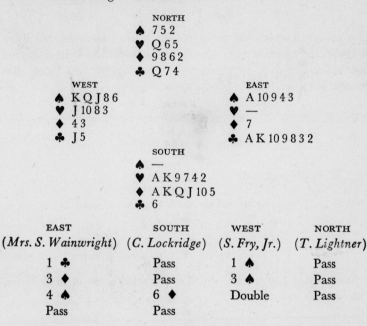

	NORTH	
	♠ 7 5 2	
	♥ Q 65	
	♦ 9 8 6 2	
	♣ Q 7 4	

WEST		EAST
♠ K Q J 86		♠ A 10 9 4 3
♥ J 10 8 3		♥ —
♦ 4 3		♦ 7
♣ J 5		♣ A K 10 9 8 3 2

	SOUTH	
	♠ —	
	♥ A K 9 7 4 2	
	♦ A K Q J 10 5	
	♣ 6	

EAST	SOUTH	WEST	NORTH
(*Mrs. S. Wainwright*)	(*C. Lockridge*)	(*S. Fry, Jr.*)	(*T. Lightner*)
1 ♣	Pass	1 ♠	Pass
3 ♦	Pass	3 ♠	Pass
4 ♠	6 ♦	Double	Pass
Pass	Pass		

Psychics all over. The humorous story is that West opened the jack of clubs which was permitted to hold the trick (dummy's queen should have been played). West then deliberated as to what to return—and declarer exposed his hand, saying "They're all mine." West now led a heart.

23. A trap-pass brings a gorgeous result.

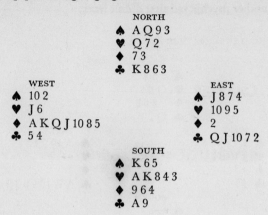

NORTH
♠ A Q 9 3
♥ Q 7 2
♦ 7 3
♣ K 8 6 3

WEST
♠ 10 2
♥ J 6
♦ A K Q J 10 8 5
♣ 5 4

EAST
♠ J 8 7 4
♥ 10 9 5
♦ 2
♣ Q J 10 7 2

SOUTH
♠ K 6 5
♥ A K 8 4 3
♦ 9 6 4
♣ A 9

North-South vulnerable.

SOUTH	WEST	NORTH	EAST
1 ♥	Ah pa-as	1 ♠	Pass
1 NT	Ah pa-as	2 NT	Pass
3 NT	Ah pa-as	Pass	Pass

West was a Southerner who had the good sense to keep saying "ah pa-as."

CHAPTER 7

REVOLUTIONARY BIDS GAIN FAVOR

During the period 1936–50, there were few significant changes in the prevailing standard American way of bidding, despite the fact that in these fifteen years dozens of "new" systems were offered to the bridge-playing public.[1] The reason for the continuing rejection was simply that none of these systems fitted the basic theory accepted by constituted authority. True, there were introduced—and accepted or tolerated by quite a number of bridge players—various revolutionary bidding gadgets to be used in special situations (such as, for example, the Stayman Convention), situations which normal methods had proved unable to cope with satisfactorily. But, by and large, the great majority of these specialized inventions made no impact on the conventional mode of bidding: it was like the flies that alight on a horse's back, to be swept off immediately by a swish of the horse's tail, only to return again promptly, to be swept off again, etc. Annoying, perhaps, to the powers-that-were, but quite endurable.

However, these "gadget inventors," like the flies, were stubborn and persistent. They retreated, improved upon and polished their

---

[1] The 4-3-2-1 point-count system of bidding—which came into existence in 1947–48—was really not a system, but merely an improved method of evaluating the worth of a hand. The orthodox principles of bidding remained undisturbed.

gadgets, retested them in the crucible of experience, and returned undaunted to redisplay their wares. They were determined to make inroads on the status quo (although it never will be known whether they were motivated by a sense of altruism or by the glorification of their ego). Although constituted authority had always branded these gadget inventors as impractical idealists, the fact is that many of them were—in my opinion—most practical, and their ideas were sound and wholesome. Developments of the past decade have attested to the fact that the bidding devices they introduced and reintroduced throughout the decades have become integrated into the new, modern systems that have emerged to challenge the standard American bidding system.

Let us inspect some of the principal revolutionary bidding gadgets that were sniping at orthodox methods throughout the years 1936–50. After briefly viewing these radical bids, we will then observe how (and why) they were assimilated into the four modern "revolutionary" American systems of bidding which have come into prominence during the 1951–60 decade. The systems[2] are:

1. Roth-Stone System (1953)
2. Stayman System (1956)
3. Bulldog System (1956)
4. Kaplan-Sheinwold System (1958)

These four systems are listed in the order of their appearance, based on the year in which they first appeared *in print* as delineated from the unknown year in which they were originally conceived.

The unorthodox and revolutionary bids which follow have, either individually or in combination, become embodied into the founda-

[2] The publications in which these systems are presented are:

a) Roth-Stone: *Bridge Is a Partnership Game,* by Alvin Roth and Tobias Stone, E. P. Dutton and Co., New York, 1958.

b) Stayman: *The Complete Stayman System of Contract Bidding,* by Samuel M. Stayman, Rinehart & Company, Inc., New York, 1956.

c) Bulldog: *Precision Power Bidding,* by William Hanna and Douglas Steen, George Coffin, publisher, Waltham, Mass., 1956.

d) Kaplan-Sheinwold: *How to Play Winning Bridge,* by Edgar Kaplan and Alfred Sheinwold, Fleet Publishing Co., 1958.

tion and/or superstructure of the four modern systems. As will be observed, some of these bids have been rejected by one or more of these systems; others have been accepted by each of the four systems. And so, each of these bids, formerly considered as a crackpot concept of an impractical mind, has become a useful citizen, and a respected member, of the community of influential and winning bridge bids.

1. THE WEAK OPENING TWO BID (EXCEPT TWO CLUBS)

This type of bid (in diamonds, hearts, or spades) denotes a hand of this kind:

♠ x x
♥ A K J x x x
♦ J x x
♣ x x

Bid 2H

The reason for its development and advocacy lies in the obvious infrequency of hands that rate the strong two bid. (For hands that warrant the strong two bid, the artificial bid of two clubs is used by the proponents of the weak two bid. The two-club bid is discussed in the next chapter.)

The origin of the weak two bid can be traced back to Harold Vanderbilt's Club System (in the early 1930's), which employed an artificial one-club bid for its strong bid, and used an opening two bid in a suit as a weak bid—so weak, in fact, that it was almost a psychic bid. But the credit for the development of the modern version of the weak two bid belongs to Howard Schenken, who introduced it to the world during the early 1940's.

About 25 percent of the American Contract Bridge League's 110,000 members employ the weak two bid, as opposed to the strong, game-forcing two bid. As will be evidenced in the next chapter, each of the four modern systems uses the weak two bid in lieu of the strong two bid.

2. THE WEAK JUMP OVERCALL

The types of hands used for this bid are:

	(1)		(2)
♠	A Q 10 x x x	♠	x x
♥	x x	♥	x
♦	x x	♦	K 10 x x
♣	x x x	♣	Q J 10 x x x

Bid 2S over
1C, 1D, or 1H

Bid 3C over
1H or 1S

In standard practice, the single jump overcall (1H . . . *2S*) has, through the years, denoted a strong suit within a strong hand, and required just a little strength in partner's hand to yield a game. It is the belief of the proponents of the weak jump overcall that, first, the type of hand described by the standard jump overcall occurs infrequently, and furthermore, when it does arise, it can be depicted by making a take-out double first, and then following up with a strong rebid. Hence, the substitution of the frequently occurring "weak" jump overcall type of hand for the "wasted" strong jump overcall type of hand. (Charles Goren has accepted the weak jump overcall as a substitute for the strong jump overcall, and has recently incorporated it into his system.) The prime purpose of the weak jump overcall is to pre-empt the opponents' bidding space, while simultaneously giving partner a concise and precise picture of the weak jump overcaller's hand. Each of the four modern systems has integrated the weak jump overcall into their systems. Of the 110,000 members of the American Contract Bridge League, over 30 percent use the weak jump overcall instead of the strong jump overcall.

3. THE WEAK ONE NO-TRUMP OPENING BID (12–14 POINTS)

This bid is made on hands of the following types:

♠	Q x x	♠	x x x	♠	x x
♥	K x x	♥	A Q x x	♥	K J x
♦	A x x x	♦	K J x x	♦	A x x x x
♣	A x x	♣	Q x	♣	K Q x

The weak no-trump opening bid can trace its ancestry almost to Adam and Eve: as early as 1928, Ely Culbertson introduced an alternative theory of light no-trumps (although he always favored the strong no-trump). This light no-trump was used by many experts throughout the ensuing years, but it was not accepted as standard by the world-at-large. In 1952, when Culbertson came out in favor of the 16–18 point no-trump (the strong no-trump, expressed in points rather than honor tricks), he reintroduced the optional light no-trump, which was based on a holding of 13–15 points. The light no-trump was advocated only for nonvulnerable openings. Culbertson's range was rejected, and the 12–14 range became the accepted one for the light or weak no-trump opening.

Not only Culbertson, but authorities such as S. Garton Churchill and Theodore Lightner, and their disciples (plus dozens of other authorities, experts, and their disciples) have always advocated the use of a weak no-trump opening (in the area of 13 points) under favorable vulnerability conditions.

But it was not until the 1950's that the bid came of age, and for the first time became not only a systemic bid, but also became the *foundation* of a system (the Kaplan-Sheinwold System).

Of the 110,000 members of the American Contract Bridge League, about 15 percent use a weak no-trump opening in contrast to the strong no-trump opening. The Kaplan-Sheinwold System uses the weak no-trump in all positions, regardless of vulnerability; both the Stayman and the Bulldog Systems employ the 12–14 point weak no-trump if not vulnerable; the Roth-Stone System uses only the strong no-trump (16–18).

4. THE WEAK JUMP RESPONSE

Written history traces the origin of this bid back to 1934, although undoubtedly it was used before then. In the Eastern Championships of that year, Harry Fishbein jumped to two spades over partner's opening one-club bid with the following hand:

♠ Q 9 7 5 4 3 2
♥ 9 4
♦ 8 2
♣ 7 3

It is assumed that Mr. Fishbein and his partner had agreed to use the weak jump response, and that his bid was not a slip of the tongue. The bid was used through bridge's formative years by a few of the experts who played in closely-knit partnerships, but it was not until Roth and Stone incorporated it into their system that it became a recognized bid (as opposed to a whim). As is apparent, the bid is made strictly for pre-emptive purposes, while simultaneously warning partner against bidding again. The Roth-Stone illustration of the type of hand required for the bid is:

♠ x x
♥ Q J 9 x x x
♦ x
♣ x x x x

Over partner's 1D opening,
bid *2H*

At the present time, the weak jump response has not been accepted by either the public or by the Stayman and Kaplan-Sheinwold Systems. (Bulldog, however, does employ it.) The primary reason for the rejection is that it is felt that the strong jump response on the very good responding hands (19 or more points) greatly facilitates slam bidding. Consequently, our modern system makers are reluctant to dispense with a big money-maker and replace it with a speculative bid.

Of the 110,000 American Contract Bridge League members, 10 percent employ the weak jump response instead of the strong jump response.

5. THE CONTROLLED, OR DISCIPLINED, PSYCHIC OPENING BID

Each of the four systems has incorporated the psychic opening bid as an orthodox systemic bid. But it is a controlled psychic, in contrast to the hit-or-miss variety employed in bridgedom's early days. Generally, the bid is made in first or second position with a hand containing 3-6 high-card points, most or all of which are concentrated in the suit bid. For example:

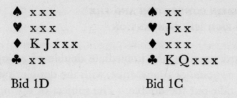

♠ x x x	♠ x x
♥ x x x	♥ J x x
♦ K J x x x	♦ x x x
♣ x x	♣ K Q x x x
Bid 1D	Bid 1C

The purpose of this modern-type psychic is threefold: (1) to inform partner that opener holds a hopeless hand; (2) to inform partner that opener can stand a lead only in the suit bid; and (3) to confuse the enemy.

Of the 110,000 members of the American Contract Bridge League, 12 percent stated that they use frequent psychs. As to how many of these use the systemic controlled or disciplined psych, as described above, is pure conjecture.

6. THE INVERTED MINOR SUIT RAISE

In standard practice, the direct single raise of partner's minor suit (1C . . . 2C; 1D . . . 2D) has always described a very weak hand; and the double raise (1C . . . 3C; 1D . . . 3D) has always indicated a strong hand.

In the Kaplan-Sheinwold System—and to a great extent in the Stayman System—the reverse holds true: the direct single raise of partner's minor suit shows a strong hand, while the direct double raise is a pre-emptive bid denoting weakness. For example, the direct double raise is made on hands of the following type:

♠ x
♥ x x x
♦ K x x x
♣ Q J x x

Over 1C, bid 3C (weak)

At the present time, neither the Roth-Stone nor the Bulldog systems have adopted this revolutionary bid. Of the 110,000 members of the American Contract Bridge League, 5 percent employ the Kaplan-Sheinwold version of the inverted single and double raises in the minor suits.

7. THE FISHBEIN CONVENTION AND THE
   MODIFIED FISHBEIN CONVENTION

In standard practice, the immediate double of an opening three bid is called *optional* or *cooperative*, with the doubler's partner being expected to take-out the double. (The subject of opening three bids is discussed in the next section.) In the Fishbein Convention, the immediate double of an opening three bid is a *penalty double;* when a take-out is desired, the left-hand opponent of the pre-emptor bids the adjacent higher-ranking suit at the lowest possible level, as an artificial bid (3D . . . *3H;* 3H . . . *3S,* etc.) The Fishbein Convention is, of course, not an obstructionist or deceptive bid. It is what might be classified as a counterattack to obstructionism. Neither Roth-Stone, Bulldog, nor Kaplan-Sheinwold employ this convention. However, Stayman does use it over an opening three-spade bid *only*—that is, a double of three spades is for penalties; and Bulldog employs a version of the Fishbein Convention known as "Modified Fishbein."

Modified Fishbein, like orthodox Fishbein, treats the immediate double of a pre-empt as a penalty double (including the immediate double of a weak no-trump opening or a weak opening two bid). But where a take-out is desired, the bid used artificially is the lowest possible minor suit (3H . . . *4C;* 3C . . . *3D*).

The Fishbein Convention, or Modified Fishbein, is employed by 25 percent of the 110,000 members of the American Contract Bridge League.

8. THE "DADDY" OF ALL OBSTRUCTIONIST BIDS: THE OPENING
   PRE-EMPTIVE BID OF THREE, FOUR, OR FIVE IN A SUIT

Ever since contract bridge came into being, constituted authority has advocated the use of an opening bid of three, four, or five in a suit as a barrier against the opponents. With few exceptions, all bridge authorities—both past and present—have agreed that an opening pre-emptive bid should be based on a long suit within a hand that is relatively weak in high cards, a hand that does not qualify for an opening bid of one in a suit. All concurred that the purpose of the bid was to impair, sever, or destroy the opponents' lines of communication.

From the early days of Culbertson to the present, the prime criterion in determining whether a hand warranted an opening pre-emptive bid was this pinpointed element of safety: one should be prepared, if he were doubled at his pre-emptive contract, to lose a maximum of 500 points, assuming his partner to be completely devoid of winning tricks. This criterion was introduced by Culbertson, and it served as a bible for pre-emptive situations. It became known as the Rule of Two and Three: have within two tricks of your contract if you are vulnerable, and within three tricks of your contract if not vulnerable. That is, if you go down two, doubled and vulnerable, at your pre-emptive contract, the loss will be 500 points; and if you go down three tricks, doubled and not vulnerable, the loss will also be 500 points.

The examples given to illustrate the Rule of Two and Three have always been of this type:

Vulnerable

♠ x	♠ K Q J 10 x x x x
♥ K Q J x x x x	♥ x
♦ J 10 9 x	♦ x x
♣ x	♣ x x
Bid 3H	Bid 3S

Not Vulnerable

♠ x x	♠ x x
♥ x x	♥ x x
♦ K Q J 10 x x x	♦ x
♣ x x	♣ Q J 10 9 x x x x
Bid 3D	Bid 3C

The rule was logically sound and mathematically valid. A game is worth, on the average, about 500 points. The purpose of a pre-emptive opening bid is to prevent the opponents from reaching a game contract which, if bid in the right suit (or no-trump), they can probably make. It is losing tactics, however, to keep them out of a game if, by doubling, they can collect more in penalties than the game would be worth to them. Hence the gearing of a pre-empt to a loss of no more than 500 points (or, to be more precise, to exactly 500 points). One's loss, if doubled and defeated by that amount, is only as much as he would have lost anyway if the opponents had bid and made their game without interference.

But this Rule of Two and Three was rarely adhered to in actual practice—not even by the authorities who advocated it and recommended it in their textbooks as the perfect criterion.[3] And it is obvious that as the years rolled on, opening pre-emptive bids—especially three bids—became weaker and weaker. Even as far back as fifteen years ago, there was not one good player who would not have opened, *not vulnerable* (against vulnerable or nonvulnerable opponents) with three diamonds, holding:

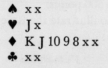

♠ x x
♥ J x
♦ K J 10 9 8 x x
♣ x x

As is obvious, if three diamonds is doubled, and partner has nothing, the contract will go down four tricks for a loss of 700 points.

Or, for that matter, is there a good player who, vulnerable, would not open with four hearts against vulnerable opponents with:

♠ x
♥ A Q J 10 9 8 7 6
♦ Q x
♣ x x

Yet, if the four-heart bid is doubled, and partner has nothing, the pre-emptor will go down 800 points, which is more than the mathematical equivalent of a game.

[3] It should be noted that the Roth-Stone System does not subscribe to the Rule of Two and Three. For opening three bids, these are the system's criteria: (1) nonvulnerable, a reasonable expectation of winning within four tricks of the pre-emptive bid; (2) vulnerable versus nonvulnerable opponents, a reasonable expectation of winning within two tricks of the pre-emptive contract; (3) vulnerable versus vulnerable opponents, a reasonable expectation of winning within three tricks of the pre-emptive contract. It should also be noted that Roth and Stone maintain that the above requirements are even more effective in rubber bridge than in duplicate bridge.

Admittedly, if this were a perfect world and all the bridge players in it were perfect, then the theoretical pre-emptive losses of 700 and 800 points, respectively, would, in the long run, result in the opening pre-emptive bidder becoming a loser. But to assume perfection is to ignore reality.

Why have opening pre-emptive bids, ignoring the mathematics of the situation, become weaker and stayed that way? Why has the almost solid suit of the pre-emptor of years gone by, depreciated or degenerated into a split or ragged suit? Why is it that, in a National Tournament held in 1958, 47 out of 52 players (not vulnerable against vulnerable opponents) opened with three spades on:

In my opinion, the answer lies in this: in experience, the realistic bridge players have lowered the textbook requirement for a pre-emptive bid (The Rule of Two and Three) because an opening three bid that denoted weakness would either almost invariably goad the opponents into action, even without the necessary values, and often into water beyond their depth; or it would be made with the assurance and comfort of knowing that the next opponent could not double for penalties and make that penalty stick.[4] In brief, the pre-emptive bid, despite its acknowledged weakened state, became a wondrous and most practical gadget—and has remained that way. And the pre-emptive bidder, in taking advantage of the situation that the opponents seemed to think he was immortal and couldn't be hurt, became unafraid to step in where even angels fear to tread; and, in so doing, he deprived the opponents of the low-level bidding space which they needed for the interchange of information.

Why, then, the distrust by constituted authority of the new pre-emptive and harassing bids such as: (1) the weak two bid; (2) the

---

[4] As was pointed out earlier in this chapter, the double of an opening three bid has always been viewed as an optional or cooperative double, with the doubler's partner being expected to take-out the double unless he had good cause to leave it in. In only rare instances did the pre-emptive three-bidder stay doubled for penalties—and so the pre-emptor emerged unscathed, with no punishment for his transgression.

weak jump overcall; (3) the weak no-trump; (4) the weak jump response; (5) the controlled or disciplined opening psychic bid? Has the value of pre-emption become null and void? Why have so many self-styled theorists delivered rousing philippics against the new pre-emptive weak bids? Is there a bridge player in the world who claims never, or seldom, to have been greatly embarrassed, let alone seriously obstructed, by an adverse pre-emptive bid such as the weak opening bid of three or four in a suit, the weak two bid, the weak jump overcall? Surely these new obstructionist bids which have been accepted as practical by many of our best—and winning— bridge players, and have become integrated into their systems, must have great merit, or at least some good features. Yet, the fact remains that, generally speaking, these bids are viewed with suspicion, as radical bids which are trying to change our way of life and, as such, should be denounced by polite society. Admittedly, they *are* trying to change our way of life. But is it not conceivable that the change may be for the better? In view of the increasing success and usage of these bids, don't they warrant a critical "look-see"?

Let us now examine the specific details of these revolutionary bids at greater length, while at the same time observing the reasons behind their adoption by the modern systems of bidding.

CHAPTER 8

REVOLUTIONARY BIDS USED BY THE MODERN SYSTEMS

In this chapter, we will discuss and analyze the reasons that motivated Roth-Stone, Stayman, Bulldog, and Kaplan-Sheinwold to break away from the ways of their elders. It will then be understood *why* they have adopted the revolutionary bids introduced in the preceding chapter and have embodied them as major components of their systems. At the same time they also did away with the former meaning of certain time-honored bids and substituted for the displaced meanings a significance that was the complete antithesis of what the bids had traditionally stood for.

1. THE WEAK TWO BID

Despite the efforts of Howard Schenken to popularize the weak two bid after he introduced it in 1940–41, bridge players refused to accept it at that time, and stuck by the strength-showing, game-forcing two bid. It was not until the Roth-Stone System was created that the weak two bid found itself out of the mire and finally on the way to public acceptance.

Actually, in ascribing credit to Roth and Stone, I am being most unfair to Schenken, Stayman, and undoubtedly others. While it is true that Roth and Stone resurrected the weak two bid and were a most dynamic force in bringing it into an active, fruitful life, they are entitled to but a share in the glory. As early as 1951—two years before the Roth-Stone System appeared in print—Sam Stayman had accepted the weak two bid as an integral part of his system and had defined and explained the bid in an earlier work of his, *Expert Bidding at Contract Bridge*.[1] But since it was not until 1956 that the *Complete Stayman System of Bidding* was published—in contrast to the Roth-Stone System which first appeared in book form in 1953—"legal seniority" for the reanimation of the weak two-bid is accorded to Roth-Stone. Undoubtedly Stayman, Roth, Stone, and other practical theoreticians were aware of the utility of the weak two bid long before they ever dreamed of propagandizing for its employment via the written word. And, further, it might well be that the weak two bid was starting on the road to popular acceptance on its own momentum at the same time that Roth and Stone were making it a system bid; and that this push—making it available in published form for all to study and apply—was all that was needed to give it impetus and to convince its slightly uncertain would-be users that it was a recommended and approved gadget.

The reason for the emergence of the weak two bid is a simple and logical one, as has been noted: the strong, forcing-to-game type of two bid arises once in a blue moon. And, if one accepts the fact of the obvious infrequency of hands that rate a strong two bid opening, why waste a perfectly good type of bid on something that comes up about once a month even with those who play daily? Why not employ a better and much more frequent use for this call?

The Schenken weak two bid, by the way, was not made on the type of hand that most players would call weak. It denoted a hand of less *high-card* strength than an opening bid, the type of hand that virtually everybody would have liked to open with one of a suit—and probably would have if they were not afraid of incurring the displeasure of partner if the bid led to a disastrous result. ("You didn't have an opening bid, partner!")

Here are some illustrations of the Schenken-type weak two bid:

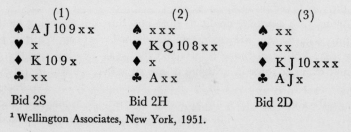

(1)	(2)	(3)
♠ A J 10 9 x x	♠ x x x	♠ x x
♥ x	♥ K Q 10 8 x x	♥ x x
♦ K 10 9 x	♦ x	♦ K J 10 x x x
♣ x x	♣ A x x	♣ A J x
Bid 2S	Bid 2H	Bid 2D

[1] Wellington Associates, New York, 1951.

As can be evidenced, the above weak two bids show not only a respectable suit, but also guarantee a little something on the side. In those early years, the introduction of the weak two bid opened the gates to a great deal of "honest" deceit; for the opponents, not fully understanding what the bid represented and being unaccustomed to it, either screamed—when they became the victims—"we wuz robbed"; or they had no set defense against it, and often pushed themselves in above their heads because they thought the bid was weaker than it actually was. But time took care of that; and both the weak two bid and the defenses against it have become standard, commonplace practice, at least in tournament circles.

In the Schenken (standard) version of the weak two bid, only the opening bids of two diamonds, two hearts, or two spades are weak. The two-club opening bid is reserved for that rockcrusher type of hand which would, in orthodox practice, be opened with a forcing two bid in the bidder's best suit. And, of course, artificial bids have been devised for the responses and rebids over the strong opening two-club bid so that both responder and opener can accurately describe their holdings.

A. *The Roth-Stone Justification for the Employment of the Weak Two Bid*

Both Roth and Stone perceived the tremendous advantage of the weak two bid as a bid that does things to the opponents: that opening with a two bid takes that first, relatively safe, round of bidding away from them, while the two-bidder's side, even if they have the better cards, can spare the loss of that round of bidding, since the opening two-bidder has pretty specifically described his holdings. And, if the opponents have slightly better, or much better, hands, they have to start trying to find out about it at the two or three level. Based on the above reasoning, the weak two bid became a standard bid in the Roth-Stone System, except that the weak two bid became a weaker two bid than that advocated by Schenken and his followers. Before presenting the requirements for the Roth-Stone weak two bid and their opinions as to its tremendous advantages, here are some examples of the Roth-Stone weak two bid:

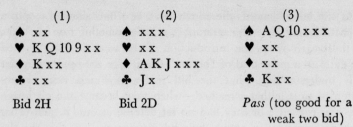

(1)	(2)	(3)
♠ x x	♠ x x x	♠ A Q 10 x x x
♥ K Q 10 9 x x	♥ x x	♥ x x
♦ K x x	♦ A K J x x x	♦ x x
♣ x x	♣ J x	♣ K x x
Bid 2H	Bid 2D	*Pass* (too good for a weak two bid)

Requirements for the Weak Two Bid

1. 7–10 points in high cards *nonvulnerable;* 9–11 points in high cards *vulnerable.*
2. A 6-card suit, or a strong 5-card suit.
3. Strength concentrated mainly in suit bid.
4. If a minor suit, it usually denies a 4-card major.
5. Usually no singleton.

In duplicate play, there are *no* forcing bids in the Roth-Stone System. *All two bids are weak, including clubs.* According to the authors, experience has proved that the weak two-club bid occurs ten times more often than does the strong two-club bid. Nevertheless, in rubber-bridge play or total-point play, the two-club opening bid is used by the system to describe a powerful hand, the bid being unconditionally forcing to game. In rubber bridge, the forcing two-club bid is essential, since the emphasis (and payoff) is on games and slams, not part-scores.

According to Roth and Stone, these are the advantages of the weak two bid:

1. It gives an accurate description of the opener's hand.
2. It acts as a harassing pre-emptive bid against the opponents, and either jams up or destroys their lines of communication.
3. It allows the partner of the weak two-bidder great latitude via the employment of deceptive responses. Since the opener's rebids are forced (as defined and illustrated in their book), and with very few exceptions the opener is not permitted to bid a game, the responder can make it extremely difficult for the opponents by:

(a) Bidding "anything" without the fear of being raised to game.

(b) Bidding the opponents' strong suits without fear of being passed by opener.

(c) Taking premature sacrifices, leaving the opponents to guess what is going on, especially if the outstanding strength is more or less equally divided in the opponents' hands, in which case there is no way of knowing whether opener's partner has a good hand or a bad one.

So, according to the system, by the judicious application of the frequently arising weak two bid, a highly effective psychological technique is created and utilized as a replacement for the infrequently occurring, and thereby wasted, strong two bid. And the modern system makers—Stayman, Bulldog, and Kaplan-Sheinwold —have followed in the footsteps of Roth and Stone. The weak two bid has been amalgamated into their systems (although, as will be observed in the remainder of this section, all of them employ the forcing two-club opening at all times to depict the rockcrusher type of hand).

B. *The Stayman Justification for the Employment of the Weak Two Bid*

According to Stayman (as with Roth-Stone), long experience with the strong two bids indicated that the opening bid of two in a suit occurred so infrequently that it was an impotent weapon; and that the use of an opening bid of two hearts or two spades has much greater utility as a pre-emptive bid than as a forcing bid. So the strong two bid in a major was replaced by the weak two bid, with the two club and two diamond opening bids being used as the forcing bids.[2]

---

[2] The strong opening bids of two clubs and two diamonds are both artificial and forcing. The two-club opening bid is made on a hand of intermediate strength (19–23 points), and is forcing for one round. The precise strength of the bid is revealed on opener's first rebid. The two-diamond opening denotes a stronger hand, and is forcing to game except if opener rebids two no-trump (2D . . . 2H . . . 2NT). The negative response to the two-club opening is two diamonds; the negative response to the two-diamond opening is two hearts. Suffice to say, Mr. Stayman has interrelated the various rebids and responses after an opening bid of two clubs or two diamonds to attain maximum efficiency.

The requirements for the weak opening two bid are:

1. A hand that does not qualify for an opening bid of one.
2. A good suit, generally 6 cards or longer.
3. A hand that figures to win 5 to 7 tricks, depending on vulnerability.

To illustrate:

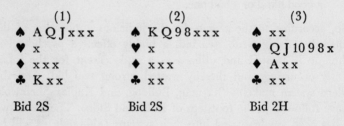

(1)	(2)	(3)
♠ A Q J x x x	♠ K Q 9 8 x x x	♠ x x
♥ x	♥ x	♥ Q J 10 9 8 x
♦ x x x	♦ x x x	♦ A x x
♣ K x x	♣ x x	♣ x x
Bid 2S	Bid 2S	Bid 2H

A raise to three of the suit by responder, whether over an intervening bid or not, is pre-emptive in nature, and is not to be interpreted as a move to invite game. Since the responder's hand may be one of several types, and since he may conceivably be laying a trap for the opponents, the responder alone should decide about sacrificing if and when the adversaries reach game. Precisely how responder can "fool around" can be observed in the illustrative deals presented in the next chapter.

The only forcing response is two no-trump. Any other bid can be dropped by opener. Responder may drop the opener's rebid if he so desires, even if responder's initial bid was the forcing two no-trump bid. Hence, responder's original bid of two no-trump can be a psychic. The psychic two no-trump is always safe, since opener is not permitted to carry responder's initial response to game. However, much more often than not, the two no-trump response will be made on a good hand, to seek further information regarding game or slam possibilities.

Thus, the weak two bid lends itself not only to pre-emption and harassment but also to chicanery and deceit. From a psychological point of view, the opponents often find the weak two bid an irresistible inducement to overcall, and not infrequently the responder is given an opportunity to take attractive—and lucrative—penalty action. For example:

NORTH	SOUTH
♠ K Q 10 x x x	♠ x
♥ x	♥ Q 10 9 x
♦ K x x	♦ A Q x x
♣ x x x	♣ K Q J x

NORTH	EAST	SOUTH	WEST
2 ♠	3 ♥	Double	

In situations comparable to the above, since responder has full knowledge that opener's hand is weak defensively, opener should not make the mistake of nullifying responder's action. When responder doubles for penalties, opener should not take out the double by running back to his suit. Responder's judgment should be respected, even if his actions seem "screwy." Responder may or may not be "fooling around," but he is always aware of the precise limited range of opener's hand. The responder should always be the one to make the final decisions, since he knows opener's hand and opener knows nothing about the responder's hand.

C. *The Bulldog Justification for the Employment of the Weak Two Bid*

As in the other modern systems, Bulldog recognizes the rarity of the strong, forcing two-bid type of hand; and, as a consequence, it employs the weak two bid in spades, hearts, and diamonds as a replacement for the strong two bid, reserving the two-club opening as a forcing bid when a hand has game-going possibilities. The weak two bid is employed regardless of vulnerability (although the weakness of the bid is naturally influenced by vulnerability conditions). The requirements for the weak two bid are:

1. Any 6-card suit, or a good 5-card suit with a 4-card side minor.
2. Weakness in the side major or majors.
3. 5–12 points in high cards, depending on vulnerability and seat.

Examples of a nonvulnerable opening bid of two hearts are:

♠ x x	♠ x x
♥ K 10 9 x x x	♥ Q J 10 x x
♦ K x x	♦ K x
♣ J x	♣ Q 9 x x

On borderline hands, where the choice is between opening with one of a suit and two of a suit, *the weak two bid, in any seat, should be given preference over an opening bid of one.*

The responder to a weak two bid may choose to pass, to build the obstructive barrier higher, or to take constructive action. A pass is recommended on a weak hand lacking either a powerful suit of its own or a fit with partner, or on a hand of medium strength when game by either partnership appears unlikely (i.e., there is no need to try for game or to obstruct the opponents).

Possible obstructionist actions include:

1. a single raise, pre-emptive
2. a double raise, pre-emptive (can also be strong)
3. a simple change of suits, a sign-off
4. a call of two no-trump, *forcing* (it can denote either a strong hand, or it can be a bluff bid)

The above obstructionist actions often lead the way to chicanery. For example, a change of suit, even if it is a nonforcing sign-off, can profitably be used as a psychic. To illustrate:

Partner bids *two hearts,* not vulnerable. On the above hand, Bulldog recommends a two-spade response! It is assumed that the opponents have at least a game, probably a slam, and that if two spades is played and goes down as many as eight (minus 400), the minus score will still be less than what the opponents could have scored by taking the bid. Of course, if the opponents double, the responder will scurry back to the haven of a heart contract.

In the Roth-Stone and Kaplan-Sheinwold Systems, the simple change of suit response is a force, but is also used for psychic purposes. Bulldog (like Stayman) prefers the nonforcing style primarily for one major reason: it enables the responder to "correct" to a better contract. For example, responder can bid two spades over two hearts with a hand such as:

♠ K Q J 10 x x
♥ x
♦ A x x
♣ x x x

Although there are several constructive actions that the partner of the weak two bidder can take, one is unique to Bulldog. This is the artificial, forcing two no-trump response and the opener's rebids to it. This two no-trump bid is made with most hands that require further information from the opening bidder. (As noted above, it can also be used as a bluff bid.) Opener has the following rebids available:

1. three clubs with a minimum
2. three diamonds with a minimum (but not the requirements for #3 and #4, below)
3. three hearts after having opened two spades, to show a maximum and the ace or the guarded king in hearts
4. three of the originally bid major suit with a minimum in shape (distribution)

D. *The Kaplan-Sheinwold Justification for the Employment of the Weak Two Bid*

Just as their modern revolutionary contemporaries have done, Kaplan and Sheinwold have accepted the weak two bid as a most practical weapon, and have integrated this bid into their system. As in the other systems, the two club opening is reserved for their big hands; the two-diamond, two-heart, and two-spade openings are all weak. The requirements for their weak two bid are approximately the same as in the other systems:

1. 9–11 points, including distribution, with no more and no less than 1½ to 2 quick tricks (AK-2; AQ-1½; A-1; KQ-1; Kx-½).
2. The suit must be *exactly* 6 cards in length, and it must be semisolid: playable opposite a singleton in partner's hand.

To illustrate:

♠ K Q J x x x
♥ K x x
♦ x x
♣ x x

This is a typical two-spade opening. One would just as soon keep the opponents out of the auction; but if they bid, partner can count on you for a trick or two on defense.

In response to the weak two bid, any new suit by responder is a one-round force, as in the two no-trump response; the raise of opener's suit (2H . . . Pass . . . *3H*) is pre-emptive; a direct jump to game in opener's suit (2S . . . Pass . . . *4S*) can denote either the ability to make a game, or it can be pre-emptive. That is, if partner opens with two spades, a raise to four spades is recommended on:

♠ A 10 x x
♥ x
♦ x x
♣ J x x x x

The pre-emptive four-spade response leaves as little room as possible for the adversaries to find their best spot.

All the above is with reference to first- and second-hand weak two bids, made before partner has passed. Third or fourth weak two bids can be quite unorthodox; for no longer are you trying to describe your hand to partner, who figures to pass no matter what you have. The prime purpose of the weak two bid in third and fourth position is to impede the opponents; and, as a consequence, the suit bid can be quite ragged, and the point-count normally required in first or second position fades into oblivion (until the next deal).

Actually, the prime criterion in third or fourth position for deciding whether a hand should be opened with a weak two bid is the character of the opposition. "Book" bids are superseded by one's judgment—and the urge to live dangerously often finds its outlet in third or fourth position. For example, the following is a recommended opening two-spade bid in third position.

♠ K J x x x x
♥ x x
♦ A 10 x x
♣ x

As first or second hand, one would pass the above because of the raggedness of the suit; he would fear that the hand might play better in a different suit. But once partner has passed, one's sole concern should be to buy the hand cheaply, or to disrupt the opponents' communication, not to find his own maximum contract.

2. THE WEAK JUMP OVERCALL

Since the origin of contract bridge, the jump overcall (1H . . . 2S) has always portrayed a strong hand. When this bid is made, partner is invited to go on with 1-plus honor tricks or roughly 6 points. The type of hand with which this strong jump overcall is made in standard practice is this:

1. Over an opening bid of 1D, overcall with 2S on:

♠ A Q 10 9 x x x
♥ x
♦ x x
♣ A K x

2. Over an opening bid of 1S, overcall with 3C on:

♠ x x
♥ Q x
♦ K J
♣ A K Q J x x x

A. *The Roth-Stone Justification for the Employment of the Weak Jump Overcall*

Since the above-described specific types of holdings were rarely possessed in the overcalling seat, Roth and Stone felt that the strong jump overcall (like the strong two bid) was a wasted bid; for either (1) their supersound nonjump overcall or (2) the take-out double followed by a strong rebid by the doubler could adequately describe the strong, standard jump-overcall type of holding possessed by the person in the overcalling seat. Why not then (they felt) adapt the jump overcall to denote the far more frequently occurring weak type of overcalling hand?

Here are some illustrations of the Roth-Stone weak jump overcall. The opening bid is *one diamond,* vulnerable. You, second hand, nonvulnerable, hold:

(1)	(2)	(3)
♠ x x	♠ A Q 10 x x x	♠ Q 10 9 x x x
♥ x	♥ x x	♥ x
♦ K 10 x x	♦ x	♦ x x
♣ Q J 10 x x x	♣ x x x x	♣ Q J x x
Bid 3C	Bid 2S	Bid 2S

Requirements for the Weak Jump Overcall

Nonvulnerable	*Vulnerable*
1. A maximum of 9 points in high cards.	1. A maximum of 11 points in high cards.
2. The strength *usually* concentrated in the suit bid.	2. The strength concentrated in the suit bid.
3. A reasonable expectation of winning within 4 tricks of the pre-emptive contract.	3. A reasonable expectation of winning within 3 tricks of the pre-emptive contract (within 2 tricks if opponents are non-vulnerable).
4. A probable broken suit and a warning to partner to avoid doubling or bidding further except at his own risk.	4. A reasonably good suit.

Actually, there are quite a few valid and cogent reasons for the use of the jump overcall to describe a weak hand rather than a strong hand. First, it enables the bridge player to exercise great liberties without promising high cards. He is permitted to bid on hands with which he is ordinarily required to pass—and this becomes a virtue if partner is not misled and the partnership remains on relatively safe ground; and, secondly, it results in unnatural free bids by the opponents who refuse to stay "fixed" and are goaded into unwarranted positive action; thirdly, it disrupts or destroys the opponents' lines of communication; and, fourthly, it gives the partner a fairly accurate picture of the pre-emptive two-bidder's hand, serving as both a warning and as a guide for a premature sacrifice.

B. *The Stayman Justification for the Employment of the Weak Jump Overcall*

As an illustration of Sam Stayman's realistic approach to bidding, one has but to reflect for a moment on his statement that every bid is a compromise. He fully recognizes that any specific type of bid is effective on certain occasions, but at the same time the bid removes from one's repertory another bid that could be equally effective; and, in such case, one has to decide which of the alternative bids is more frequent in occurrence, and to utilize the more frequent bid as the more practicable bid. Simultaneously, it becomes necessary to eliminate the more infrequent bid if one is to reap the maximum benefits of the more useful bid. This was the criterion used when Stayman and his teammates abandoned the strength-showing jump overcall (1H . . . 2S) so as to use the jump overcall for pre-emptive purposes. As early as the first World Championships in 1950 (won by the United States) this revolutionary weak jump overcall was used to good effect by Sam Stayman.

Mr. Stayman's point of view on this subject can be observed in the following quotations from his book:

Currently, most players use the same methods to show a good hand when an opponent opens the bidding: they double informatorily, overcall in notrump, or make a jump overcall. This is splendid in theory, except that it keeps a fine bidding tool on a part-time job. We have found that there are few occasions to use the jump overcall with a good hand. And even when these occasions have arisen, a double followed by a suit bid has done the job as well or better. Since the jump overcall could not earn its keep as a strength-showing device, we have assigned a function to it that puts it to work more frequently and usefully. We use the single-jump overcall (1D . . . 2S, etc.):

(1) as a pre-emptive bid with equal vulnerability, or when the opponents are vulnerable and we are not.

(2) to show a good hand when we are vulnerable against nonvulnerable opponents.[3]

Whether the uninitiated reader approves of this weak bid or not, the fact is that Stayman, Schenken, Helen Sobel, John Crawford, George Rapee, etc., all consider it as a most potent and practical weapon. Since each of these players is a high-stakes rubber-bridge player, in addition to being a top-flight tournament player, it must be assumed that if their employment of the weak jump overcall had been demonstrated to be ill-advised, they would have relegated it to the scrap heap a long time ago. Not only have they not done so, but they seem to have grown more enamoured of it.

C. *The Bulldog Justification for the Employment of the Weak Jump Overcall*

A jump overcall to the two-level (1C . . 2S) and a direct jump in the opponents' suit (1D . . . 3D) are pre-emptive bids made on weak hands, regardless of vulnerability. The primary function of these bids is to harass and/or create chaos. To attain this end, they usurp the normal avenues of bidding communication. They require only that one possess sufficient trick-taking power in distribution to avoid a cataclysmic defeat. As an example, a non-vulnerable overcall of 2S over 1C is warranted on these hands:

♠ Q J x x x x	♠ K J 10 9 x x
♥ x x	♥ x
♦ K J 10	♦ J x x x
♣ x x	♣ x x

Note that each of the above hands approximates a weak two bid. However, any single jump overcall to the *three-level* denotes a strong hand. These bids are strongly invitational to a three no-trump or a major suit game. To illustrate:

(1)	(2)
♠ x x x	♠ x x
♥ K x	♥ A Q J 10 x x
♦ x	♦ Q 10
♣ A K J 10 x x x	♣ A Q x

[3] Stayman: *op. cit.*

(1) Over an opening 1S bid, jump to *3C*.

(2) Over an opening 1S bid, jump to *3H*.

All multi-jump overcall (1D . . . *3S;* 1H . . . *4C,* etc.) are pre-emptive and disruptive. For example, over an opening one-diamond bid, a nonvulnerable jump overcall of *three spades* is recommended with:

♠ K Q 10 x x x x

♥ x x x

♦ x

♣ J x

With another spade, or with the addition of the queen of clubs at the expense of a red card (Q J x of clubs), *four spades* would become the proper jump overcall.

D. *The Kaplan-Sheinwold Justification for the Employment of the Weak Jump Overcall*

As in the three other modern systems, the simple jump (1D . . . 2S) overcall is a weak pre-emptive bid. No point-count requirements are set for this type of overcall, since it is a tactical gambling bid rather than a descriptive one; and judgment—reinforced by knowledge derived from experience—becomes the key factor in determining if and when the bid should be used. Nevertheless, the lack of a mathematical mandate does not result in any mis-conception as to the type of hand required for the bid; nor does this lack lead to the abuse of the bid by its systemic wielders. Of course, correct tactical deployment of the pre-emptive jump overcall does necessitate a perceptive understanding of the authors' purpose in integrating this bid into their system. I trust the brief presentation that follows will give the reader some insight into the prime intent and practical functioning of the weak jump overcall—but if it doesn't, their book will.

The weak jump overcall puts partner on notice immediately that the overcaller is not looking for game. As a result, one does not have to worry that partner will get him into trouble. Also, the jump overcall makes it easier for partner to sacrifice against an enemy game contract, since the bid guarantees that the defensive strength of the hand is limited. And, most important, the weak pre-emptive jump bid does a most effective job of disrupting the opponents' communication. As an example, let us examine the following hand:

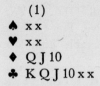

(1)
♠ x x
♥ x x
♦ Q J 10
♣ K Q J 10 x x

Your right-hand opponent opens with *one spade*. If it disturbs you to pass—well, it should. But what do you accomplish by overcalling with two clubs—other than to put partner into a guessing situation as to whether you have a really good hand, an intermediate type of overcalling hand, or whether you're overcalling to direct a lead? Would you not have bid two clubs with each of the following hands?

(2)	(3)	(4)
♠ x x	♠ x x	♠ x x x
♥ x x	♥ A Q x	♥ A
♦ K J x	♦ x x	♦ A x x
♣ A K Q J x x	♣ A Q J x x x	♣ K Q 10 x x x

How can your partner possibly know, if you make a two-club overcall with each of the above four hands, whether you're interested in a game or are merely making a nuisance bid? Furthermore, and most important, a two-club overcall over one spade on Hand (1) takes away little bidding room, but a *three*-club overcall robs the enemy of one full level, and a crucial level at that.

Isn't it your desire on Hand (1) to deprive the opponents of bidding space, while at the same time to inform partner that you possess a pretty bad hand? Surely, the jump to three clubs accomplishes your objectives perfectly. Hence, the three-club overcall, as a concretization of the Kaplan-Sheinwold principle that one should jump with the weaker hand to crowd the bidding for the opponents, and to go slow with the stronger hand to leave the partnership more space for investigation. As always, there is a risk in this—but experience has demonstrated the long-run efficiency of this principle.

How does one determine whether to make a simple overcall or a jump overcall? The solution lies in the answer to the question one should pose: "Why am I in the bidding?" If you want to bid because there is a genuine prospect that the hand belongs to your side, possibly for a game—as on Hands (2), (3), and (4) above— then make the simple nonjump overcall. But if you want to bid in order to jam up the opponents' communication, or to find a sacrifice, then jump. As was mentioned, there are no hard-and-fast rules governing overcalls; it is up to one's judgment. As a matter of fact, many hands are susceptible to both treatments. For example, you hold:

♠ x x
♥ x x
♦ K Q J 10 x x
♣ A x x

If you are in second seat, and the first-hand opponent opens with one heart, it is probably best to bid two diamonds. Admittedly, this is a skinny overcall, but there is a decent chance that partner may have sufficient controls in the side suits to produce three no-trump.

But if you are in third or fourth seat, and your opponent opens with one heart, the situation has changed. Partner is now a passed hand, and it is much less likely that he can produce the stoppers and tricks required to make three no-trump. With your prospects for game having diminished appreciably, *three diamonds* now becomes the recommended bid, to take advantage of the pre-emptive value of the jump.

As a general criterion, one can guide himself by quick tricks in determining whether a hand calls for pre-emptive jump overcalls or not. With 2½ quick tricks or more, one should almost never use the pre-emptive jump (if you do, partner will be misled as to your defensive strength). It is with hands that contain a maximum of 1½ quick tricks, plus considerable playing strength distributionally, that constitute the ideal weak jump overcalling hands. As with all pre-emptive bids, the pattern to look for is offensive, not defensive, strength.

The partner of the pre-emptive overcaller has an easy job, for which he is well paid if his guiding slogan is "speech is silver, silence is golden." When a weak jump overcall is made, it must be remembered that the overcaller does not want to hear from his partner. He is not describing his hand to you for you to take action based on his bid. The primary, if not exclusive, aim of his bid is to prevent the adversaries from proceeding to their best contract at their own leisurely pace. He has usurped the space normally reserved for the good-card holders, possibly at great risk. To take away the opponents' bidding room, he is deliberately overbidding, gambling against a double. And if the next opponent does not double, partner has won his gamble!

So, unless you have absolutely clear-cut action to take, pass and be content with whatever advantage partner's bid had given your side. Don't penalize partner for making a weak bid—if you do, he'll learn to hate you.

In my opinion, there is no doubt whatsoever as to the practicability of the weak jump overcall as a quality substitute for the strong jump overcall. Nor, for that matter, is there any doubt in my mind about the practicability of the weak two bid as a replacement for the strong two bid, if one reserves the use of the opening two-club bid as a forcing bid. If there are any fundamental disadvantages to either of these bids—and to all the weakness bids—they lie in human frailty: its users too often deviate from the prescribed limits of the bids; that is, its users cannot contain themselves at times and frequently make a weak jump overcall (or open a weak two bid) on hands that are either too good or not good enough, thereby achieving great success in misleading partner. Thus, if there are any serious faults in the weak jump overcall or the weak two bid, the blame should be attributed to the sins of the users rather than to the sins of the bids themselves.

3. THE WEAK NO-TRUMP (12–14 POINTS)

A. *The Stayman Justification for the Employment of the Weak No-trump*[4]

Sam Stayman points out that the opening bid of one no-trump is one of the most respected weapons in the arsenal of an offensive pair.

---

[4] The Roth-Stone System does not employ the weak no-trump. The Bulldog System employs the weak no-trump only when not vulnerable. When vulnerable, Bulldog employs a 17–19 point no-trump, as opposed to the standard 16–18 point no-trump.

Even when the bid requires no greater strength than the opening suit-bid, the initial no-trump call somehow cows the adversaries and keeps them silent. Traditionally, the initial bid of one no-trump had denoted a hand of more than nominal opening strength. During the past decade, the accepted point-count requirement for the one no-trump opening bid has been 16–18 points. When the bid of one no-trump carries the authority of so much count, there is sufficient reason for the opponents to lean back in their chairs and ponder only about what suit to open against the final contract. For with so much strength massed in one hand, and the other partner an unknown force to be reckoned with, the chances of scoring a game against a strong no-trump opening bid are extremely slight.

There are, of course, certain disadvantages to the opening bid of one no-trump. By-passing, as it does, the entire bidding space of the one-level, it makes approach bidding all but impossible. There is also the danger that the opening may be exposed to severe penalties if the opponents possess the major share of the remaining high cards. But this is a hazard that can be discounted, not because it does not exist, but because it lurks in every decision to embark on a bidding journey. Certainly the risk in bidding is warranted by the game or slam bonus which is the bidder's objective. The opening bid of one no-trump has great intimidating value, and the barrier set up against the opponents is difficult to surmount because it involves substantial risk for the player who is sufficiently daring to challenge for possession of the bidding field. In experience, one cannot help but agree that the advantages of the 16–18 point no-trump far outweigh its disadvantages.

Nevertheless, there is also much to be said for establishing the strength of the opening no-trump bid at 12–14 points (the weak no-trump). At first glance, it may appear that a bid of one no-trump with a hand no stronger than an opening suit-bid of one is insupportable. But, on analysis, many sound reasons can be revealed to buttress the claims of those who hold it to be a most effective bidding tool.

As against the argument that it exposes the bidder to serious penalty is the answer that the bid makes contention difficult for the opponents who must step into the auction at the two-level. The adversary who sits to the left of an opening no-trump knows that if he bids, he may find himself caught between a sledge hammer and an anvil, and the loss may be tremendous. But if he passes, he may be surrendering with a hand that might yield game. The opponent to the right is no better off, for even when responder has passed the bid of one no-trump, there is no assurance that he does not hold 11 or 12 points, in which case the defenders will be exposing their necks to decapitation if they construe his silence as a display of weakness.

The 12–14 point no-trump has practical advantages other than its pre-emptive value. The one-level is ordinarily employed for the investigation of hand distributions, the aim being to uncover a trump suit—preferably a major—in which the partnership stands its best chance of producing a game or a part-score. When the bidding starts at the very lowest level—at one club, for example—a great deal of information may be exchanged by two players before they have reached one no-trump, the terminal point of the one-level. This is all highly desirable when exploration is necessary, because the players have distributions that require delineation. But there is one great disadvantage to the initial low-level bid. It permits an opponent to make an overcall on a hand of marginal strength, and this liberty of action that he enjoys leads frequently to a bidding contest that puts the opening bidder and his partner out of business.

No great harm results from competition when the defenders are badly outclassed, because the offensive pair will simply ignore the defenders and continue on its way to a selected contract. When, however, the division of wealth is such that it does not give the opener and his partner a decisive superiority, there is a tremendous advantage in being able to keep the opponents silent. The opening bid of one no-trump accomplishes this many times when an opening suit bid of one might not. Confronted with the necessity of entering at the two level if he wishes to contest, and aware of the fact that opener's partner may be waiting to ambush him, the defender may decide that it is safer to stay out of the bidding and await more promising days. Thus, many hands will be purchased economically by the declarant pair. And often, when he feels reluctant to sit back with a strong hand, the defender will step out into the two level to be entrapped by two strong hands.

The opening bid of one no-trump, based on a balanced hand of

12–14 points, has little or no distributional assistance to offer partner. Almost invariably, the opener would rebid one no-trump if he were to open with a suit bid of one. By bidding one no-trump at once, he informs his partner that his 12–14 points are in high cards scattered throughout the four suits. This makes penalty action by responder a lot easier when an overcall intervenes, for he need not fear that a large part of the opener's hand will be valueless defensively. Another advantage is that makable no-trump contracts at game may be reached when the combined hands hold 25 points divided almost evenly between the two hands, neither one of which contains a full opening bid.

There is, of course, greater risk in the 12–14 no-trump than in the 16–18 point one, but this apparent greater susceptibility to penalties is largely illusory. If responder has 6 points, the pair would have reached one no-trump had opener bid one of a suit; and if the responder has less than 6 points, a pass to an opening suit-bid would have revealed opener's plight, and exposed him to what might have been a severe penalty. The opening bid of one no-trump provides a certain amount of protection when the responder is very weak. Since his pass may contain as much as 11 points, the opponent who bids after him cannot tell whether the responder was just short of game strength or has a very poor hand. Furthermore, if the opponents do take penalty action, responder may frequently be able to rescue when he holds a 5- or 6-card suit, with the assurance that opener will furnish some consolidating strength in his suit.

The Stayman System takes the position in the center of the two popular no-trump standards by advocating the use of either or both. Not vulnerable, the requirements may be set at 12–14; vulnerable, 16–18 points. With this dual range, one may enjoy the advantage of the weak no-trump as a barrier when the risks of penalty are slight; and take refuge in the strong no-trump when punishment may be severe.[5]

It is not Stayman's intent to foist either no-trump range on any bridge player. He points out that there is much to be said for the

[5] During the past two years, Mr. Stayman has modified these ranges somewhat, and is currently testing these new ranges in competitive play. Vulnerable, he is employing the range of 15–17 points in all positions. Not vulnerable, in first, second, and fourth positions, 12–14; in third position, 11–14, or 10–14 with a 5-card club suit.

employment of either standard to the exclusion of the other throughout his system; and he urges the student to use whichever no-trump
seems best suited to his style and temperament. Another Stayman
suggestion strikes me as being a most logical compromise: to use
the weak no-trump at matchpoint (duplicate) play, where a bottom
on one board is offset by a top on another regardless of the swing
in total points; and to use either the weak or the strong no-trump
according to vulnerability conditions when total points (rubber
bridge) govern the play.

In Stayman's opinion, if he were forced at gun-point to choose
one range to the exclusion of the other, he would select the weak
no-trump as the more effective, and as the no-trump calculated to
give greater mobility to the offensive pair.

B. *The Kaplan-Sheinwold Justification for the Employment of the Weak No-trump*

The very core of the Kaplan-Sheinwold System is the weak no-
trump opening. According to the authors, with their disciples serving
as corroborative statistical witnesses, about one out of every four
hands is opened with one no-trump!

Before discussing the reason that the authors have established the
weak no-trump as the System's foundation, and the advantages and
disadvantages of the bid, let us define the bid and the situations in
which it is used: The weak no-trump *must be bid* on all balanced
hands which contain 12–14 high-card points. It is used in all positions, at all times, regardless of vulnerability conditions.

By a balanced hand is meant, specifically, either a 4-3-3-3 distribution, a 4-4-3-2 distribution, or a 5-3-3-2 distribution *if* the 5-card
suit is a minor suit. The doubleton, in either the 4-4-3-2 or 5-3-3-2,
may well consist of nothing more than x x.

To illustrate the weak no-trump:

♠ A K x x	♠ K x	♠ K x x
♥ J 10 x	♥ Q 10 x	♥ x x x
♦ A x x	♦ Q 10 x x	♦ A Q x x x
♣ x x x	♣ A J x x	♣ K x

There is just one exception to the statement that "the weak no-
trump *must be bid*": one may, if he desires, *pass* a bare 12-point

hand if he is vulnerable and the opponents are not; but under no circumstances may this type of hand be opened with one of a suit.

What are the advantages of the weak no-trump which have resulted in its being established as the base of the Kaplan-Sheinwold System? Why has the system eliminated, as an opening bid, the strong 16–18 point no-trump and replaced it with the weak 12–14 point no-trump?[6] Here are their reasons:

1. Since the weak no-trump type of hand occurs about once in every four deals, and the strong no-trump only about once in every 15 or so deals, there is certainly great logic in employing the weak no-trump for its pre-emptive effect if the results are demonstrated to be more beneficial. Putting it another way, one needs the pre-emptive effect of the one no-trump opening on bad hands, not on the good ones which can always be handled with consummate ease. This is in line with the Kaplan-Sheinwold principle of using high bids for weak hands and low bids for strong hands whenever this principle can be followed with reasonable safety. In the opinion of the authors, the weak no-trump has become an ideal pre-emptive type of bid. If the opponents wish to compete, they must enter the bidding at the two level, which is certainly more dangerous than coming in at the one level.

2. It facilitates the handling of the 4-3-3-3, 4-4-3-2, and 5-3-3-2 top-heavy hand that one frequently passed because no convenient or economic rebid existed. For example:

(a)	(b)	(c)	(d)
♠ A K x x	♠ Q x x	♠ A x x x	♠ x x
♥ A x x	♥ Q x x	♥ J x x	♥ Q x x
♦ J 10 x	♦ K Q x x	♦ x x x x	♦ A K x x x
♣ x x x	♣ A x x	♣ A K	♣ K x x

The advantage of opening the above hands with one no-trump is this: it affords a satisfactory method of opening certain 12–13

---

[6] We are not discussing here the relative merits of the weak no-trump (12–14) versus the strong no-trump (16–18). This subject was examined in the preceding section, with Stayman analyzing the pros and cons. However, lest the reader develop the feeling that the strong no-trump has been retired, let me state that in the Kaplan-Sheinwold System, they have a precise way of showing—via opener's rebid—the type of hand that standard American bidding opens with one no-trump. The latter is described a few pages hence.

point hands which would (1) otherwise have to be passed, or (2) even if they were uncomfortably opened with one of a suit, would be rebid one no-trump anyway, leading to the same contract but giving the opponents the opportunity of bidding at the one level. Not only is this pre-emptive advantage attained via the one no-trump opening, but it enables partner to become the captain of the team, thereby making for simple controlled bidding, since responder has quite accurate private knowledge of the combined strength and distribution held by his side. Many hands are thus played at a safe one no-trump contract, and quite a few risky two no-trump contracts are avoided. In addition, it achieves the pre-emptive advantage claimed for the weak two bid without encountering the difficulties that are sometimes faced by partner in handling the latter.

3. The weak no-trump opening capitalizes on the limit-bid theory explicitly. Partner will not disturb the no-trump (in quest of a game) unless he has at least 12 points. If he bids a suit at the two level, then he is obviously looking for a better contract with an unbalanced hand. The responses of two diamonds, two hearts, and two spades to one no-trump are all sign-offs, and command a pass from opener. The two-club response is the Stayman Convention.

4. Danger is created for a protective reopening by fourth hand after two passes, due to the fact that opener's partner may easily be lying in ambush with 10 or 11 points after passing to his partner's opening one no-trump bid.

5. Psychologically, the phrase *weak no-trump* often induces an adversary to overcall on a shaky holding, giving the responder a chance for a good penalty double. On the other hand, good players have learned that it is foolish to overcall a 16–18 point no-trump, knowing that since it is almost impossible to score a game against this bid, it's a bad risk to stick one's neck out for a partial at best. This is in line with a disadvantage of the strong no-trump: it warns the opponents not to commit suicide; and thus, the chief source of substantial gains, the penalty double, is lost.

6. A cumulative pre-emptive situation is built up when the opening no-trumper's partner responds with two of a suit, especially a major. While the opening bidder must pass this response, still it may

contain from 0–11 points; and thus, a defensive bidder might be walking into as many as 25 adversely held points, sometimes at the three level. Conversely, failure to compete may allow the sign-off bidder to take a cheap sacrifice, while the defenders could make a partial, or even game, with a possible combined holding of up to 28 points.

7. The opening no-trumper's partner enjoys an advantage in defensive play, and finds numerous penalty-double situations where this advantage pays off.

8. The weak no-trump dovetails perfectly with the accepted concept—by Culbertson, Goren, and all the other experts—that the best place to play a mediocre hand is at one no-trump. With an ordinary hand, the responder will pass; and the opposition will be in the dark as to the distribution and lie of the cards. The partnership should always reach the best contract at the two level. With strong hands, the bidding is also greatly facilitated, since responder knows opener has exactly 12–14 high-card points.

9. The no-trump opening will tend to inhibit a no-trump game by the opposition even though they have a sound play for that contract. The opponents will be psychologically deterred from making the no-trump bid after that denomination has been first named by the opening bidder. This will hold true even against the finest players; and unless the adversaries understand completely the balance-of-power principle, they will find themselves playing part-score contracts when they ought to be in game.

10. There is the unique advantage of more successfully playing many close contracts in no-trump, due to the strength being fairly evenly divided between the opening no-trumper and his partner. It has been found that, probably due to excellent communication facilities between the two hands, more actual tricks can be developed from the same number of points than is the case when the preponderance of the strength is concentrated in one hand.

11. And, lastly, but of prime importance, there is a justifiable implication of a sound hand when the opening bid is one of a suit rather than one no-trump. This is neither the time nor the place to discuss and analyze the systemic coordination of the opening bid of one in a suit with opener's various types of rebids, or to illustrate how responder's apparently unorthodox rebids are actually logical

and sound.[7] One major example should clearly demonstrate how the use of the weak no-trump as the system's key opening bid has drastically (and dramatically) altered many time-honored concepts regarding the significance of opener's first rebid.

Look at the two following bidding sequences:

	(1)				(2)	
N		*S*		*N*		*S*
1 ♣		1 ♥		1 ♦		1 ♠
1 NT				*1 NT*		

In standard American bidding, throughout the ages, the above one no-trump rebid has always denoted a minimum opening bid which was made on a balanced hand. But in the Kaplan-Sheinwold System, this interpretation is impossible, for if opener had a minimum balanced hand he would have opened with the weak no-trump (12–14)! Hence, in the Kaplan-Sheinwold System, the one no-trump rebid by opener shows 15–17 points, within a balanced hand.[8] Obviously, the Kaplan-Sheinwold responder now requires fewer points than in standard systems to make a second forward-going response. All these necessary readjustments between opener and responder have, of course, been carefully studied and observed in practice, and the finished products have become embodied into the system as new, modern, iconoclastic concepts.

Let us now turn our attention to the presumed detrimental aspects of the weak no-trump.

The prime objection to the use of the weak no-trump in all positions regardless of vulnerability is that the bid, when made while vulnerable, is too easy to double for penalties and to punish severely. In theory, this seems to be a justifiable criticism, and one could create thousands of hypothetical illustrative hands where a vulnerable weak no-trump bidder is punished severely for his "sin." But, in actual practice, it seldom happens. The unbelievably few severe

---

[7] For those who are interested in learning all the precise details of the functioning of the Kaplan-Sheinwold System, they can be studied in the system book, *How to Play Winning Bridge* (op cit.).

[8] When opener has a balanced hand containing 18–20 points, he will tend to jump to two no-trump. Thus, opener's *rebid* of either one no-trump or two no-trump takes care of all hands which, in standard practice, are opened with a strong no-trump (16–18 points).

penalties taken in many years of experimentation[9] with the weak no-trump is due to various safety factors which are available. One of these is the rescue by responder or opener in a 5-card or longer suit. Another is the exclusive use of the redouble by either partner as an SOS after an opposing double and penalty pass. Still another is the fact that reopening doubles are risky, for if the opening bidder's partner has the balance of strength, he will be waiting with the ax over the forced response of the doubler's partner. And still another is the immediate resort to the Stayman Convention by responder even when the latter has a horrible hand, the intent being to ward off the impending doom which would otherwise surely envelop him. When the outstanding high-card strength—even to the extent of 26 points—is more or less evenly divided in the opponents' hands, neither of them can afford to step in with assurance, for the Stayman bidder *may* have a fair hand. Even when the use of the Stayman Convention has been revealed as a phony—by the user passing the opener's response, whether it be two diamonds, two hearts, or two spades—the partnership will be in a suit, and suits are always harder to double for penalties since neither of the opponents usually has trumps stacked against the bidder. Thus the weak no-trumper's team generally escapes unscathed. Here is a typical illustration of the above, taken from the author's book:

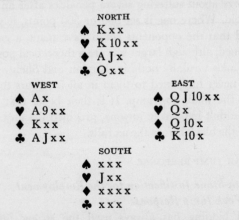

```
                        NORTH
                        ♠ K x x
                        ♥ K 10 x x
                        ♦ A J x
                        ♣ Q x x
        WEST                            EAST
        ♠ A x                           ♠ Q J 10 x x
        ♥ A 9 x x                       ♥ Q x
        ♦ K x x                         ♦ Q 10 x
        ♣ A J x x                       ♣ K 10 x
                        SOUTH
                        ♠ x x x
                        ♥ J x x
                        ♦ x x x x
                        ♣ x x x
```

[9] Not only by the weak no-trump predecessors of Kaplan and Sheinwold and their disciples, but by dozens of our contemporary top-flight experts and their disciples in the United States and Europe.

NORTH	EAST	SOUTH	WEST
1 NT	Pass	2 ♣	Pass
2 ♥	Pass	Pass	Double
Pass	2 ♠	Pass	2 NT
Pass	3 NT	Pass	Pass
Pass			

It will be observed that if South had passed one no-trump, West would have doubled. This would have been left in by East, and any subsequent retreat to a suit, or an SOS redouble by North or South, would then have been doubled also. But when South promptly bid the Stayman two clubs, he created a situation in which West's later double of North's two-heart contract announced not heart strength, but general overall strength. In this situation, East, in order to leave the double in, needed heart strength specifically—and he didn't have it. East and West, of course, bid and made three no-trump, but they lost a chance to inflict a disastrous penalty on the weak no-trumper's side.

Just as one swallow doesn't make a summer, so one illustration doesn't prove or disprove a theory. Nevertheless, it is the opinion of the weak no-trumpers—based on many swallows and many illustrations from life—that if one is reasonably agile, there is no need to worry about suffering severe penalties after an opening one no-trump bid. Where one is set 300 or 500 points, it will generally be revealed that the opponents could have made a game. And, as was mentioned, although larger sets are a theoretical possibility when responder holds virtually nothing, Kaplan and Sheinwold maintain that it has never happened to them in all the years that they have been using the weak no-trump. It is their belief that major catastrophes shouldn't happen to anyone, provided the user learns to get his neck off the block before the ax falls.

4. THE WEAK JUMP RESPONSE

A. *The Roth-Stone Justification for the Employment of the Weak Jump Response*

Standard bidding has always used the strong jump response (1D . . . 2S) to denote a magnificent hand that guaranteed at least a game, and in contemporary times has been considered by most players as a slam try. Roth and Stone, however, feel that the weak jump response has greater utility than does the strong jump response. Here is the type of hand with which Roth-Stoners make a weak jump-shift response:

Partner opens with one diamond, and you bid *two hearts* with the following hand:

♠ x x
♥ Q J 9 x x x
♦ x
♣ x x x x

Their reasons for employing the weak jump-shift response are these: scientific bidding has progressed to a point where it is comparatively simple to bid the good hands without using the strong jump-shift response. However, serious problems still arise with (1) hands containing a long suit but fewer than 6 points, and (2) hands with a suitable first-round response but no adequate rebid. In the opinion of Roth and Stone, the weak jump-shift response provides practical assistance to the holders of hands of these two types, while taking care of the tremendous responding hands by normal bidding means.

The Roth-Stone requirements for the weak jump-shift response are:

1. not more than 6 points in high cards
2. a 6-card or longer suit, or a fairly good 5-card suit (if the latter, only at the two level—not at the three level)
3. usually no more than 2 cards in partner's suit, particularly if the latter's suit is a major suit

It is my belief that the weak jump-shift response as a substitute for the strong jump-shift response is a less effective weapon. First, it is recognized and accepted by most authorities that the precise type of holding required for the weak jump-shift response occurs quite infrequently as compared with the strong jump-shift slam-try type of holding. It is admitted, of course, that hands of the latter type do not arise too often either. But when the powerful responding hands do present themselves, the immediate strong jump-shift response identifies slam aspirations; and generally, not only is the bidding of a small or a grand slam facilitated but also the partnership can stop at game instead of winding up at five hearts or five spades that might be in jeopardy.

While the Roth-Stone contention that scientific bidding has progressed to a point where it is comparatively simple to bid the good hands without using the strong jump-shift response is true—*if* the scientific bidding is performed by scientists—as yet the masses have not reached the stage where they are capable of scientific, inferential, delicate-judgment bidding. Therefore, to replace a weapon that is efficient within its intended range by a weapon that seems to provide no appreciable advantage considering its infrequency of use, is to substitute harassing and annoying of the enemy at the expense of attacking them and beating their brains out via the bidding of a slam.

That the employment of the weak jump-shift response rather than the strong jump-shift response is not justified at the present stage of bridge's development seems to be confirmed by the fact that neither Stayman nor Kaplan-Sheinwold has seen fit to embody this bid into their systems; they have preserved the strong jump-shift response as an aggressive weapon.

B. *The Bulldog Justification for the Employment of the Weak Jump Response*

In the Bulldog System, as in Roth-Stone, the jump-shift response is a pre-emptive bid used to denote a weak hand and a long suit. However, there is one exception: *the nonvulnerable three-club response,* which shows a strong hand and which is forcing even if the opener has psyched (this bid will be discussed in the section which follows, on psychic opening bids). Vulnerable, the three-club response is a natural pre-empt, as are all other jump-shift responses. Here is an example of the weak jump-shift response. Partner opens *one heart,* vulnerable or not vulnerable, and responder holds:

♠ x x
♥ J x
♦ Q J 9 x x x x
♣ x x

Bid 3D

In the opinion of the authors, the weak jump-shift response is a powerful harassing weapon which is not only an effective danger signal and near sign-off for the opener, but also a high hurdle for the opponents to clear should they possess the majority of good cards. With the nonvulnerable three-club response available over opener's possible psychic one-club, one-diamond, one-heart, or one-spade opening, to depict a strong hand, the authors feel that a tremendous advantage accrues to the users of the jump-shift response as a preemptive bid.

5. THE PSYCHIC OPENING BID

Ever since the birth of contract bridge in 1925, the psychic opening bid has been used as a "monkeyshines" bid: its intended result was to deceive the opponents through creating in their minds the illusion that the psychic bidder possessed some specific asset which, in reality, he did not possess. As has been stated, and evidenced, it is highly questionable as to whether the psychic opening succeeded in its purpose as much as half the time. But hope springs eternal; and its wielders, evidently undismayed by the psychic's complete uncertainty of success, have nevertheless employed it throughout the years, whenever the time seemed propitious; or just for a lark, to see what would happen; or to interject some color to counteract a dull run of cards. Sometimes success crowned their efforts, and sometimes dire consequences ensued.

As has been observed, these psychics were, in the main, a hit-or-miss affair, the bidder never knowing until it was all over whether his bid had been beautifully inspirational or downright stupid. But in the Roth-Stone System—and in each of the other modern systems—order and design replaced chaos and anarchy: the psychic opening bid became a controlled or disciplined weapon.

A. *The Roth-Stone Justification for the Employment of the Controlled or Disciplined Opening Psychic Bid*

The Roth-Stone System is the first system that advocates a psychic —an opening bid without the customary requirements—and incorporates this bid into the bidding structure. This bid is *not* designed to deceive the opponents. It is a specialized bid, employed in first or second position, and used to inform partner as to which suit should be led.

Where an opening bid has been demonstrated to be a psychic by opener passing his partner's response (that is, by not providing the "guaranteed" rebid), it has in effect told this story: "I have a psychic. My high cards are mainly in the suit I have bid, and I can stand no other lead."

The requirements for this disciplined bid are:

1. It is made only in first or second position.
2. At least a 4-card suit and 3–6 points in high cards, with the strength concentrated exclusively, or almost exclusively, in the suit bid (no worse than Q 10 x x).
3. A balanced hand with no singleton or void.
4. It is usually made when not vulnerable. A vulnerable psychic is permitted only when the opponents are also vulnerable.

Since the psychic opening is part of the system, the standard responses of two no-trump (13–15) and three no-trump (16–18) have been eliminated, except when the opener's side is vulnerable and the opponents are not. In their place have been substituted the response of two no-trump to show 20–21 points and the response of three no-trump to show 22 or more points.

Unless partner responds with two no-trump or a double raise of opener's suit, the psychic opener must pass at his first opportunity. Over a two no-trump response from partner, if the psycher has a maximum psych (5 or 6 points), he will rebid either three no-trump or three of his suit. If opener has 3 or 4 points (a minimum psych), he will pass. Conversely, over a two no-trump response, any bid by opener *other than three no-trump or a rebid of his suit at the three level,* confirms a legitimate opening. And, with a regulation opening bid, slam is assured after a two or three no-trump response from partner.

The double raise of opener's major suit as constituting a semiforce, even if opener has psyched, is a new extension of the system and is designed, of course, to further protect the responder when the latter holds a tremendous hand (20 or more points) with a fit in opener's suit. Over 1H . . . *3H* or 1S . . . *3S,* opener will pass with a minimum psych. But if opener has 5 or 6 points, he will bid three no-trump, confirming a maximum psych which requires responder to bid a game in the agreed-upon suit: To illustrate:

	You	Partner
You hold:		
♠ A Q 10 9 8	1 ♠	3 ♠
♥ x x	?	
♦ x x x		
♣ x x x		

You will bid three no-trump, which, while confirming a psychic, denotes a maximum holding and shows a willingness to play a game. Partner must now bid four spades.

As to whether the advantages of the Roth-Stone psychic opening outweigh is disadvantages is open to question. But, regardless of how one feels about the practical efficiency of the bid, the fact is that the modern revolutionary systems which came into being after Roth-Stone (Stayman, Bulldog, Kaplan-Sheinwold) have all integrated the opening psychic into their systems of bidding. It must be presumed, then, that since Roth, Stone, Stayman, Hanna, Steen, Kaplan, and Sheinwold are all known to be excellent players—and were so before their systems made their way into print—that they would not have fused the controlled or disciplined psychic opening bid into their systems unless it had proven in experience to be a most practical weapon.

It should be noted that, according to Roth and Stone, the psychic bid should be limited primarily to match-point play (as opposed to rubber-bridge or total-point play) where so much stress is placed on the overtrick and where, should the psychic backfire, the loss is one board and not one's life.

B. *The Stayman Justification for the Employment of the Controlled or Disciplined Opening Psychic Bid*

As a tactical bid, the effectiveness of the psychic opening lies in what it accomplishes, when it succeeds; and when it fails, in the uncertainty it plants in the minds of the adversaries who may, forever after, regard with suspicion every adverse action that has the appearance of irregularity. But the psychic bid, when used intemperately and promiscuously, is an evil; for when it backfires, the losses can be staggering. Yet, as Stayman points out, when it is not used at all, a partnership gives away certain advantages that may make the difference between success and failure.

In the Stayman System, the prepared (controlled or disciplined) psychic opening bid is accepted practice. However, an opening psychic must conform to certain prescribed standards:

1. Only hands containing 3–6 points qualify, of which at least 2 points must be in the suit bid.
2. The suit that is bid must be from 4 to 6 cards in length, preferably at least a 5-carder.
3. The hand must contain no second suit with greater than 4-card length.

By attaching the above specifications, two basic purposes are served. First, if the psychic is discovered and exposed, as is often the case, the bidder's partner may, nevertheless, make the indicated opening lead to strength, so important at no-trumps, and of prime importance in duplicate where every trick saved has significance. Second, a player may occasionally embark on harassing maneuvers without taking the chance that he has made it impossible for his own pair to proceed to a sound contract.

The Stayman System makes allowance for the recognition of an opening psychic bid in situations where the great strength in the responder's hand makes it appear a possibility that the opening bid is not of the genuine, regular, normal variety. Whereas a psychic opener may pass responses that are ordinarily forcing, such as one-over-one, etc., *he is required to respond to a jump-shift response.* The important thing for both members of the partnership is to be made aware directly that the opening bid was a phony.

When an opening bidder has received a jump-shift response, he shows that his opening bid is psychic by making *the cheapest possible rebid in his original suit or no-trump.* For example:

1. SOUTH		2. SOUTH	
♠ K J 10 x x		♠ x x	
♥ x x		♥ K J 10 x x	
♦ x x x		♦ x x x	
♣ x x x		♣ x x x	

SOUTH	NORTH	SOUTH	NORTH
1 ♠	3 ♣	1 ♥	2 ♠
3 ♠		2 NT	

If the opening bid is normal, the rebid is *anything other* than the cheapest rebid in no-trumps or in the original suit. For example:

	1. SOUTH			**2.** SOUTH
♠	A x x		♠	x x
♥	x x		♥	A K J x x
♦	A J 10 x		♦	A Q x
♣	A x x x		♣	x x x

SOUTH	NORTH		SOUTH	NORTH
1 ♦	2 ♥		1 ♥	2 ♠
3 ♣			3 ♥	

As can be observed, the prepared Stayman psychic opening bid is a disciplined bid, and has been developed into a little system of its own. But, as with all bids that are unconventional and untruths, the psychic is a dangerous weapon unless handled with care by both opener and responder. It should not be employed with a partner who is unaccustomed to psychics and does not expect them.

C. *The Bulldog Justification for the Employment of the Controlled or Disciplined Opening Psychic Bid*

For the same reasons as advanced by Roth-Stone and Stayman, Bulldog believes that the controlled psychic opening bid is a most useful weapon. The requirements for the bid are:

1. It is usually made when not vulnerable.
2. The hand has fewer than 7 high-card points.
3. The bidder is always prepared for a lead in the suit he bids, and hence, a 2-point high-card minimum in this suit (Q 10 x x).

Just as in the other systems, a little artificial system is developed to protect the psycher's partner should the latter possess a tremendous hand. The logic here is indisputable: since the psychic bidder must always pass until his tactic has become exposed, certain specialized bids must be introduced to protect partner when he holds overwhelming strength.

In the Bulldog System, *a three-club response is an absolute force.*

Although artificial, it implies sufficient strength to justify a three-level bid even opposite a psych. The three-club bid denotes at least 20 points with a fit in opener's suit, or at least 23 points without a fit, and implies a game opposite a maximum psychic bid.

The three-club response asks: "Partner, are you psyching?" Opener answers three diamonds if he has psyched, in effect saying: "Yes, you've caught me red-handed!" All other rebids are natural and confirm a legitimate opening bid—in which case a slam is just about guaranteed.

When the responder holds a shapeless 20–23 points—and naturally suspects a psychic—he makes the strongly encouraging jump to *two no-trump* (comparable to the Roth-Stone response). Any of six artificial rebids are then permitted opener, whereby the latter can identify his holding: maximum psych, minimum psych, legitimate opening, etc. Speaking as a former history student, I don't recall any historical epoch when as much attention was paid to the "poor" as is paid to Bulldog's psychic opening bidder. (Since the opening psychic bid is made only when not vulnerable, the three-club response as a force applies only when not vulnerable. Vulnerable, as a jump-shift response, the three-club bid is a normal, pre-emptive weakness bid.)

There are two schools of Bulldog—the Western and the Southern. Both advocate a very light opening bid, but the Southern school's requirements are much lower than the Western school's. So the Southern school has dispensed with the opening psychic bid (though reluctantly), since it was becoming difficult to differentiate the very light opening bid from the psychic opening bid.

D. *The Kaplan-Sheinwold Justification for the Employment of the Controlled or Disciplined Opening Psychic Bid*

As in the three other modern systems, the opening psychic bid has become a component part of the Kaplan-Sheinwold System. Here are the requirements for the bid:

1. a biddable suit, at least 4 cards long, and usually 5-card length, headed by an ace, king, or queen
2. 3–6 points in high cards
3. no ace or king in a side suit

The following are typical examples, all of which would also be opened as psychics in each of the other three systems:

♠ x x	♠ x x	♠ x x x
♥ K J x x x	♥ x x x	♥ x x x
♦ x x x	♦ J x x	♦ K Q J x
♣ x x x	♣ Q 10 x x x	♣ x x x
Bid 1H	Bid 1C	Bid 1D

In the opinion of the authors, the psychic opening can be a very effective weapon. Not that it tends to frighten the sophisticated opponents out of the auction, for when one has a miserable hand, the opponents will surely have more than enough strength to act in positive fashion. But what the bid does is to jostle the opponents out of their normal, accustomed auction into a strange and uncomfortable situation. An excellent illustration of this viewpoint is presented in the next chapter.

The price for disturbing the enemy's bidding on their big hands, via a psychic, is not paid in disastrous sets when the psychic boomerangs. Surprisingly, perhaps, the authors view the psychic opening as one of the safest of all orthodox bids. Almost invariably, the opponent who sits behind the psychic bidder doubles for take-out, or overcalls, and the psychic bidder is out of trouble unless his partner gets too active. But if his partner is cognizant of the possibility of a psychic, he will learn to view the opening bid with suspicion and tread cautiously. Of course, occasional trouble will develop— as it has in the past—when responder cannot confirm whether the opening bid was legitimate or counterfeit. But the fact remains that, in experience, the psychic opening has paid handsome dividends to Kaplan-Sheinwold adherents.

6. THE INVERTED MINOR SUIT RAISES

In standard practice, the single raise of a minor suit opening (1C . . . *2C;* 1D . . . *2D*) has always denoted a weak hand, while the double raise (1C . . . *3C;* 1D . . . *3D*) has always been made on a strong hand. In the Kaplan-Sheinwold System, the raise of one club to two clubs and the raise of one diamond to two diamonds is *forcing.* The raise of one club to *three clubs* and the raise of one diamond to *three diamonds* is weak. In tournament circles, this has become known as the "inverted minor raises." Why this departure from orthodox practices, and the inverted use of the minor suit raises?

A. *The Kaplan-Sheinwold Justification for the Employment of the Inverted Minor Suit Raises*

First, it should be noted that there is precedent for this treatment in standard American practice. Through the years, the double raise in a major suit (1S . . . *3S;* 1H . . . *3H*) has always denoted a strong hand, while the triple raise has denoted a weak hand (1S . . . *4S;* 1H . . . *4H*). In other words, the higher raise indicated a weak hand, while the lower raise indicated a strong hand. This is in consonance with the Kaplan-Sheinwold basic principle that pre-emptive effects are necessary with bad hands, not with good ones; and that consequently they support in both theory and practice, the thesis of using high bids for weak hands and low bids for strong hands whenever it is consistent with reasonable safety.

In a letter to the *Bridge World* in 1955,[10] Edgar Kaplan was already convinced that the standard, orthodox usage of the single and double minor suit raises was quite useless. He stated:

> . . . it is just plain foolish to play one club by you, two clubs by partner, as a bad hand (I'm referring to the two-club raise, of course), and to treat the double raise to three clubs as a good hand. Exactly the reverse is logical. When I hold:

♠ x x
♥ Q x x
♦ x x x
♣ K J x x x

I want to be able to bid three clubs over partner's one club and force the opponents to guess whether and when to come in at the three level. When I hold:

♠ x x
♥ A Q x
♦ Q x x
♣ A 10 x x x

[10] *The Bridge World,* August 1955.

I want to be able to force with two clubs over one, to save a round of bidding for the investigation of three no-trump or of slam. It makes no sense at all to crowd the bidding on hands that clearly belong to you, and to keep the auction low on hands which you are afraid belong to the enemy. The pre-emptive jump raise and the strong single raise should definitely be used in the minors. . . . In the majors this can also be very effective, especially in conjunction with five-card majors, to enable you to jump on three-card support. . . .

It is interesting to note that exactly four years later, in a poll conducted by the *Bridge World* of 96 of the nation's top-ranking experts, one of the questions asked was: "What do you think of the Kaplan-Sheinwold idea of playing *strong* single raises in the minors, with one diamond—pass—three diamonds purely pre-emptive? I like this treatment. . . . I dislike this treatment. . . ."

Of the American standard and independent experts, this was their viewpoint: 59 like this treatment; 32 dislike it. There were 5 "no comments." The conclusion is, of course, obvious: the majority of experts, in accepting the Kaplan-Sheinwold concept of the most utilitarian use of the single and double raises in the minors, honestly believe that swimming against the tide of tradition will yield better results.

In terms of the precise requirements of the system, the weak double raise is based on 5–8 points in high cards, with no freakish distribution that may yield a reasonable play for game in the minor suit. It must be based on 5 or more trumps, since the opener often has only a 3-card suit. It must deny a 4-card major, since no 4-card major is ever bypassed. In effect, it warns partner that there is no game if opener has the usual 15–17 points.

The single raise, point-wise, begins where the double raise ends: the minimum value is 9 points in high cards, enough to yield a play for game if partner has toward the upper end of the expected 15–17 points. The maximum value is some 20-odd points, enough for an immediate jump in a new suit. The forcing single raise in a minor suit denies a 4-card major. As always, the first duty of the responder is to show a major suit if he can.

How and what opener rebids after either the single or double raise is not in the province of this text. Suffice to say, the Kaplan-Sheinwold System has worked out the necessary interrelationships, with the result that inverted minor suit raises have become a smoothly functioning machine.

Neither Roth-Stone nor Bulldog has incorporated this bid into their systems. Stayman, however, has paid it tribute by using the double raise (1C . . . 3C; 1D . . . 3D) as a nonforcing bid, reserving the double raise for hands of this type:

♠ x
♥ Q x x x
♦ x x x
♣ K J x x x

Bid *3C* over 1C

Now let us view these modern, revolutionary bids in action, as they arose in championship competition. Look at them closely as they parade in review in top-flight play—and I'm certain that, despite conscious or subconscious prejudices against them, you will find yourself applauding as they pass before you.

CHAPTER 9

THE REVOLUTIONARY BIDS PARADE IN REVIEW IN CHAMPIONSHIP PLAY

THE ROTH-STONE SYSTEM

1. *The Weak Two Bid*

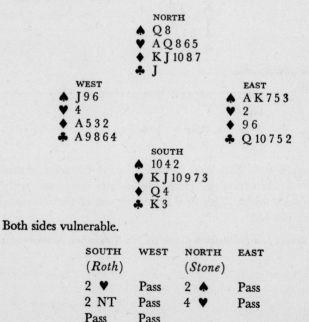

```
                        NORTH
                     ♠ Q 8
                     ♥ A Q 8 6 5
                     ♦ K J 10 8 7
                     ♣ J
        WEST                                 EAST
     ♠ J 9 6                              ♠ A K 7 5 3
     ♥ 4                                  ♥ 2
     ♦ A 5 3 2                            ♦ 9 6
     ♣ A 9 8 6 4                          ♣ Q 10 7 5 2
                        SOUTH
                     ♠ 10 4 2
                     ♥ K J 10 9 7 3
                     ♦ Q 4
                     ♣ K 3
```

Both sides vulnerable.

SOUTH (Roth)	WEST	NORTH (Stone)	EAST
2 ♥	Pass	2 ♠	Pass
2 NT	Pass	4 ♥	Pass
Pass	Pass		

Responder to a weak two bid indulges in "shenanigans," and his shrewd operations keep the opponents out of a spade game. North-South are down one. No chance for the two-spade response to go bad, since opener is not allowed to make any embarrassing rebid.

Source: *The Bridge World,* September, 1956. National Team Championships, 1951.

2. *The Weak Two Bid*

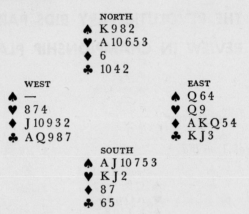

```
                    NORTH
                 ♠ K 9 8 2
                 ♥ A 10 6 5 3
                 ♦ 6
                 ♣ 10 4 2
     WEST                          EAST
  ♠ —                          ♠ Q 6 4
  ♥ 8 7 4                      ♥ Q 9
  ♦ J 10 9 3 2                 ♦ A K Q 5 4
  ♣ A Q 9 8 7                  ♣ K J 3
                    SOUTH
                 ♠ A J 10 7 5 3
                 ♥ K J 2
                 ♦ 8 7
                 ♣ 6 5
```

Both sides vulnerable.

SOUTH (*Roth*)	WEST	NORTH (*Stone*)	EAST
2 ♠	Pass	4 ♠	Pass
Pass	Pass		

At the other table East-West arrived at a five-diamond contract, which they made with ease. Here, four spades was made with a successful heart finesse. This deal illustrates one of the advantages of the weak two bid.

Source: *Bridge Is a Partnership Game,* op. cit. Vanderbilt Championships, 1959.

3. *The Weak Jump Overcall*

```
                        NORTH
                    ♠ x x
                    ♥ 10 9 x
                    ♦ x x
                    ♣ K J 10 9 x x
        WEST                            EAST
    ♠ A K Q x x                     ♠ J 10 x x
    ♥ x x                           ♥ K Q J x
    ♦ K Q J x x                     ♦ 10 9 x
    ♣ x                             ♣ x x
                        SOUTH
                    ♠ x x
                    ♥ A x x x
                    ♦ A x x
                    ♣ A Q x x
```

East-West vulnerable.

WEST	NORTH	EAST	SOUTH
	(*Mrs. Kemp*)		(*A. Roth*)
1 ♠	3 ♣	3 ♠	5 ♣
5 ♠	Pass	Pass	Double
Pass	Pass	Pass	

The weak jump overcall is a harassing and deceptive bid. Roth knew that his partner had a club suit and nothing else, hence he could see that the five-club contract figured to go down just three tricks. Of course, it was impossible for West to know that South was taking a premature sacrifice. Had North passed originally, it would have been impossible for North-South to get together in clubs. Or, if North had made a two-club overcall, South would not have sacrificed, since North, in this case, might well have had the little defensive strength needed to defeat four spades.

Source: *Bridge Is a Partnership Game,* op. cit. Masters Pairs Championship, 1952.

4. *The Weak Jump Overcall*

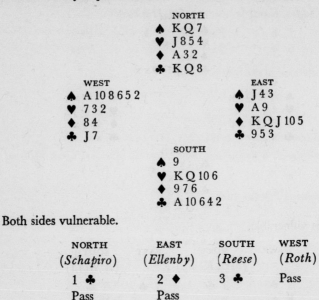

NORTH
♠ K Q 7
♥ J 8 5 4
♦ A 3 2
♣ K Q 8

WEST
♠ A 10 8 6 5 2
♥ 7 3 2
♦ 8 4
♣ J 7

EAST
♠ J 4 3
♥ A 9
♦ K Q J 10 5
♣ 9 5 3

SOUTH
♠ 9
♥ K Q 10 6
♦ 9 7 6
♣ A 10 6 4 2

Both sides vulnerable.

NORTH (*Schapiro*)	EAST (*Ellenby*)	SOUTH (*Reese*)	WEST (*Roth*)
1 ♣	2 ♦	3 ♣	Pass
Pass	Pass		

The harassing effect of the weak jump overcall. The fact is that Reese and Schapiro—two of the world's best players—were shut out of their best contract.

Source: *The Bridge World,* March, 1955. International Match between the United States and England for the World's Championship, 1955.

5. *The Weak Jump Response*

NORTH
♠ A K J x x x
♥ A x x
♦ A K x x
♣ —

SOUTH
♠ x
♥ x x
♦ Q 10 9 x x x
♣ J 10 x x

East-West vulnerable.

NORTH	EAST	SOUTH	WEST
(*Mrs. Kemp*)		(*H. Harkavy*)	
1 ♠	Pass	3 ♦	Pass
6 ♦	Pass	Pass	Pass

At the other table the bidding went:

NORTH	EAST	SOUTH	WEST
1 ♠	Pass	Pass	Pass

Seven diamonds were made by Mr. Harkavy.

Source: *Bridge Is a Partnership Game,* op. cit. National Team of Four, 1950.

6. *The Opening Psychic Bid*

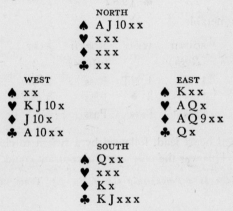

NORTH
♠ A J 10 x x
♥ x x x
♦ x x x
♣ x x

WEST
♠ x x
♥ K J 10 x
♦ J 10 x
♣ A 10 x x

EAST
♠ K x x
♥ A Q x
♦ A Q 9 x x
♣ Q x

SOUTH
♠ Q x x
♥ x x x
♦ K x
♣ K J x x x

East-West vulnerable.

NORTH	EAST	SOUTH	WEST
(*Mrs. E. Kemp*)		(*H. Harkavy*)	
1 ♠	1 NT	Pass	2 NT
Pass	3 NT	Pass	Pass
Pass			

With the otherwise abnormal spade lead, three no-trump was down one. The psychic is a lead-directing bid, to achieve results such as the above.

Source: *Bridge Is a Partnership Game,* op. cit. National Open Team of Four, 1952.

7. The Opening Psychic Bid

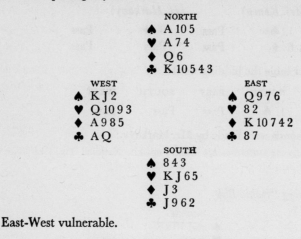

```
                    NORTH
                 ♠ A 10 5
                 ♥ A 7 4
                 ♦ Q 6
                 ♣ K 10 5 4 3
    WEST                        EAST
 ♠ K J 2                     ♠ Q 9 7 6
 ♥ Q 10 9 3                  ♥ 8 2
 ♦ A 9 8 5                   ♦ K 10 7 4 2
 ♣ A Q                       ♣ 8 7
                    SOUTH
                 ♠ 8 4 3
                 ♥ K J 6 5
                 ♦ J 3
                 ♣ J 9 6 2
```

East-West vulnerable.

SOUTH (Roth)	WEST	NORTH (Stone)	EAST
1 ♥	1 NT	Pass	2 ♦
Pass	3 ♦	Pass	3 NT
Pass	Pass	Pass	

The directed heart lead, followed by a switch to clubs, defeated the contract. This was the only way the contract could be defeated.

Source: *Bridge Is a Partnership Game,* op. cit. Team of Four, 1957, Pittsburgh.

8. The Opening Psychic Bid

```
                    NORTH
                 ♠ K Q J 10 x x
                 ♥ K x
                 ♦ A x
                 ♣ A Q x

                    SOUTH
                 ♠ x x x
                 ♥ x x x
                 ♦ x x x
                 ♣ K 10 8 x
```

Neither side vulnerable.

SOUTH	WEST	NORTH	EAST
(*T. Stone*)		(*A. Roth*)	
1 ♣	Double	4 ♠	Pass
Pass	Pass		

West was known to be a sound bidder and an honest opponent, and Roth correctly deduced that Stone was psyching. The game at four spades figured to be a virtual laydown, since South was marked for the king of clubs, and a lead toward the king of hearts could always be made. The game is otherwise just about impossible to bid with any assurance of its being made.

Source: National Men's Team-of-Four Championship.

9. *The Opening Psychic Bid*

NORTH
♠ x x
♥ x x
♦ J x x
♣ Q J 9 8 7 x

SOUTH
♠ K x x
♥ A K Q 10
♦ K Q x x
♣ K x

Both vulnerable.

NORTH	EAST	SOUTH	WEST
(*Mrs. Kemp*)		(*Roth*)	
1 ♣	1 ♠	2 ♣!	Pass
Pass	Pass		

Again, the recognition of the psychic opening, which necessitates keen judgment. When East made a vulnerable overcall, South suspected a psychic; and, if that were the case, North had to pass any response that South made. Therefore South could not afford to scout around for another bid. If it were not a psychic, then the free bid of two clubs was virtually forcing. Also, since North-South were vulnerable, the assumption was made that North had a respectable club suit. Of course, if North bid again, South would have driven to a slam.

Source: National Open Pairs, 1952.

10. *The Opening Psychic Bid*

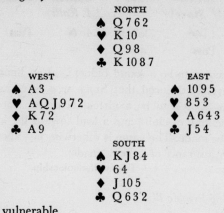

NORTH
- ♠ Q 7 6 2
- ♥ K 10
- ♦ Q 9 8
- ♣ K 10 8 7

WEST
- ♠ A 3
- ♥ A Q J 9 7 2
- ♦ K 7 2
- ♣ A 9

EAST
- ♠ 10 9 5
- ♥ 8 5 3
- ♦ A 6 4 3
- ♣ J 5 4

SOUTH
- ♠ K J 8 4
- ♥ 6 4
- ♦ J 10 5
- ♣ Q 6 3 2

North-South vulnerable.

EAST	SOUTH	WEST	NORTH
(*Roth*)		(*Mrs. Seligman*)	
1 ♦ !	Pass	1 ♥	Pass
Pass	1 ♠	2 ♥	2 ♠
3 ♥ !	Pass	4 ♥	Pass
Pass	Pass		

Roth's opening bid was proven psychic when he passed Mrs. Seligman's response. His subsequent raise indicated merely the possession of a winning trick—and, of course, he knew that Mrs. Seligman had a tremendous hand since otherwise she would not have bid again when partner was known to be "busted."

Source: National Mixed Pair Championships, 1952.

11. *The Opening Psychic Bid*

NORTH
- ♠ —
- ♥ A K Q J 6 4
- ♦ A 7
- ♣ A Q 7 3 2

SOUTH
- ♠ 6 3 2
- ♥ 8 7 3
- ♦ 10 8 5
- ♣ K J 9 8

Neither side vulnerable.

SOUTH	WEST	NORTH	EAST
(*F. Karpin*)		(*A. Roth*)	
1 ♣	Pass	7 ♣	Pass
Pass	Pass	Pass	

From North's position, South was almost surely on a psychic opening. This would give South at least the K 10 x x of clubs, and no king of diamonds on the outside. Note that seven hearts is unmakable.

Source: *The Bridge World,* February, 1954. Washington Open Pair Championship, 1953.

THE STAYMAN SYSTEM

12. *The Weak No-trump*

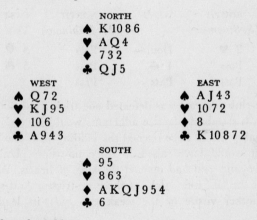

```
                      NORTH
                   ♠ K 10 8 6
                   ♥ A Q 4
                   ♦ 7 3 2
                   ♣ Q J 5
      WEST                              EAST
   ♠ Q 7 2                           ♠ A J 4 3
   ♥ K J 9 5                         ♥ 10 7 2
   ♦ 10 6                            ♦ 8
   ♣ A 9 4 3                         ♣ K 10 8 7 2
                      SOUTH
                   ♠ 9 5
                   ♥ 8 6 3
                   ♦ A K Q J 9 5 4
                   ♣ 6
```

Neither side vulnerable.

NORTH	EAST	SOUTH	WEST
(*S. Stayman*)			
1 NT	Pass	3 NT	Pass
Pass	Pass		

At the other table, four diamonds was the opening bid, down one. Stayman fulfilled his three no-trump contract.

Source: National Team-of-four championships, 1953.

13. *The Weak Two Bid*

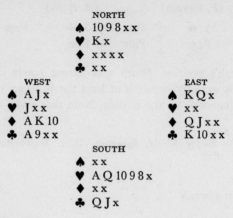

NORTH
- ♠ 10 9 8 x x
- ♥ K x
- ♦ x x x x
- ♣ x x

WEST
- ♠ A J x
- ♥ J x x
- ♦ A K 10
- ♣ A 9 x x

EAST
- ♠ K Q x
- ♥ x x
- ♦ Q J x x
- ♣ K 10 x x

SOUTH
- ♠ x x
- ♥ A Q 10 9 8 x
- ♦ x x
- ♣ Q J x

Both sides vulnerable.

SOUTH	WEST	NORTH	EAST
(*S. Stayman*)		(*M. Rubinow*)	
2 ♥	Double	Pass	3 ♥
Pass	4 ♣	Pass	5 ♣
Pass	Pass	Pass	

The five-club contract was defeated one trick. Had South passed originally (as standard practice adherents would have done), West unquestionably would have opened the bidding with one no-trump, which East would have raised to three no-trump. Unless North were clairvoyant, and had opened the king of hearts, West would have taken the first nine tricks at three no-trump. And so, we can observe another virtue of the weak two bid: its lead-directing feature.

Source: Rubber bridge, 1960.

14. *The Weak Two Bid*

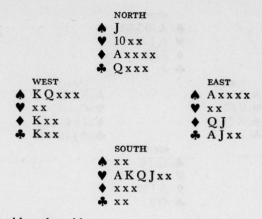

NORTH
♠ J
♥ 10 x x
♦ A x x x x
♣ Q x x x

WEST
♠ K Q x x x
♥ x x
♦ K x x
♣ K x x

EAST
♠ A x x x x
♥ x x
♦ Q J
♣ A J x x

SOUTH
♠ x x
♥ A K Q J x x
♦ x x x
♣ x x

Neither side vulnerable.

SOUTH	WEST	NORTH	EAST
		(*S. Stayman*)	
2 ♥	Pass	2 NT	Pass
3 ♥	Pass	Pass	Pass

The three-heart contract suffered a 1-trick set. East-West can make four spades. North's two no-trump response was forcing, but when he passed three hearts, it was obvious that his response had been a psychic bid. Of course, East should have come in with three spades at that point. However, the fact remains that he didn't. If North had passed the opening two-heart bid, undoubtedly East would have stepped in with two spades.

Source: National Championships, 1959.

15. *The Psychic Response*

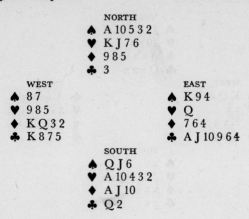

NORTH
♠ A 10 5 3 2
♥ K J 7 6
♦ 9 8 5
♣ 3

WEST
♠ 8 7
♥ 9 8 5
♦ K Q 3 2
♣ K 8 7 5

EAST
♠ K 9 4
♥ Q
♦ 7 6 4
♣ A J 10 9 6 4

SOUTH
♠ Q J 6
♥ A 10 4 3 2
♦ A J 10
♣ Q 2

North-South vulnerable.

In one room, the bidding went:

SOUTH	WEST	NORTH	EAST
1 ♥	Pass	1 ♠	2 ♣
Pass	3 ♣	3 ♥	4 ♣
4 ♥	5 ♣	Double	Pass
Pass	Pass		

North-South was plus 100 points.

In the other room, the bidding went:

SOUTH	WEST	NORTH	EAST
		(S. Stayman)	
1 ♥	Pass	2 ♣	Pass
2 ♥	Pass	3 ♥	Pass
4 ♥	Pass	Pass	Pass

North-South was plus 620 points.

Source: Team-of-four match, London, 1953.

16. *The Psychic Response*

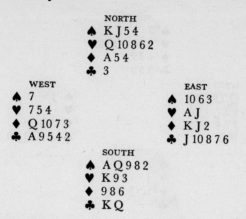

NORTH
♠ K J 5 4
♥ Q 10 8 6 2
♦ A 5 4
♣ 3

WEST
♠ 7
♥ 7 5 4
♦ Q 10 7 3
♣ A 9 5 4 2

EAST
♠ 10 6 3
♥ A J
♦ K J 2
♣ J 10 8 7 6

SOUTH
♠ A Q 9 8 2
♥ K 9 3
♦ 9 8 6
♣ K Q

Both sides vulnerable.

At most tables the bidding went 1S . . . *3S* . . . 4S, down one with the normal diamond opening. At the table where Stayman was North, the bidding went:

SOUTH	NORTH
1 ♠	2 ♦
2 ♠	4 ♠

West elected to open a heart, and 11 tricks were made. Note that North has the *values* for his bid, so that the deception of partner can't prove costly.

Source: Masters Pairs, 1954.

17. *Psychological Bidding*

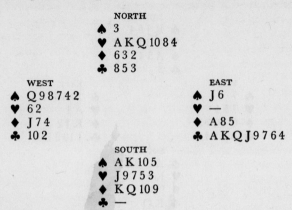

NORTH
♠ 3
♥ A K Q 10 8 4
♦ 6 3 2
♣ 8 5 3

WEST
♠ Q 9 8 7 4 2
♥ 6 2
♦ J 7 4
♣ 10 2

EAST
♠ J 6
♥ —
♦ A 8 5
♣ A K Q J 9 7 6 4

SOUTH
♠ A K 10 5
♥ J 9 7 5 3
♦ K Q 10 9
♣ —

North-South vulnerable.

EAST	SOUTH	WEST	NORTH
(*L. Tarlo*)	(*S. Stayman*)	(*Gardener*)	(*Rapee*)
1 ♣	Double	1 ♠	4 ♥
5 ♣	5 ♥	Pass	Pass
6 ♣	Pass	Pass	6 ♥
Pass	Pass	Pass	

There was, of course, nothing to the play. This was a bidding coup, pure and far from simple.

When Rapee jumped to four hearts, he showed a long independent suit. Stayman could depend almost 100% on a six-card or seven-card suit headed by ace-king or ace-king-queen. Hence Stayman could be almost certain that his side could make six hearts.

A less devious player would have jumped at once to six hearts, or he might have cue-bid the clubs. Subtle Sam Stayman simply satisfied himself with a bid of five hearts.

The reason for this apparent lack of enterprise may be found in Tarlo's bid of five clubs. Tarlo was not vulnerable and obviously had a big enough club suit to sacrifice at seven clubs against any slam that North and South bid confidently.

Stayman had two reasons for bidding only five hearts. If that were the final contract, it might be more profitable than doubling seven clubs (it would have been—780 points as against 600). If East went on to six clubs when North and South had shown willingness to play the hand at only five hearts, it would seem that the Americans were quite uncertain of six hearts when they finally bid it. Hence East might fail to sacrifice.

Stayman got the chance to add a turn of the screw when Tarlo did (quite logically) sacrifice at six clubs. Instead of bidding six hearts, Stayman passed!

This was a forcing pass, compelling Rapee to bid six hearts or double. Actually Rapee bid six hearts. He had suspected what was going on during the previous round of bidding but had not been quite sure. The forcing pass convinced him that he had been right—and also told him why Stayman had passed instead of bidding six hearts himself.

Stayman wanted the slam to come from his partner so that East would be uncertain about how much defense his partner had. If Stayman had bid the slam, West's failure to double would oblige East to sacrifice. When Rapee bid the slam, East was unwilling to sacrifice against a slam that his partner might be able to set. Hence he passed, and the weak West hand had to speak last.

This was beautiful co-operative jockeying by Stayman and Rapee, and it is hard to see what Tarlo and Gardener could have done about it. Tarlo could feel sure of winning a trick with his ace of diamonds, and had some reason to hope that his partner also could win a trick or two against a slam that was bid so haltingly.

Certainly Tarlo wanted to create a swing, since his team was behind. If six hearts was a normal contract, the American players in the other room would sacrifice at seven clubs. Hence Tarlo could not hope to gain a swing by doing the same thing. There was some hope if six hearts could be beaten, for then the English team might make a plus score in both rooms.

When six hearts is passed around to Gardener, what should he do? Should he bid seven clubs on the theory that his partner's pass is forcing? But the pass isn't really forcing. Tarlo might have enough to set six hearts without wanting to locate strength definitely by a double. Or perhaps the reluctantly bid slam might be set partly by the aid of West's queen of spades—or possibly even the jack of diamonds.

There is certainly nothing to guide Gardener to the best action. This, of course, is exactly what Rapee and Stayman had been hoping for when they bid their slam in so peculiar a fashion.

At the other table England bid the slam in aggressive fashion—but this was no hand for aggressive bidding:

EAST	SOUTH	WEST	NORTH
(*Silodor*)	(*Konstam*)	(*Crawford*)	(*Dodds*)
1 ♣	2 ♣	Pass	3 ♥
5 ♣	6 ♥	Pass	Pass
7 ♣	Double	Pass	Pass
Pass			

Seven clubs doubled went for only 600 points. Six hearts was worth 1530 points (with honors). The American team thus gained 930 points on the hand.

Source: First International team-of-four match, 1950. United States versus England. The description of the deal is quoted verbatim from *The Bridge World*, December, 1950.

THE BULLDOG SYSTEM

18. *The Weak Two Bid*

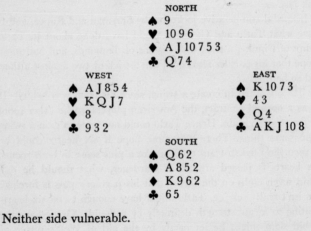

NORTH
♠ 9
♥ 10 9 6
♦ A J 10 7 5 3
♣ Q 7 4

WEST
♠ A J 8 5 4
♥ K Q J 7
♦ 8
♣ 9 3 2

EAST
♠ K 10 7 3
♥ 4 3
♦ Q 4
♣ A K J 10 8

SOUTH
♠ Q 6 2
♥ A 8 5 2
♦ K 9 6 2
♣ 6 5

Neither side vulnerable.

NORTH	EAST	SOUTH	WEST
(*W. Hanna*)		(*S. Lazard*)	
2 ♦	Pass	3 NT	Pass
Pass	Pass		

The two-diamond opening is routine, and East, without a convenient bid, passed. South had a choice of continuing destructive tactics: three diamonds, four diamonds, or three no-trump. His choice was well rewarded, for the opponents remained silent; and when West opened the king of hearts against three no-trump (probably the correct lead, although not the most successful), South went down only two—for minus 100—for a near-top on the board.

Source: Open Pairs Tournament, Houston, Texas, July 1954.

19. *The Weak Two Bid*

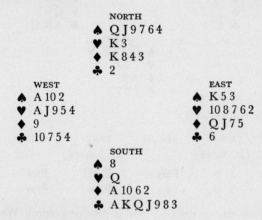

NORTH
- ♠ Q J 9 7 6 4
- ♥ K 3
- ♦ K 8 4 3
- ♣ 2

WEST
- ♠ A 10 2
- ♥ A J 9 5 4
- ♦ 9
- ♣ 10 7 5 4

EAST
- ♠ K 5 3
- ♥ 10 8 7 6 2
- ♦ Q J 7 5
- ♣ 6

SOUTH
- ♠ 8
- ♥ Q
- ♦ A 10 6 2
- ♣ A K Q J 9 8 3

Neither side vulnerable.

NORTH (*A. Binder*)	EAST	SOUTH (*W. Hanna*)	WEST
2 ♠	Pass	2 NT	Pass
3 ♥	Pass	3 NT	Pass
Pass	Pass		

In response to the exploratory two no-trump bid, North showed his maximum plus the guarded king of hearts by bidding three hearts. Now South was sure of the no-trump game and bid it. Had North denied a heart control, South would have tried for a club game.

Although today several pairs would reach the no-trump game by a third seat opening of three no-trump (pre-emptive), no other pair reached three no-trump when this deal occurred, in 1952.

Source: Los Angeles Regional Open Pairs Championship, 1952.

20. *The Psychic Opening*

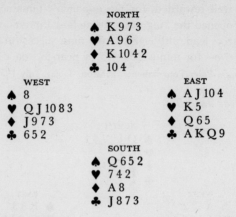

NORTH
♠ K 9 7 3
♥ A 9 6
♦ K 10 4 2
♣ 10 4

WEST
♠ 8
♥ Q J 10 8 3
♦ J 9 7 3
♣ 6 5 2

EAST
♠ A J 10 4
♥ K 5
♦ Q 6 5
♣ A K Q 9

SOUTH
♠ Q 6 5 2
♥ 7 4 2
♦ A 8
♣ J 8 7 3

Neither side vulnerable.

WEST	NORTH	EAST	SOUTH
(*D. Steen*)		(*S. Lazard*)	
1 ♥	Pass	2 NT	Pass
3 ♥	Pass	Pass	Pass

The two no-trump response was a psychic control. West's rebid is a close decision between three hearts (a minimum psyche with shape) and four hearts (a maximum psyche with shape). The defense did not slip and West was held to nine tricks. The score of plus 140 was worth 11 out of 12 match points, as most East-West pairs ended up in three no-trump and going down 1 to 3 tricks. Thus, the psychic opening can have constructive as well as destructive merit.

Source: Texas Regional Men's Pairs, Houston, Texas, 1954.

21. *The Psychic Opening*

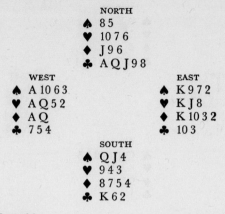

NORTH
♠ 8 5
♥ 10 7 6
♦ J 9 6
♣ A Q J 9 8

WEST
♠ A 10 6 3
♥ A Q 5 2
♦ A Q
♣ 7 5 4

EAST
♠ K 9 7 2
♥ K J 8
♦ K 10 3 2
♣ 10 3

SOUTH
♠ Q J 4
♥ 9 4 3
♦ 8 7 5 4
♣ K 6 2

East-West vulnerable.

SOUTH	WEST	NORTH	EAST
(*W. Hanna*)		(*D. Steen*)	
1 ♠	1 NT	Pass	3 NT
Pass	Pass	Pass	

Normally, a suit psychic is made in a suit of four cards or longer, but the pre-emptive value of the spade bid swung the decision in this deal. After the routine one no-trump overcall, Steen decided not to bid two clubs but instead to await developments. His wisdom was proved, for, after East naturally raised to the no-trump game, he was able to defeat the contract by taking the first 5 club tricks.

At table 2, West opened with one no-trump (after South passed), and the partnership reached the normal four-spade contract (via the Stayman Convention). The play was routine.

Source: All-Western Knockout Teams, Denver, Colo., 1954.

22. *The Weak Jump Overcall*

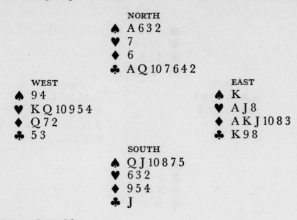

```
                    NORTH
                 ♠ A 6 3 2
                 ♥ 7
                 ♦ 6
                 ♣ A Q 10 7 6 4 2
   WEST                                EAST
 ♠ 9 4                               ♠ K
 ♥ K Q 10 9 5 4                      ♥ A J 8
 ♦ Q 7 2                             ♦ A K J 10 8 3
 ♣ 5 3                               ♣ K 9 8
                    SOUTH
                 ♠ Q J 10 8 7 5
                 ♥ 6 3 2
                 ♦ 9 5 4
                 ♣ J
```

East-West vulnerable.

EAST	SOUTH	WEST	NORTH
	(*W. Hanna*)		(*S. Lazard*)
1 ♦	2 ♠	Pass	4 ♠
Double	Pass	5 ♥	5 ♠
Double	Pass	Pass	Pass

South's jump overcall is typical of the pre-emptive use of this bid. North bid four spades, hoping to play it there, but he was willing to go to five both as a sacrifice and as a bid to make, for if South had a reasonable spade suit, there should be some play for the latter contract.

The play involved only guessing the location of the spade king. South went up with the ace of spades on the first lead of the suit. The rest was easy.

At the other table, the North-South pair never bid spades, and East-West were allowed to play the hand at four hearts, which they made.

Source: National Masters Knockout Teams Championships, Chicago, 1959.

23. *The Weak Jump Response*

NORTH
♠ A 9 2
♥ A J 8 3
♦ 7
♣ A K 6 5 4

WEST
♠ Q 10 8 5
♥ Q 9 7 5 2
♦ A 8 2
♣ Q

EAST
♠ K J 6
♥ K 10 4
♦ K 4 3
♣ J 10 8 3

SOUTH
♠ 7 4 3
♥ 6
♦ Q J 10 9 6 5
♣ 9 7 2

Neither side vulnerable.

NORTH (*W. Hanna*)	EAST	SOUTH (*D. Steen*)	WEST
1 ♣	Pass	2 ♦	Pass
Pass	Pass		

On this deal, the pre-emptive jump response served two purposes. First, it immediately located the best contract for the North-South partnership. In play, two diamonds were made, for a plus score of 90, and 10 out of 12 match-points (losing only to East-West sets). And second, it kept the East-West partnership from locating their part-score in hearts. At most tables, the bidding went:

NORTH	EAST	SOUTH	WEST
1 ♣	Pass	Pass	Double
Pass	1 NT	2 ♦	2 ♥
Pass	Pass	Pass	

Source: Los Angeles Regional Open Pair Championships, 1953.

THE KAPLAN-SHEINWOLD SYSTEM

24. *The Weak No-trump*

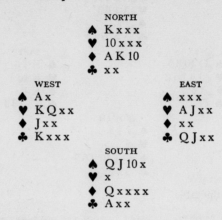

```
                    NORTH
                  ♠ K x x x
                  ♥ 10 x x x
                  ♦ A K 10
                  ♣ x x

   WEST                          EAST
 ♠ A x                         ♠ x x x
 ♥ K Q x x                     ♥ A J x x
 ♦ J x x                       ♦ x x
 ♣ K x x x                     ♣ Q J x x

                    SOUTH
                  ♠ Q J 10 x
                  ♥ x
                  ♦ Q x x x x
                  ♣ A x x
```

North-South vulnerable.

WEST	NORTH	EAST	SOUTH
1 ♣	Double	Pass	2 ♣
Pass	2 ♠	3 ♣	4 ♠
Pass	Pass	Pass	

This contract was made by Sheinwold and Kaplan's teammates. At the other table the bidding went:

WEST	NORTH	EAST	SOUTH
(*A. Sheinwold*)		(*E. Kaplan*)	
1 NT	Pass	Pass	Pass

With a heart lead, seven tricks were made. Which of the vulnerable opponents should risk a vulnerable bid over 1 NT?

Source: National Team-of-four Championships, 1957.

25. *The Weak No-trump*

NORTH
♠ A 7
♥ K Q 6 4
♦ A 8 4
♣ 10 5 3 2

WEST
♠ Q 10 8 3
♥ A 9 5
♦ Q 7
♣ K Q 8 6

EAST
♠ K J 4 2
♥ 10 3
♦ K 9 6 5
♣ A J 7

SOUTH
♠ 9 6 5
♥ J 8 7 2
♦ J 10 3 2
♣ 9 4

East-West vulnerable.

NORTH	EAST	SOUTH	WEST
1 NT	Pass	2 ♣	Pass
2 ♥	Pass	4 ♥ !	Pass
Pass	Pass		

This contract went down two, for 100 points (it could have been three, for minus 150). The opponents have a cold game in spades.

Source: Rubber Bridge, 1955.

26. *The Psychic Opening*

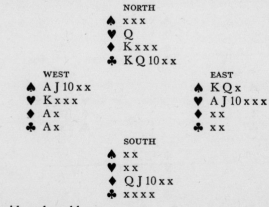

NORTH
♠ x x x
♥ Q
♦ K x x x
♣ K Q 10 x x

WEST
♠ A J 10 x x
♥ K x x x
♦ A x
♣ A x

EAST
♠ K Q x
♥ A J 10 x x x
♦ x x
♣ x x

SOUTH
♠ x x
♥ x x
♦ Q J 10 x x
♣ x x x x

Neither side vulnerable.

At the table where the teammates of Kaplan and Sheinwold sat
East and West, the bidding went:

SOUTH	WEST	NORTH	EAST
Pass	1 ♠	Pass	2 ♥
Pass	4 ♥	Pass	4 NT
Pass	5 ♠	Pass	5 NT
Pass	6 ♦	Pass	7 H
Pass	Pass	Pass	

At Kaplan and Sheinwold's table, the bidding went:

SOUTH	WEST	NORTH	EAST
(*A. Sheinwold*)		(*E. Kaplan*)	
1 ♦ !	Double	Redouble	2 ♥
Pass	4 ♥	Pass	Pass
Pass			

The opponents were not fooled by the psychic. But the bid dis-
torted the opponents' normal auction. West never got to bid his
spade suit. But when Kaplan's teammates held the East-West hands,
the system's 5-card spade opening made it easy for them to bid
the grand slam, since responder could count on five spade tricks.

Source: Team-of-four match, 1955.

27. *The Weak Jump Overcall*

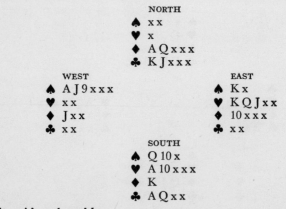

NORTH
♠ x x
♥ x
♦ A Q x x x
♣ K J x x x

WEST
♠ A J 9 x x x
♥ x x
♦ J x x
♣ x x

EAST
♠ K x
♥ K Q J x x
♦ 10 x x x
♣ x x

SOUTH
♠ Q 10 x
♥ A 10 x x x
♦ K
♣ A Q x x

Neither side vulnerable.

The most common auction was:

SOUTH	WEST	NORTH	EAST
1 ♥	1 ♠	2 ♦	Pass
2 NT	Pass	3 ♣	Pass
5 ♣	Pass	Pass	Pass

At the table where Kaplan and Sheinwold were sitting East-West:

SOUTH	WEST (*E. Kaplan*)	NORTH	EAST (*A. Sheinwold*)
1 ♥	2 ♠	3 ♦	Pass
3 NT	Pass	Pass	Pass

With the spade lead by West, North-South went down two.

At the tables where five clubs became the final contract, 11 tricks were made easily.

Source: Goldman Pair Championships, 1957.

28. *The Pre-emptive Response to an Overcall*

```
                      NORTH
                    ♠ A K J x x
                    ♥ J x x
                    ♦ A Q x
                    ♣ x x
      WEST                          EAST
    ♠ x x x                       ♠ x x
    ♥ A Q x x                     ♥ K x x x
    ♦ x                           ♦ J 10 9 x
    ♣ A K 10 x x                  ♣ Q x x
                      SOUTH
                    ♠ Q x x
                    ♥ x x
                    ♦ K x x x x
                    ♣ J x x
```

Both sides vulnerable.

WEST	NORTH	EAST	SOUTH
1 ♣	Double	Pass	1 ♦
1 ♥	1 ♠	2 ♥	2 ♠
4 ♥	Pass	Pass	Pass

The four-heart contract was fulfilled.

At the other table, with Kaplan sitting North and Sheinwold sitting South, the bidding went:

WEST	NORTH	EAST	SOUTH
1 ♣	1 ♠	Pass	2 ♠
Pass	Pass	Pass	

The "crowding" two-spade contract was made.

Source: Team-of-four match, 1957.

29. *A Pre-empt on a Pre-empt*

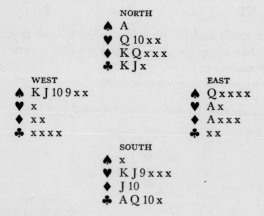

```
                NORTH
            ♠ A
            ♥ Q 10 x x
            ♦ K Q x x x
            ♣ K J x
   WEST                          EAST
♠ K J 10 9 x x               ♠ Q x x x x
♥ x                          ♥ A x
♦ x x                        ♦ A x x x
♣ x x x x                    ♣ x x
                SOUTH
            ♠ x
            ♥ K J 9 x x x
            ♦ J 10
            ♣ A Q 10 x
```

North-South vulnerable.

WEST	NORTH	EAST	SOUTH
(*E. Kaplan*)		(*A. Sheinwold*)	
3 ♠	Double	5 ♠!	6 ♥
Pass	Pass	Pass	

South's bid was perfectly reasonable—he had a very strong hand opposite partner's double, and no room was available for investigation. Any lower bid by East would have enabled a check for aces.

Source: Team-of-four match, 1956.

30. *Inverted Minor Raises*

NORTH
♠ J x
♥ K x x
♦ Q J x x
♣ K Q x x

SOUTH
♠ A x x x
♥ x
♦ A K x x
♣ J x x x

Both sides vulnerable.

SOUTH	NORTH
(*E. Kaplan*)	(*R. Hirschberg*)
1 ♦	2 ♦
2 ♠	2 NT
3 ♦	Pass

At the other table, the bidding went:

SOUTH	NORTH
1 ♦	3 ♦*
3 ♠	3 NT
Pass	

* Not a good bid, but it is in accord with "tradition," even though it is a trifle light. Three no-trump went down three.

Source: Vanderbilt Team-of-four championships, 1956.

31. *Inverted Minor Raises*

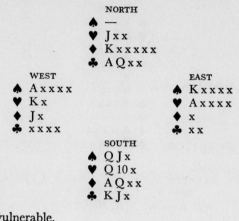

NORTH
♠ —
♥ J x x
♦ K x x x x x
♣ A Q x x

WEST
♠ A x x x x
♥ K x
♦ J x
♣ x x x x

EAST
♠ K x x x x
♥ A x x x x
♦ x
♣ x x

SOUTH
♠ Q J x
♥ Q 10 x
♦ A Q x x
♣ K J x

East-West vulnerable.

SOUTH (*R. Freeman*)	WEST	NORTH (*M. Michaels*)	EAST
1 ♦	Pass	2 ♦	Pass
3 NT	Pass	Pass	Pass

This deal arose in a team of-four event. When the board was replayed, North-South arrived at a five-diamond contract. This was defeated one trick when West made the inspired opening of the king of hearts, and, two tricks later, ruffed the third round of hearts.

When Mr. Freeman played the board, at three no-trump, the normal spade opening was made, and the contract was fulfilled with ease.

Source: District of Columbia Championships, 1958.

CHAPTER 10

DECEPTION AND OBSTRUCTIONISM
IN CHAMPIONSHIP PLAY (1949–60)

The dating of the birth of the "modern age of bridge" as 1949, is an arbitrary choice. The only justification is that in 1949 the newly crowned king, Charles H. Goren, accepted the mandate of the people in decreeing: "Death to the Honor Trick Method!" and "Long Live the Point-Count Method!" Although the supersession of honor tricks by point-count was not a revolutionary change, it was the first major break with the traditional way of evaluating the worth of a hand, a way that had existed from the birth of contract bridge in 1925. Goren depicts this introduction of the new era—a modern era—in these words:

For a great many years I have advocated the point count for all phases of No Trump bidding, and to a limited extent where trump suits were involved. It may have been surprising to many of my readers therefore that I should have delayed so long publishing a book on the point count for suit bidding, though it became apparent that a great many players in all parts of the continent found this method of presentation to their liking.

The answer is a simple one. As I have ofttimes stated, I never ask my students to serve as guinea pigs. Consequently I determined to postpone publication of my complete work until such time as I was able to cure most of the defects and iron out all the fallacies that were inherent in the different versions of the point count method that had heretofore been hastily offered to the public in various parts of this country and England.

It required a great deal of study and experimentation. But . . . I was able to develop a scale of values which will work effectively in an over-whelming majority of hands. . . .[1]

The deals in this chapter are classified into various types of psychics: psychic opening bids, psychic responses, psychic over-calls, etc. Again, the reader should bear in mind that the word *psychic,* as used throughout this text, has the connotation of "bid-ding what you don't have, or bluffing, in order to create an illusion of strength, or to conceal a weakness; or not bidding what you have, in order to create a mirage for the adversaries." These deals, if they were to be given more dignity, might be classified as psy-chological bids, lead-inhibiting bids, harassing bids, etc., which, in purpose and effect, they actually are.

Appended to each deal is the word *beneficial* or *detrimental.* The reference here is to whether the specific psychic bid was successful or unsuccessful in its intent to harass, confuse, or mislead the op-position. Of course, a one-word conclusion is hardly a satisfactory criterion in adjudging the virtue of a bid; nor can the utilitarianism of a bid be measured by its result in one isolated instance. Never-theless, when one evaluates the success or failure of a particular psychological bid, certainly the consideration of the final result must be weighted heavily. Yet, if a psychic bid succeeded in muddling the opposition to such an extent that it drove them to a bad, or inferior, contract which was made by either a series of inspired guesses or by misdefense, are we to label the psychic bid as a failure? Or should the latter perhaps be classified within the category of "the operation was successful, but the patient died"?

The resolution of these questions I toss into the lap of the reader, who, in turn, can pass it on to the laps of the gods, whose business it is to render such decisions. My designation of *beneficial* or *detri-mental* in reference to each of the psychic bids pertains to the *intended purpose* of the bid: to cause the adversaries to misbid or misplay their hands, or to misdefend if the psyching side ob-tained the contract. If it succeeded in this purpose, I call the psychic bid beneficial; if it failed, I call it detrimental.

Here they are, then, the deals that feature the psychological strategy of the sophisticated modern era of bridge.

[1] *Point Count Bidding in Contract Bridge,* by Charles H. Goren, Simon and Schuster, New York, 1949.

1. THE PSYCHIC OPENING—BENEFICIAL

(Rubber Bridge, 1952)

NORTH
♠ Q J x x x
♥ Q x
♦ A 10 x x x
♣ x

WEST
♠ 8 x x
♥ K x x
♦ K x
♣ K 9 x x x

EAST
♠ 9 2
♥ J 10 9
♦ Q J 9 x
♣ A 10 x x

SOUTH
♠ A K 10
♥ A 8 x x x
♦ x x
♣ Q J x

North-South vulnerable.

NORTH	EAST	SOUTH	WEST
Pass	1 ♣	Double	1 NT
2 ♠	Pass	Pass	Pass

The fact that South should have bid again is immaterial. The psychic opening, plus the response of one no-trump, plus the fact that North has passed originally, resulted in the makable game of four spades not being reached.

2. PSYCHIC OPENING—BENEFICIAL

(French vs. British, 1958)

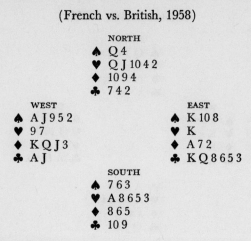

NORTH
- ♠ Q 4
- ♥ Q J 10 4 2
- ♦ 10 9 4
- ♣ 7 4 2

WEST
- ♠ A J 9 5 2
- ♥ 9 7
- ♦ K Q J 3
- ♣ A J

EAST
- ♠ K 10 8
- ♥ K
- ♦ A 7 2
- ♣ K Q 8 6 5 3

SOUTH
- ♠ 7 6 3
- ♥ A 8 6 5 3
- ♦ 8 6 5
- ♣ 10 9

Neither side vulnerable.

NORTH (*Trezel*)	EAST (*J. Sharples*)	SOUTH (*Jais*)	WEST (*R. Sharples*)
Pass	1 ♣	1 ♠	Double
Pass	Pass	1 NT	2 NT
Pass	3 ♣	Pass	3 ♠
Pass	4 ♦	Pass	6 ♦
Pass	6 ♠	Pass	Pass
Pass			

The psychic was exposed, but declarer misguessed the location of the queen of spades. Six clubs was makable with no finesse.

3. PSYCHIC OPENING—BENEFICIAL

(Rubber bridge, 1949)

```
                        NORTH
                        ♠ A Q 2
                        ♥ 8 2
                        ♦ K 6 5 3
                        ♣ Q 7 6 4
        WEST                                    EAST
        ♠ K J 9 5 4 3                           ♠ 10 6
        ♥ A 7                                   ♥ K 4
        ♦ A Q 7                                 ♦ 9 8 4 2
        ♣ J 9                                   ♣ A K 10 8 2
                        SOUTH
                        ♠ 8 7
                        ♥ Q J 10 9 6 5 3
                        ♦ J 10
                        ♣ 5 3
```

East-West vulnerable.

SOUTH	WEST	NORTH	EAST
1 ♥	1 ♠	1 NT	2 ♣
Pass	2 ♠	Pass	Pass
Pass			

Had South passed, East-West would have arrived at four spades. The psychic kept them out of it.

4. PSYCHIC OPENING BID—DETRIMENTAL

(Italy vs. U.S., 1957)

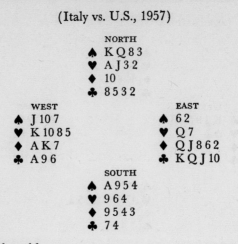

<pre>
                    NORTH
                 ♠ K Q 8 3
                 ♥ A J 3 2
                 ♦ 10
                 ♣ 8 5 3 2
      WEST   EAST
   ♠ J 10 7   ♠ 6 2
   ♥ K 10 8 5   ♥ Q 7
   ♦ A K 7   ♦ Q J 8 6 2
   ♣ A 9 6   ♣ K Q J 10
                    SOUTH
                 ♠ A 9 5 4
                 ♥ 9 6 4
                 ♦ 9 5 4 3
                 ♣ 7 4
</pre>

Both sides vulnerable.

NORTH (*H. Ogust*)	EAST (*Avarelli*)	SOUTH (*Koychou*)	WEST (*Belladonna*)
Pass	Pass	1 ♥	Pass
3 ♥	Pass	Pass	Double
Pass	Pass	Pass	

Down 1100!

5. PSYCHIC OPENING—DETRIMENTAL

(International Match, 1951, Italy vs. U.S.)

NORTH
♠ 4 3 2
♥ A 7 5 3
♦ A 10 3 2
♣ 6 3

WEST
♠ J 10
♥ 10 9 4 2
♦ Q 9 7 4
♣ 10 4 2

EAST
♠ 9 8 7 5
♥ 8
♦ K J 6 5
♣ A Q 9 5

SOUTH
♠ A K Q 6
♥ K Q J 6
♦ 8
♣ K J 8 7

Neither side vulnerable.

WEST (*S. Stayman*)	NORTH	EAST (*H. Schenken*)	SOUTH
1 ♠	Pass	3 ♠	Double
Pass	Pass	Pass	

Down 1100! Could have been set 1300, but how could the opponents defend correctly?

**6. PSYCHIC OPENING REVEALED TO ALL, BUT PARTNER
CONTESTS FOR A PARTIAL—DETRIMENTAL**

(National Team Championships, 1951)

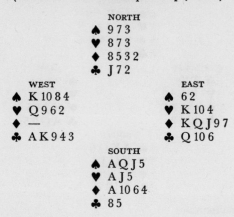

```
                        NORTH
                        ♠ 9 7 3
                        ♥ 8 7 3
                        ♦ 8 5 3 2
                        ♣ J 7 2
      WEST                                EAST
      ♠ K 10 8 4                          ♠ 6 2
      ♥ Q 9 6 2                           ♥ K 10 4
      ♦ —                                 ♦ K Q J 9 7
      ♣ A K 9 4 3                         ♣ Q 10 6
                        SOUTH
                        ♠ A Q J 5
                        ♥ A J 5
                        ♦ A 10 6 4
                        ♣ 8 5
```

North-South vulnerable.

NORTH	EAST	SOUTH	WEST
(*T. Stone*)		(*A. Roth*)	
1 ♦ (!)	Pass	1 ♠	Pass
Pass	Double	2 ♦	2 ♠
Pass	Pass	3 ♦ (!)	Pass
Pass	Double	Pass	Pass
Pass			

Stone decided to open with a first-hand psychic, vulnerable against nonvulnerable opponents.

Roth blames himself for not passing two spades. He knew that Stone had a psychic when he failed to provide his guaranteed rebid over one spade—he just thought that Stone might have had better diamonds and he was afraid that his side was being robbed of a part-score. Nevertheless, as Roth admits, it was too risky to bid three diamonds. DOWN 1100!

7. A PSYCHIC ONE NO-TRUMP OPENING—DETRIMENTAL

(Masters Team-of-Four Championships, 1953)

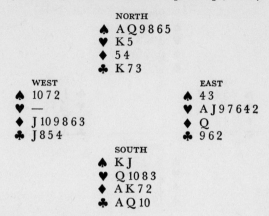

```
                         NORTH
                       ♠ A Q 9 8 6 5
                       ♥ K 5
                       ♦ 5 4
                       ♣ K 7 3
       WEST                              EAST
     ♠ 10 7 2                          ♠ 4 3
     ♥ —                               ♥ A J 9 7 6 4 2
     ♦ J 10 9 8 6 3                    ♦ Q
     ♣ J 8 5 4                         ♣ 9 6 2
                         SOUTH
                       ♠ K J
                       ♥ Q 10 8 3
                       ♦ A K 7 2
                       ♣ A Q 10
```

North-South vulnerable.

WEST	NORTH	EAST	SOUTH
(*S. Stayman*)	(*I. Erdos*)	(*H. Schenken*)	(*M. Schleifer*)
1 NT(!)	2 ♠	4 ♥	Double
Pass	Pass	Pass	

A cause célèbre. Down 1100.

At the other table, North-South arrived at six spades, which was defeated with a heart lead and a heart continuation. Six no-trump was makable.

8. PSYCHIC OPENING AND PSYCHIC REBID TO NO AVAIL—DETRIMENTAL

(Rubber bridge, 1949)

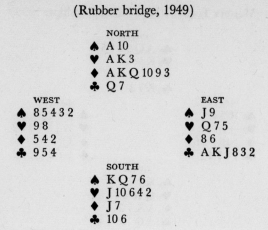

NORTH
- ♠ A 10
- ♥ A K 3
- ♦ A K Q 10 9 3
- ♣ Q 7

WEST
- ♠ 8 5 4 3 2
- ♥ 9 8
- ♦ 5 4 2
- ♣ 9 5 4

EAST
- ♠ J 9
- ♥ Q 7 5
- ♦ 8 6
- ♣ A K J 8 3 2

SOUTH
- ♠ K Q 7 6
- ♥ J 10 6 4 2
- ♦ J 7
- ♣ 10 6

North-South vulnerable.

NORTH	EAST	SOUTH	WEST
1 ♣	Pass	1 ♥	Pass
2 ♠	Pass	3 ♠	Pass
6 NT	Double	Pass	Pass
Pass			

Down 1400!

9. PSYCHIC OPENING—DETRIMENTAL

(World Championships, Sweden vs. U.S., 1953)

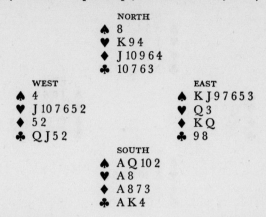

NORTH
- ♠ 8
- ♥ K 9 4
- ♦ J 10 9 6 4
- ♣ 10 7 6 3

WEST
- ♠ 4
- ♥ J 10 7 6 5 2
- ♦ 5 2
- ♣ Q J 5 2

EAST
- ♠ K J 9 7 6 5 3
- ♥ Q 3
- ♦ K Q
- ♣ 9 8

SOUTH
- ♠ A Q 10 2
- ♥ A 8
- ♦ A 8 7 3
- ♣ A K 4

Neither side vulnerable.

NORTH (*Crawford*)	EAST (*Lilliehook*)	SOUTH (*Stayman*)	WEST (*Anulf*)
1 ♥	2 ♠	2 NT	Pass
Pass	Pass		

North's psychic induced a feeble bid on South's part. South should instead have doubled the overcall or risked a bid of three no-trump. The weakish jump overcall may have interfered.

10. SEMI-PSYCHIC OPENING LEADS TO TROUBLE—DETRIMENTAL

(Masters Pair Championship, 1950)

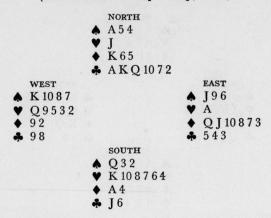

```
                          NORTH
                        ♠ A 5 4
                        ♥ J
                        ♦ K 6 5
                        ♣ A K Q 10 7 2
        WEST                              EAST
      ♠ K 10 8 7                        ♠ J 9 6
      ♥ Q 9 5 3 2                       ♥ A
      ♦ 9 2                             ♦ Q J 10 8 7 3
      ♣ 9 8                             ♣ 5 4 3
                          SOUTH
                        ♠ Q 3 2
                        ♥ K 10 8 7 6 4
                        ♦ A 4
                        ♣ J 6
```

Both sides vulnerable.

SOUTH	WEST	NORTH	EAST
1 ♥	Pass	3 ♣	Pass
3 ♥	Pass	4 NT	Pass
5 ♣	Pass	6 NT	Pass
7 NT	Pass	Pass	Double
Pass	Pass	Pass	

A semi-psychic opening, followed by a "lie" in responding to Blackwood Convention. Then the thought that if partner could bid six no-trump with no aces in the South hand, then South could bid the grand slam.

After the hand had been played and North had taken an 800-point set, he quietly asked South: "How about a Coke?" "Okay," answered the dejected South. When North returned a few minutes later, he was carrying a Coke and a beer. As South reached for the beer, North drew it back, remarking: "I thought you wanted a Coke?" Whereupon South retorted: "Gosh, partner, can't you recognize a psych?" The answer is obvious.

11. PSYCHIC OPENING—DETRIMENTAL

(Duplicate bridge, International Open Pairs in England, 1957)

NORTH
♠ 8 5
♥ K Q J 5
♦ A K 8 5
♣ J 6 3

WEST
♠ J 9 7 2
♥ 9 7 4 2
♦ 9 4
♣ Q 10 4

EAST
♠ 6 3
♥ 6 3
♦ Q J 7 3 2
♣ K 9 8 2

SOUTH
♠ A K Q 10 4
♥ A 10 8
♦ 10 6
♣ A 7 5

North-South vulnerable.

EAST	SOUTH (*H. S. Brown*)	WEST	NORTH (*M. Cohn*)
1 ♦	Double	Pass	2 ♦
Pass	3 ♠	Pass	4 ♦
Pass	4 ♥	Pass	5 ♥
Pass	6 ♥	Pass	Pass
Pass			

A psychic opening spurs opponents on—to a fine contract.

A diamond was opened, taken by the ace, after which the king of diamonds was played, followed by a third diamond, declarer ruffing with his ace. Trumps were then drawn, and the finesse for the jack of spades lost, but declarer now had 12 tricks.

12. PSYCHIC RESPONSE—BENEFICIAL

(International Match, 1958. Italy vs. U.S.)

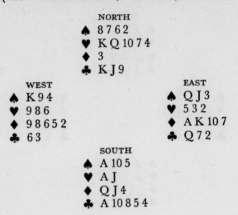

NORTH
- ♠ 8 7 6 2
- ♥ K Q 10 7 4
- ♦ 3
- ♣ K J 9

WEST
- ♠ K 9 4
- ♥ 9 8 6
- ♦ 9 8 6 5 2
- ♣ 6 3

EAST
- ♠ Q J 3
- ♥ 5 3 2
- ♦ A K 10 7
- ♣ Q 7 2

SOUTH
- ♠ A 10 5
- ♥ A J
- ♦ Q J 4
- ♣ A 10 8 5 4

North-South vulnerable.

WEST (*G. Rapee*)	NORTH (*Belladonna*)	EAST (*S. Silodor*)	SOUTH (*Avarelli*)
Pass	Pass	1 ♦	Double
1 ♥ (!)	2 ♦	Pass	3 ♣
Pass	3 ♥	Pass	3 NT
Pass	4 ♣	Pass	4 ♥
Pass	Pass	Pass	

The club queen was misguessed, and declarer went down one. Three no-trump is a much finer contract. The psychic muddled the bidding.

13. PSYCHIC RESPONSE TO WEAK TWO BID—BENEFICIAL

(Duplicate bridge, 1956.)

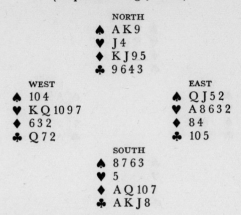

NORTH
♠ A K 9
♥ J 4
♦ K J 9 5
♣ 9 6 4 3

WEST
♠ 10 4
♥ K Q 10 9 7
♦ 6 3 2
♣ Q 7 2

EAST
♠ Q J 5 2
♥ A 8 6 3 2
♦ 8 4
♣ 10 5

SOUTH
♠ 8 7 6 3
♥ 5
♦ A Q 10 7
♣ A K J 8

North-South vulnerable.

WEST	NORTH	EAST	SOUTH
2 ♥	Pass	3 ♣	Double
Pass	Pass	3 ♦	Double
Pass	Pass	3 ♥	3 ♠
Pass	4 ♠	Pass	Pass
Pass			

East's bidding—after the weak two bid—needled North-South into a precarious contract. With misdefense, it made.

14. THE PSYCHIC RESPONSE—BENEFICIAL

(Duplicate bridge, 1959)

NORTH
♠ K Q
♥ K Q J x x
♦ A J 10 x x
♣ x

WEST
♠ J 10 8 7
♥ A 9
♦ 9 8 5 4
♣ K J x

EAST
♠ A 9 4 2
♥ 10 8 5
♦ x
♣ A Q 10 x x

SOUTH
♠ x x x
♥ x x x
♦ K Q x
♣ x x x x

Neither side vulnerable.

NORTH	EAST	SOUTH	WEST
(*Mrs. J. Bryant*)		(*FLK*)	
1 ♥	Pass	1 ♠	Pass
2 ♦	Pass	2 ♥	Pass
3 ♥	Pass	Pass	Pass

The one-spade response for fear that if I passed, the opponents would come in. Actually, the contract was made although it could have been defeated. The opponents are cold for a game at spades.

15. A PSYCHIC RESPONSE—BENEFICIAL

(Team-of-Four Championships, 1950)

```
                        NORTH
                     ♠ 6
                     ♥ A Q 10 6 2
                     ♦ A 9 6 4
                     ♣ K 6 2
   WEST                                    EAST
♠ 10 9 8 5 2                            ♠ A 7 3
♥ J 7 4                                 ♥ K 9 8 5 3
♦ Q                                     ♦ 3 2
♣ Q J 7 3                               ♣ A 10 9
                        SOUTH
                     ♠ K Q J 4
                     ♥ —
                     ♦ K J 10 8 7 5
                     ♣ 8 5 4
```

Both sides vulnerable.

NORTH	EAST	SOUTH	WEST
(*F. Hirsch*)		(*FLK*)	
1 ♥	Pass	2 ♦	Pass
3 ♦	Pass	4 ♣ *	Pass
4 ♥	Pass	5 ♦	Pass
Pass	Pass		

* A psych of the nondangerous variety, hoping to stop a club lead. It was my intent to bid five diamonds right over three diamonds, but I felt the four-club bid couldn't lose and might gain. A club lead would have beaten five diamonds.

16. A PSYCHIC RESPONSE, AND NO EXPOSURE—BENEFICIAL

(Rubber bridge, 1950)

NORTH
♠ A K x x x
♥ Q
♦ A x x
♣ A 8 x x

WEST
♠ x
♥ x x x x
♦ J x x x
♣ K x x x

EAST
♠ J x
♥ A K J 10 x x
♦ Q 10 x x
♣ Q

SOUTH
♠ Q 10 x x x
♥ x x
♦ K x
♣ J 10 9 x

North-South vulnerable.

EAST	SOUTH	WEST	NORTH
1 ♥	Pass	1 ♠	Double
2 ♥	Pass	Pass	?

What action should North take? He passed. Two hearts was made with 100 honors. North-South could have made 11 tricks at spades.

17. DECEPTIVE BIDDING BY SOUTH GIVING THE IMPRESSION
OF TAKING A SACRIFICE—BENEFICIAL

(Knockout-Team-of-Four, 1957)

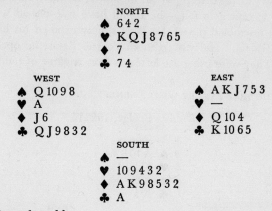

NORTH
- ♠ 6 4 2
- ♥ K Q J 8 7 6 5
- ♦ 7
- ♣ 7 4

WEST
- ♠ Q 10 9 8
- ♥ A
- ♦ J 6
- ♣ Q J 9 8 3 2

EAST
- ♠ A K J 7 5 3
- ♥ —
- ♦ Q 10 4
- ♣ K 10 6 5

SOUTH
- ♠ —
- ♥ 10 9 4 3 2
- ♦ A K 9 8 5 3 2
- ♣ A

Both sides vulnerable.

NORTH (*J. Kunkel*)	EAST	SOUTH (*Mrs. T. Michaels*)	WEST
3 ♥	3 ♠	4 ♥	4 ♠
Pass	Pass	5 ♥	5 ♠
Pass	Pass	6 ♥	Double
Pass	Pass	Pass	

18. TRAP-PASSING

A *trap-pass* is a pass made by a player who possesses a good hand,
or at least a much better hand than his pass denotes. The bid is
made in the hope that the opponents will think that the trapper
is "busted," and each opponent will then give his partner credit
for a better hand than he actually possesses. And the trapper can
then sneak in and ambush the opponents.

The following anecdote is told by Oswald Jacoby about the four
notorious psychic bidders who liked to use trap bidding. In a rubber
game, the auction went:

NORTH	EAST	SOUTH	WEST
1 ♠	Double	Redouble	

West had an eight-spot holding and instantly realized that there was something wrong with the deck. The opening spade might be legitimate, but East could only double as a psychic—with a good hand he would have trap-passed. Similarly, South would not have redoubled except as a fake—he would have trap-passed with anything that resembled power. So West simply exposed his hand and cried: "Misdeal." He was right, of course. Even the opener had psyched! They were using the leftovers from a game of pinochle.

19. PSYCHIC TRAP-PASS BY WEST—BENEFICIAL

(Rubber Bridge, 1954)

NORTH
♠ A 10 9 5 4
♥ K J 7 3
♦ A 6
♣ K 5

WEST
♠ 2
♥ Q 10 8 4
♦ Q J 10 5
♣ Q 10 8 3

EAST
♠ K Q J 7
♥ A 9 6
♦ 9 7 4
♣ A J 2

SOUTH
♠ 8 6 3
♥ 5 2
♦ K 8 3 2
♣ 9 7 6 4

North-South vulnerable.

EAST	SOUTH	WEST	NORTH
1 ♠	Pass	Pass(!)	Double
Pass	2 ♣	Double	Redouble(?)
Pass	Pass	Pass	

Down 1600!

20. A PSYCHIC RESPONSE—DETRIMENTAL

(Men's Team-of-Four Championship, 1949)

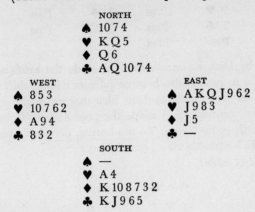

NORTH
- ♠ 10 7 4
- ♥ K Q 5
- ♦ Q 6
- ♣ A Q 10 7 4

WEST
- ♠ 8 5 3
- ♥ 10 7 6 2
- ♦ A 9 4
- ♣ 8 3 2

EAST
- ♠ A K Q J 9 6 2
- ♥ J 9 8 3
- ♦ J 5
- ♣ —

SOUTH
- ♠ —
- ♥ A 4
- ♦ K 10 8 7 3 2
- ♣ K J 9 6 5

North-South vulnerable.

SOUTH (*A. Moyse, Jr.*)	WEST	NORTH (*H. Schenken*)	EAST
1 ♦	Pass	1 ♠ (!)	Double
2 ♣	Pass	5 ♣	5 ♠
Pass	Pass	Double	Pass
Pass	Pass		

This contract was down 2, for 300 points. Six clubs is back-to-back for North-South. Who is to blame?

21. PSYCHIC RESPONSE—DETRIMENTAL

(Team-of-Four Championships, 1957)

NORTH
- ♠ A K 7
- ♥ A Q J 6 3
- ♦ A
- ♣ Q 6 4 2

SOUTH
- ♠ Q 6 2
- ♥ 5 2
- ♦ Q 9 7 4
- ♣ A K 7 3

Neither side vulnerable.

NORTH	EAST	SOUTH	WEST
		(*R. Kahn*)	
1 ♥	Pass	1 ♠	Pass
3 ♣	Pass	3 NT	Pass
Pass	Pass		

As told by Dick Kahn: "After I'd made the artificial response I was afraid to raise clubs, because partner's jump shift was probably based on good spades and the idea that we might get together on some high contract. So I made the poor and inadequate second response of three no-trump. To my horror, everybody passed."[2] (Seven clubs is makable via a heart finesse.)

At the other table:

NORTH	SOUTH
1 ♥	1 ♠
3 ♣	4 ♣
4 ♦	6 ♣
6 ♠ (!)	Pass

The six-spade contract suffered a 3-trick set—which proves that "dishonesty" can be costly.

22. A PSYCHIC RESPONSE RESULTS IN BAD LEAD—DETRIMENTAL

(Life Masters Individual Championships, 1950.)

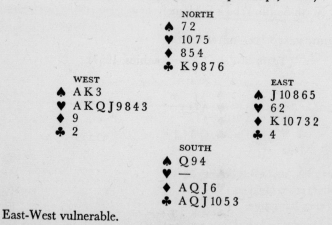

```
                    NORTH
                 ♠ 7 2
                 ♥ 10 7 5
                 ♦ 8 5 4
                 ♣ K 9 8 7 6
   WEST                              EAST
 ♠ A K 3                          ♠ J 10 8 6 5
 ♥ A K Q J 9 8 4 3                ♥ 6 2
 ♦ 9                              ♦ K 10 7 3 2
 ♣ 2                              ♣ 4
                    SOUTH
                 ♠ Q 9 4
                 ♥ —
                 ♦ A Q J 6
                 ♣ A Q J 10 5 3
```

East-West vulnerable.

[2] Taken verbatim from *The Bridge World*, September, 1957.

NORTH	EAST	SOUTH	WEST
			(*B. J. Becker*)
Pass	Pass	1 ♣	2 ♣
2 ♠ (!)	Pass	3 ♠	4 ♥
Pass	Pass	5 ♣	5 ♥
Pass	Pass	Pass	

Opening lead: a spade! It was not covered, but five was now made. If North opens his fourth-best club, South should let him hold the trick, in order to obtain a diamond shift.

23. PSYCHIC RESPONSE TO WEAK TWO BID COSTLY—DETRIMENTAL

(Duplicate bridge, 1959.)

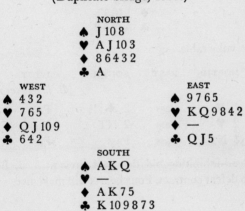

```
                    NORTH
                  ♠ J 10 8
                  ♥ A J 10 3
                  ♦ 8 6 4 3 2
                  ♣ A
      WEST                        EAST
    ♠ 4 3 2                     ♠ 9 7 6 5
    ♥ 7 6 5                     ♥ K Q 9 8 4 2
    ♦ Q J 10 9                  ♦ —
    ♣ 6 4 2                     ♣ Q J 5
                    SOUTH
                  ♠ A K Q
                  ♥ —
                  ♦ A K 7 5
                  ♣ K 10 9 8 7 3
```

Neither side vulnerable.

WEST	NORTH	EAST	SOUTH
Pass	Pass	2 ♥	Double
2 ♠	Double (1)	Pass	Pass
3 ♥	Double (2)	Pass	Pass (3)
Pass			

(1) North had met West before.
(2) Dollars from Heaven.
(3) Nervous but game.

Down 700.

24. PSYCHIC RESPONSE—NO GAIN; NO LOSS

(Vanderbilt Team of Four Championships, 1950.)

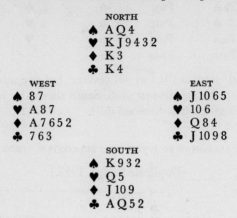

NORTH
♠ A Q 4
♥ K J 9 4 3 2
♦ K 3
♣ K 4

WEST
♠ 8 7
♥ A 8 7
♦ A 7 6 5 2
♣ 7 6 3

EAST
♠ J 10 6 5
♥ 10 6
♦ Q 8 4
♣ J 10 9 8

SOUTH
♠ K 9 3 2
♥ Q 5
♦ J 10 9
♣ A Q 5 2

Neither side vulnerable.

NORTH	EAST	SOUTH	WEST
			(*B. J. Becker*)
1 ♥	Pass	2 ♦ (!)	Pass
2 ♥	Pass	2 NT	Pass
3 NT	Pass	Pass	Pass

Psychic lead-inhibiting bid does not prevent lead. Becker led a diamond, to defeat contract. Four hearts will make five.

25. PSYCHIC RESPONSE—DETRIMENTAL, PERHAPS

(Team-of-Four, 1956.)

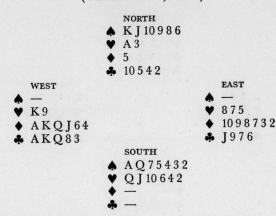

```
                          NORTH
                        ♠ K J 10 9 8 6
                        ♥ A 3
                        ♦ 5
                        ♣ 10 5 4 2
         WEST                                    EAST
       ♠ —                                     ♠ —
       ♥ K 9                                   ♥ 8 7 5
       ♦ A K Q J 6 4                           ♦ 10 9 8 7 3 2
       ♣ A K Q 8 3                             ♣ J 9 7 6
                          SOUTH
                        ♠ A Q 7 5 4 3 2
                        ♥ Q J 10 6 4 2
                        ♦ —
                        ♣ —
```

Neither side vulnerable.

NORTH	EAST	SOUTH	WEST
2 ♠ (!)	Pass	4 NT (2)	5 ♠ (3)
Pass	Pass	Pass	

(1) The weak two bid.

(2) South wanted to buy the hand at six spades, so he bid 4 NT as a display of strength.

(3) West wanted his partner to bid, so made the cue bid. This is the only hand I've ever seen where the final contract was in a suit that both declarer and dummy were void of.

North opened his singleton—and South trumped. Down 13.

At the other table, seven spades were bid and made, the heart finesse being successful.

26. PSYCHIC LEAD-INHIBITING REBID—BENEFICIAL

(Men's Pair Championships: 1950)

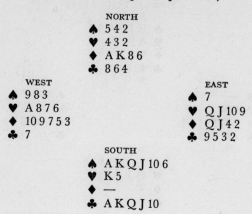

NORTH
- ♠ 5 4 2
- ♥ 4 3 2
- ♦ A K 8 6
- ♣ 8 6 4

WEST
- ♠ 9 8 3
- ♥ A 8 7 6
- ♦ 10 9 7 5 3
- ♣ 7

EAST
- ♠ 7
- ♥ Q J 10 9
- ♦ Q J 4 2
- ♣ 9 5 3 2

SOUTH
- ♠ A K Q J 10 6
- ♥ K 5
- ♦ —
- ♣ A K Q J 10

Both sides vulnerable.

SOUTH (R. Kahn)	WEST	NORTH (FLK)	EAST
2 ♠	Pass	3 ♦	Pass
4 ♦ (!)	Pass	4 ♠	Pass
4 NT	Pass	5 ♦	Pass
6 NT	Pass	Pass	Pass

Evidently Dick had decided to bid six no-trump after my positive response, and his raise to four diamonds was designed to talk the opponents into making a heart lead. He knew he couldn't get to dummy to cash whatever diamonds might be there, unless I had the nine of spades. West opened the ace of hearts, for fear that if he didn't it might be put to sleep. A spade or a club lead would have defeated the contract.

27. PSYCHIC REBID MISLEADING DEFENDERS IN BIDDING
AND PLAY—BENEFICIAL

(Team of Four, 1954)

NORTH
♠ 9 8 6
♥ Q 10 8 7
♦ 7 3 2
♣ Q 9 2

WEST
♠ Q 10 5 4 2
♥ K J 3 2
♦ Q J 4
♣ 10

EAST
♠ K 7 3
♥ —
♦ K 9 8 6 5
♣ J 8 7 5 4

SOUTH
♠ A J
♥ A 9 6 5 4
♦ A 10
♣ A K 6 3

Both sides vulnerable.

SOUTH (W. Rosen)	WEST (T. Stone)	NORTH (L. Mathe)	EAST (A. Roth)
1 ♥	Pass	2 ♥	Pass
2 ♠ (!)	Pass	3 ♥	Pass
4 ♥	Double	Pass	Pass
Pass			

This deal was reported in *The Bridge World*,[3] as follows: "Tobias
Stone, West, doubled with great firmness. Stone had the hearts and
spades behind declarer, and he was going to teach the young upstart
not to get frisky with his elders. . . . Four hearts was made when,
as hearts were being played, Roth discarded clubs. South had shown
up with two diamonds, and presumably had five hearts and four
spades—so Roth discarded clubs. . . . If Rosen hadn't hit upon the
idea of the two spade bid, Stone would not have doubled, and Roth
would not have discarded clubs."

[3] September, 1954

28. PSYCHOLOGICAL BID, A PREMATURE SAVE—BENEFICIAL

(Vanderbilt Team of Four Championships, 1953)

From East-West's point of view, who has the good cards?

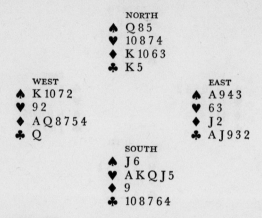

NORTH
♠ Q 8 5
♥ 10 8 7 4
♦ K 10 6 3
♣ K 5

WEST
♠ K 10 7 2
♥ 9 2
♦ A Q 8 7 5 4
♣ Q

EAST
♠ A 9 4 3
♥ 6 3
♦ J 2
♣ A J 9 3 2

SOUTH
♠ J 6
♥ A K Q J 5
♦ 9
♣ 10 8 7 6 4

East-West vulnerable.

SOUTH (*E. Kaplan*)	WEST	NORTH (*Ruth Sherman*)	EAST
1 ♥	Pass	2 ♥	Pass
4 ♥	Pass	Pass	Pass

A pre-emptive rebid, a premature sacrifice, with an outside chance of stealing the whole pot. (Three spades can be made the other way.) Down two, with 100 honors. No score.

At the other table:

SOUTH	WEST	NORTH	EAST
Pass	1 ♦	Pass	1 ♠
2 ♥	2 ♠	4 ♥	Double
Pass	4 ♠	Pass	Pass
5 ♥	Double	Pass	Pass
Pass			

Down three, 500 points, less 100 honors.

29. PSYCHIC REBID RESULTS IN BAD CONTRACT—DETRIMENTAL

(Rubber Bridge, 1953)

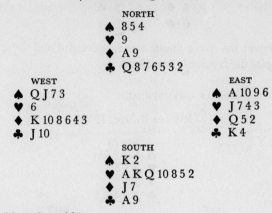

NORTH
♠ 8 5 4
♥ 9
♦ A 9
♣ Q 8 7 6 5 3 2

WEST
♠ Q J 7 3
♥ 6
♦ K 10 8 6 4 3
♣ J 10

EAST
♠ A 10 9 6
♥ J 7 4 3
♦ Q 5 2
♣ K 4

SOUTH
♠ K 2
♥ A K Q 10 8 5 2
♦ J 7
♣ A 9

Neither side vulnerable.

SOUTH	WEST	NORTH	EAST
1 ♥	Pass	2 ♣	Pass
2 ♠ (!)	Pass	3 ♣	Pass
4 ♥	Pass	4 ♠	Pass
5 ♥	Pass	Pass	Double
Pass	Pass	Pass	

30. PSYCHIC LEAD-INHIBITING REBID—BENEFICIAL,
    BUT LOSS INCURRED

(Rubber Bridge, 1959)

NORTH
♠ 9 8 x
♥ A K x
♦ Q J 10
♣ K 10 x x

SOUTH
♠ A Q J x x x
♥ x
♦ x x
♣ A Q J x

Neither side vulnerable.

SOUTH	NORTH
1 ♠	2 NT
3 ♦	3 ♠
6 ♠	Pass

A sad story: the spade finesse was unsuccessful and the slam went down despite the favorable heart lead.

31. PSYCHIC OVERCALL—BENEFICIAL

(Rubber Bridge, 1950)

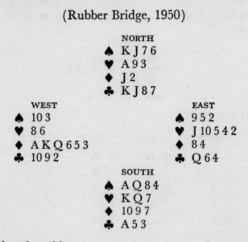

```
                    NORTH
                 ♠ K J 7 6
                 ♥ A 9 3
                 ♦ J 2
                 ♣ K J 8 7
   WEST                           EAST
 ♠ 10 3                         ♠ 9 5 2
 ♥ 8 6                          ♥ J 10 5 4 2
 ♦ A K Q 6 5 3                  ♦ 8 4
 ♣ 10 9 2                       ♣ Q 6 4
                    SOUTH
                 ♠ A Q 8 4
                 ♥ K Q 7
                 ♦ 10 9 7
                 ♣ A 5 3
```

North-South vulnerable.

SOUTH	WEST	NORTH	EAST
1 NT	2 ♣ (!)	3 NT	Pass
Pass	Double	Redouble	Pass
Pass	Pass		

Down 1000! Psychic overcall with "solid" suit in reserve.

32. THE PSYCHIC OVERCALL—BENEFICIAL

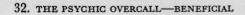

(Rubber Bridge, 1954)

                        NORTH
                        ♠ 9 7 5 4
                        ♥ Q 8 7 5
                        ♦ J 10 5 2
                        ♣ 2

    WEST   EAST
    ♠ K J 8 3   ♠ A Q 10
    ♥ K J 10 6   ♥ A 9 4 2
    ♦ K 7 6   ♦ A 8 3
    ♣ 9 3   ♣ Q 8 6

                        SOUTH
                        ♠ 6 2
                        ♥ 3
                        ♦ Q 9 4
                        ♣ A K J 10 7 5 4

Neither side vulnerable.

EAST	SOUTH	WEST	NORTH
1 NT	2 ♥	Double	Pass
Pass	2 ♠	Double	Pass
Pass	3 ♣	Double(!)	Pass
Pass	Pass		

The contagious double after a psychic.

33. A PSYCHIC OVERCALL AND A CONTAGIOUS DOUBLE—BENEFICIAL

(Masters Pairs, 1950)

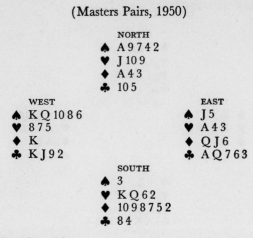

NORTH
- ♠ A 9 7 4 2
- ♥ J 10 9
- ♦ A 4 3
- ♣ 10 5

WEST
- ♠ K Q 10 8 6
- ♥ 8 7 5
- ♦ K
- ♣ K J 9 2

EAST
- ♠ J 5
- ♥ A 4 3
- ♦ Q J 6
- ♣ A Q 7 6 3

SOUTH
- ♠ 3
- ♥ K Q 6 2
- ♦ 10 9 8 7 5 2
- ♣ 8 4

Neither side vulnerable.

EAST	SOUTH	WEST	NORTH
	(*D. Warner*)		(*M. Hodges*)
1 ♣	1 ♠	Double	Pass
Pass	1 NT	Double	Pass
Pass	2 ♦	Pass	Pass
Double	Pass	Pass	Pass

Two diamonds doubled was fulfilled. A psychic overcall, with a prayer that something good would happen. Two diamonds was doubled on rhythm—a contagious double.

34. PSYCHICS BY OPPONENTS OF OPENING BIDDER
    AND A CONTAGIOUS DOUBLE—BENEFICIAL

(Duplicate bridge, 1952)

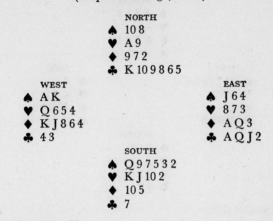

NORTH
♠ 10 8
♥ A 9
♦ 9 7 2
♣ K 10 9 8 6 5

WEST
♠ A K
♥ Q 6 5 4
♦ K J 8 6 4
♣ 4 3

EAST
♠ J 6 4
♥ 8 7 3
♦ A Q 3
♣ A Q J 2

SOUTH
♠ Q 9 7 5 3 2
♥ K J 10 2
♦ 10 5
♣ 7

North-South vulnerable.

EAST	SOUTH	WEST	NORTH
1 ♣	Pass	1 ♦	Pass
1 NT	Double	Pass	2 ♣
Double	2 ♦ (!)	Double	Pass
Pass	2 ♥	Double	Pass
Pass	2 ♠	Pass	Pass
Double	Pass	Pass	Pass

So attractive was the doubling rhythm that East-West later said
that they gave consideration to doubling North's final pass. Actually,
the contract was made by excellent play.

35. PSYCHIC OVERCALL—BENEFICIAL

(England vs. U.S.A., 1954)

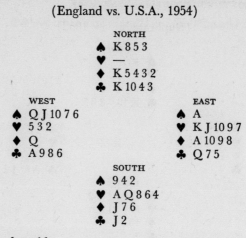

NORTH
♠ K 8 5 3
♥ —
♦ K 5 4 3 2
♣ K 10 4 3

WEST
♠ Q J 10 7 6
♥ 5 3 2
♦ Q
♣ A 9 8 6

EAST
♠ A
♥ K J 10 9 7
♦ A 10 9 8
♣ Q 7 5

SOUTH
♠ 9 4 2
♥ A Q 8 6 4
♦ J 7 6
♣ J 2

East-West vulnerable.

EAST	SOUTH	WEST	NORTH
1 ♥	1 ♠ (!)	2 ♣	4 ♠
5 ♣	Double	5 ♥	Pass
Pass	Double	Pass	Pass
Pass			

Down 800! This was a high caliber game—and the deception worked.

36. PSYCHIC OPENING AND PSYCHIC OVERCALL—
   OVERCALL BENEFICIAL

(World Championships, United States vs. Sweden, 1953.)

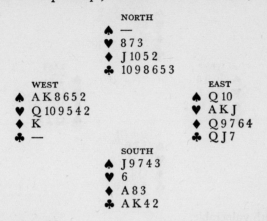

NORTH
♠ —
♥ 8 7 3
♦ J 10 5 2
♣ 10 9 8 6 5 3

WEST
♠ A K 8 6 5 2
♥ Q 10 9 5 4 2
♦ K
♣ —

EAST
♠ Q 10
♥ A K J
♦ Q 9 7 6 4
♣ Q J 7

SOUTH
♠ J 9 7 4 3
♥ 6
♦ A 8 3
♣ A K 4 2

East-West vulnerable.

NORTH	EAST	SOUTH	WEST
(*J. Crawford*)	(*Lilliehook*)	(*H. Schenken*)	(*Anulf*)
1 ♣	1 ♥	1 ♠	6 ♥
Pass	Pass	Pass	

The contract could have been defeated. Two psychics.

The opening lead was the ace of clubs. Dummy ruffed and led a trump to the ace. Declarer led the club jack, South played low, and dummy discarded the king of diamonds. East led the heart jack to dummy's queen, and returned a spade. North discarded and East won with the queen. East led the spade ten, South winning with the jack. South led the club king, dummy ruffing. Dummy led a low spade, and East ruffed. East got to dummy by ruffing a diamond, drew the last trump, and ran the spades, making the contract.

Comment: North should have doubled the slam contract, for an unusual lead (almost surely, spades); South should not have opened the club ace, and should have covered the club jack.

37. PSYCHIC OVERCALL—BENEFICIAL

(World Championships, 1955. England vs. U.S.A.)

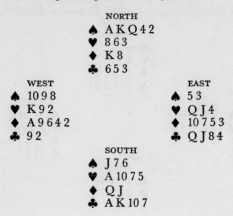

```
                        NORTH
                    ♠ A K Q 4 2
                    ♥ 8 6 3
                    ♦ K 8
                    ♣ 6 5 3
    WEST                                EAST
 ♠ 10 9 8                            ♠ 5 3
 ♥ K 9 2                             ♥ Q J 4
 ♦ A 9 6 4 2                         ♦ 10 7 5 3
 ♣ 9 2                               ♣ Q J 8 4
                        SOUTH
                    ♠ J 7 6
                    ♥ A 10 7 5
                    ♦ Q J
                    ♣ A K 10 7
```

North-South vulnerable.

EAST (*Dodds*)	SOUTH (*Ellenby*)	WEST (*Meredith*)	NORTH (*Roth*)
Pass	1 ♣	1 ♠	Double
Pass	Pass	1 NT	Pass
Pass	Double	2 ♣	Pass
Pass	Double	2 ♦	Pass
Pass	2 ♠	Pass	4 ♠
Pass	Pass	Pass	

Exposing a psychic—top-flight—and yet, three no-trump is a superior contract. With no psychic, at the other table the bidding went:

EAST (*Mathe*)	SOUTH (*Reese*)	WEST (*Bishop*)	NORTH (*Schapiro*)
Pass	1 ♣	Pass	1 ♠
Pass	1 NT	Pass	3 NT
Pass	Pass	Pass	

38. PSYCHIC RESPONSE TO PARTNER'S OVERCALL—BENEFICIAL

(Rubber bridge, 1952)

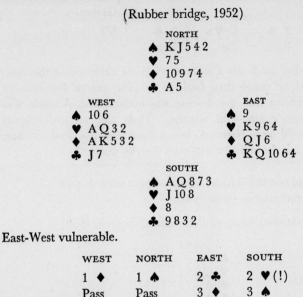

NORTH
♠ K J 5 4 2
♥ 7 5
♦ 10 9 7 4
♣ A 5

WEST
♠ 10 6
♥ A Q 3 2
♦ A K 5 3 2
♣ J 7

EAST
♠ 9
♥ K 9 6 4
♦ Q J 6
♣ K Q 10 6 4

SOUTH
♠ A Q 8 7 3
♥ J 10 8
♦ 8
♣ 9 8 3 2

East-West vulnerable.

WEST	NORTH	EAST	SOUTH
1 ♦	1 ♠	2 ♣	2 ♥ (!)
Pass	Pass	3 ♦	3 ♠
Pass	Pass	Pass	

East-West can make either five hearts or five diamonds.

39. PSYCHIC RESPONSE TO AN OVERCALL—BENEFICIAL

(Masters Pairs, 1950)

NORTH
♠ K J 2
♥ A 8 7 6 5 2
♦ K
♣ A 10 2

WEST
♠ A Q 10 7 6 5
♥ K 10
♦ 9 6 5
♣ Q 7

EAST
♠ 8 4 3
♥ —
♦ A 8 4 3
♣ K J 9 8 5 4

SOUTH
♠ 9
♥ Q J 9 4 3
♦ Q J 10 7 2
♣ 6 3

Both sides vulnerable.

WEST	NORTH	EAST	SOUTH
			(*J. Gerber*)
1 ♠	2 ♥	2 ♠	3 NT(!)
Pass	Pass	Pass	

When Gerber made his 3 no-trump bid, he expected further bid-ding, so that he could then back in to four hearts. But nothing happened—except that the defense was undermined. A spade was opened, Gerber's nine-spot winning. Then the successful heart finesse, followed by a diamond. When East took the diamond ace, he shifted to a club; and 12 tricks were thereby made.

40. A PSYCHIC DOUBLE WHICH MISLEADS DECLARER IN THE PLAY OF THE CARDS—BENEFICIAL

(National Team-of-Four Championship, 1956)

```
                        NORTH
                        ♠ —
                        ♥ Q 8 6 5
                        ♦ A K 10 9 7 4 3
                        ♣ A Q
        WEST                              EAST
        ♠ A K J 9 3                       ♠ Q 10 6 5 2
        ♥ J 10 2                          ♥ K
        ♦ 5                               ♦ 6 2
        ♣ K 8 7 2                         ♣ J 10 6 4 3
                        SOUTH
                        ♠ 8 7 4
                        ♥ A 9 7 4 3
                        ♦ Q J 8
                        ♣ 9 5
```

North-South vulnerable.

WEST	NORTH	EAST	SOUTH
1 ♠	Double	4 ♠	5 ♥
Pass	6 ♥	Double	Pass
Pass	Pass		

East's double leads declarer into leading queen of hearts, playing East for K J x or K 10 x. A spade opening, followed by two rounds of hearts. Down 3, for minus 800.

41. PSYCHIC OVERCALL PARTNER FAILS TO RECOGNIZE—DETRIMENTAL

(Rubber Bridge, 1956)

East-West vulnerable.

```
                    NORTH
                 ♠ 5
                 ♥ Q 6 2
                 ♦ K 4
                 ♣ A K Q 7 5 3 2
```

SOUTH	WEST	NORTH	EAST
		(D. R. Sims)	
Pass	1 ♠	3 NT	Double
Pass	Pass	4 ♣ (1)	Double
4 NT (2)	Pass	5 ♣	Double
5 NT (3)	Double	(4)	

(1) This I could make.
(2) My partner didn't like clubs.
(3) He still didn't.
(4) We went around again.[4]

42. THE WEAK TWO BIDS RUINS THE OPPONENTS—
(THE OVERCALL) HARASSING BID BENEFICIAL

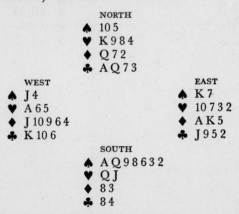

```
                    NORTH
                 ♠ 10 5
                 ♥ K 9 8 4
                 ♦ Q 7 2
                 ♣ A Q 7 3
   WEST                              EAST
♠ J 4                              ♠ K 7
♥ A 6 5                            ♥ 10 7 3 2
♦ J 10 9 6 4                       ♦ A K 5
♣ K 10 6                           ♣ J 9 5 2
                    SOUTH
                 ♠ A Q 9 8 6 3 2
                 ♥ Q J
                 ♦ 8 3
                 ♣ 8 4
```

Both sides 60 on score and vulnerable.

[4] Taken verbatim from an article by Dorothy Rice Sims in *The Bridge World*, May, 1956.

NORTH	EAST	SOUTH	WEST
Pass	Pass	2 ♠	Pass
Pass	2 NT	Pass	Pass
Double	Pass	Pass	Pass

Down 1700! (Could have been *only* 1100 by double dummy play.)

The queen of hearts opening was ducked, and the ace of hearts in dummy won the continuation of the jack. Declarer elected to lead a diamond to his ace, and then a club back to dummy's king-ten. He finessed the ten; North won with the queen and returned a spade. The defense was able to run the rest of the tricks.[5]

43. PSYCHICS AND COUNTER PSYCHICS, AND A HORRIBLE FINAL CONTRACT—OVERCALL DETRIMENTAL

(Rubber Bridge, 1951)

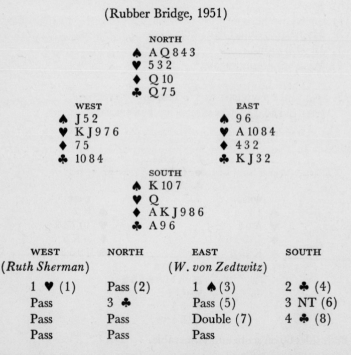

```
                        NORTH
                     ♠ A Q 8 4 3
                     ♥ 5 3 2
                     ♦ Q 10
                     ♣ Q 7 5
     WEST                                  EAST
  ♠ J 5 2                               ♠ 9 6
  ♥ K J 9 7 6                           ♥ A 10 8 4
  ♦ 7 5                                 ♦ 4 3 2
  ♣ 10 8 4                              ♣ K J 3 2
                        SOUTH
                     ♠ K 10 7
                     ♥ Q
                     ♦ A K J 9 8 6
                     ♣ A 9 6
```

WEST	NORTH	EAST	SOUTH
(*Ruth Sherman*)		(*W. von Zedtwitz*)	
1 ♥ (1)	Pass (2)	1 ♠ (3)	2 ♣ (4)
Pass	3 ♣	Pass (5)	3 NT (6)
Pass	Pass	Double (7)	4 ♣ (8)
Pass	Pass	Pass	

[5] From *All the Tricks,* by Helen Sobel, Greenberg: Publisher, Philadelphia, 1949.

The analysis is by Waldemar von Zedtwitz.

(1) Typical psychic. Ruth Sherman. She's a fine player.

(2) A Roth-Stone system player. Couldn't even think about over-calling, of course.

(3) The "obvious" bid. My partner couldn't have spades unless she had a very good hand. [Because, having bid hearts, she could only show spades by reversing, which would be a strong bid. FLK]

(4) Good bid. South was stirring things up and playing for a swing. He didn't think he could make game his way, but was angling toward three no-trump, or maybe to get doubled at three or four diamonds.

(5) Somebody was sure to bid again, but if nobody did, I didn't care much.

(6) South assumed that his partner had a heart stopper.

(7) Of course by now I knew West had opened a psychic. But if I didn't double there was a good chance that the opponents could make their contract against a spade opening. I doubled for a heart lead, and also because I didn't think South could stand it. [Three no-trump. FLK]

(8) The right bid, of course. South was still angling to get doubled at four diamonds.[6]

[As is evident, North-South can make either six spades or six diamonds. They did not make four clubs. FLK]

[6] Taken verbatim from *The Bridge World,* December, 1952.

44. PSYCHIC RAISE OF OVERCALL, CREATING IMPRESSION OF STRENGTH
AND CONVINCING OPENER'S PARTNER THAT OPENER WAS PSYCH-
ING—HARASSING AND BENEFICIAL

(National Team of Four Championships, 1956)

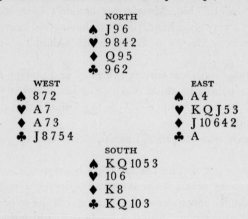

NORTH
♠ J 9 6
♥ 9 8 4 2
♦ Q 9 5
♣ 9 6 2

WEST
♠ 8 7 2
♥ A 7
♦ A 7 3
♣ J 8 7 5 4

EAST
♠ A 4
♥ K Q J 5 3
♦ J 10 6 4 2
♣ A

SOUTH
♠ K Q 10 5 3
♥ 10 6
♦ K 8
♣ K Q 10 3

East-West vulnerable.

NORTH (A. Sheinwold)	EAST (T. Stone)	SOUTH (E. Kaplan)	WEST (A. Roth)
Pass	1 ♥	1 ♠	Pass
2 ♠	Pass	3 ♠	Pass
Pass	Pass		

Sheinwold bluffed. If he had passed, Stone would have reopened
the bidding. Roth probably suspected that Stone was psyching.
Down 2. Four hearts cold. (Stone psychs even with unfavorable
vulnerability.)

45. PSYCHIC RESPONSE—BENEFICIAL, AND THEN SOME!

(International Team of Four. U.S. vs. Italy, 1951)

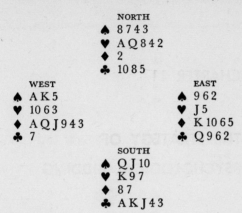

```
                         NORTH
                      ♠ 8 7 4 3
                      ♥ A Q 8 4 2
                      ♦ 2
                      ♣ 10 8 5
    WEST                                    EAST
 ♠ A K 5                                 ♠ 9 6 2
 ♥ 10 6 3                                ♥ J 5
 ♦ A Q J 9 4 3                           ♦ K 10 6 5
 ♣ 7                                     ♣ Q 9 6 2
                         SOUTH
                      ♠ Q J 10
                      ♥ K 9 7
                      ♦ 8 7
                      ♣ A K J 4 3
```

Both sides vulnerable.

WEST	NORTH	EAST	SOUTH
(*Stayman*)		(*Rapee*)	
1 ♦	Pass	1 ♥ (!)	2 ♣
2 ♥	Pass	3 ♦	Pass
3 ♠	Pass	3 NT	Pass
Pass	Pass		

South opened a low club and East stole a game.

The above deal seems inconsequential, but yet, suppose that originally Rapee had bid either two diamonds or passed. Would North-South have arrived at the easily makable four-heart contract? Probably.

CHAPTER 11

THE STRATEGY OF
PSYCHOLOGICAL BIDDING

From an objective viewpoint, there can be no doubt in anyone's mind but that the various types of "psychological" bids presented and analyzed in the preceding sections of this text are here to stay. Just as the different varieties of standard pre-emptive bids and psychics have persisted throughout the ages, so the young, new harassing and obstructionist types of bids—the weak two bid, the weak jump overcall, the weak no-trump, etc.—have arisen to reinforce their older teammates in the everlasting struggle against those who have been accustomed to an easy, comfortable, and unmolested way of life. It is my opinion that most of these new bids will, in the near future, become adopted by a great number of the world's bridge players and will be wielded with ever-increasing accuracy. To shout "death to the invaders" will not negate the validity and power of these new bids. Even if one does not choose to employ any of these radical bids, he must, in self-defense, become not only acclimated to them but also familiar with their workings. Otherwise, he will either perish at the table or be robbed of his rightful heritage—the right to show a reasonable, or maximum, profit on his good cards. How does one go about adapting himself to this drastically changing environment?

Let's be realistic about these psychological and space-consuming bids. Their purposes are (1) to confuse, outsmart, or hypnotize the opponents, (2) to disrupt the opponents' lines of communication, (3) to prevent the enemy from sauntering merrily along their accustomed paths of bidding, (4) to goad or taunt the adversaries into unwarranted positive action, (5) to scare them out of their wits, thereby rendering them incapable of thinking clearly, or rendering them impotent, or (6) generally, to throw a monkey wrench into their bidding (or thinking) machinery. And it is a fact that a certain part of the time the remaining cards will be so distributed that the "unorthodox" bid will work to perfection, as hoped for. What is the defense against the psychological bid? How can it be overcome?

Unfortunately—and paradoxically—the secret of satisfactory defense against these unorthodox bids is that there isn't any! There is no defense that will work all the time, just as there is no type of unorthodox (or orthodox) bid that will always accomplish its intended result. When confusion has become the order of the day, rational analysis becomes incapable of solving irrational goings-on with a consistently high degree of success. One is forced to guess, to speculate, to ferret out fact from fiction—and misinterpretation or sheer guesswork becomes inevitable at times. For example, let us look at the following deal:

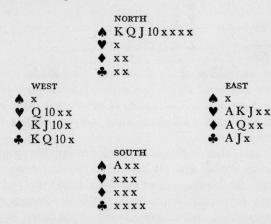

NORTH
♠ K Q J 10 x x x x
♥ x
♦ x x
♣ x x

WEST
♠ x
♥ Q 10 x x
♦ K J 10 x
♣ K Q 10 x

EAST
♠ x
♥ A K J x x
♦ A Q x x
♣ A J x

SOUTH
♠ A x x
♥ x x x
♦ x x x
♣ x x x x

North opens with *three spades,* both sides being vulnerable. What do you, sitting East, do? Probably you double, in which case you will get to four hearts; or perhaps, if either you or partner is clairvoyant, optimistic, and sufficiently aggressive, to the easily makable contract of six hearts. But, had you been the dealer, your one-heart opening bid would probably have elicited a three-heart response from partner, in which case the slam would undoubtedly have been arrived at. North's bid, of course, deprived you of the valuable bidding space needed to exchange information with partner. As a result, you were forced to guess as to your immediate action, and subsequent action, if any. In a sense, you were lucky: you caught your partner with a good hand. Tomorrow, in the same circumstances, when you double North's opening three spade bid, you may run into this (as have all of us):

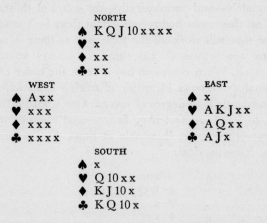

```
                    NORTH
              ♠ K Q J 10 x x x x
              ♥ x
              ♦ x x
              ♣ x x
 WEST                                EAST
♠ A x x                            ♠ x
♥ x x x                            ♥ A K J x x
♦ x x x                            ♦ A Q x x
♣ x x x x                          ♣ A J x
                    SOUTH
              ♠ x
              ♥ Q 10 x x
              ♦ K J 10 x
              ♣ K Q 10 x
```

With the interchange of the South and West hands, you, sitting East, become a doomed man if you utter the word *double* over the opening three-spade bid. And South, of course, will make his presence heard and felt via a reverberating *double* over any bid that East or West makes.

Here we have, then, a simple textbook pre-emptive opening bid, which mystifies nobody and yet has the potential of creating much chaos. What is the solution to East's problem (and yours and mine)? Petition for a law to prohibit pre-emptive bids—or learn to cultivate a healthy respect for, and an appreciation of, the power of the bid, which conveys a precise message to partner while simultaneously keeping the opponents from arriving at a rational and logical contract.

The weak two bid, the weak jump overcall, the weak no-trump, etc., are all dedicated and geared to destroying the enemy while maintaining a most practical and harmonious relationship with partner. Speaking objectively, when one is faced with the decision as to what to do over a pre-emptive or harassing bid, he is quite frequently forced to guess—and a fair percentage of the time he will guess wrong.

To the current devotees and the future disciples of these new-type obstructionist, harassing, and "fancy" unorthodox bids, let me issue a very necessary word of warning:

> The great majority of points at bridge are won by finding your right contract, and not by either pushing the enemy into the wrong one or by indulging in capricious bidding on your good cards.

When you have an obvious, sound, constructive bid to make, make it instead of seeking a bid that *might* confuse the opponents, but that might also lead to your own self-destruction by confusing partner. Go after your own contract by describing your hand to partner. In brief, don't fool around with your good hands, which are your bread and butter. If you elect to employ any type of pre-emptive or harassing bid, such as described in this text, stay within the prescribed limits of the particular bid. Don't deviate merely because you have learned to love to plague or annoy the opponents. These new obstructionist bids can operate efficiently only if their specifically designated range is not violated. Once the range is violated, one has set forth on the road to creating three formidable enemies at the table: not only your two opponents, but also your partner. In these Frankenstein circumstances, each of them is capable of inflicting a deathblow. And if there is no kibitzer available, there goes your bridge game.

PART II

THE PLAY

CHAPTER 12

THE NECESSITY FOR DECEPTIVE PLAY

Just as the knowledge and application of deceptive bidding tactics are essential if one aspires to become a good bridge player, so the knowledge and application of deceptive techniques in play must be included in the good bridge player's arsenal of weapons. But, as in the field of bidding, deception must not be viewed as a substitute for technical skill. Rather, it must supplement technical skill, since technical skill in itself is not sufficient to yield optimum results. In combination, working as a unit, technical skill and deceptive tactics form a well-rounded bridge personality, geared to the attainment of maximum efficiency.

That deception in play is mandatory if winning results are to be achieved is concurred in by everyone. Even those who are categorically opposed to deception in bidding agree that in *play* deception is a must; and that when all seems lost, the effective application of deception, camouflage, and chicanery can often alter one's seemingly apparent destiny, and hence should be applied. So deceptive tactics in play must be utilized not merely for self-protection but, in the long run, for self-preservation.

Actually, no justification is really required to demonstrate the necessity for the application of deceptive techniques in play. The first law of nature is self-preservation. And when observation reveals that one is doomed to defeat if the opponents play properly, one's only salvation lies in the hope that he can trick them into playing incorrectly. Such "deceit" is available to both the declarer and the defenders. Generally speaking, more often than not the practice of deception brings better results when declarer applies it, since a defender, by a deceptive play, may easily mislead his partner as to the true state of affairs. Of course, to deceive partner without deceiving declarer is not deception—it is sabotage. And yet, there are situations where a defender deliberately (and properly) misleads partner to gain a desired result! A deal illustrating this latter point is presented on page 279. From the viewpoint of declarer's deceptive tactics, he has no worry about fooling partner, since partner is making sandwiches or mixing drinks.

Deceptive play takes many varied forms: a tricky lead based on an interpretation of the bidding, a false-card, a high card thrown off unnecessarily, a discard made at a time when it will greatly confuse an opponent, the winning of a trick with a high card when one could have won it with a low card, a trick refused for a reason the opponent can only guess at, etc. The purpose of each of these deceptive plays is, of course, to create an incorrect impression in the mind of the opponent you are trying to deceive—to make him believe that a mirage is actually reality, with the hoped-for effect that he will then think and plan as you want him to do.

Let us take a look at two simple deals that arose in actual competition. Both contain identical false-carding plays, one being employed by declarer and the other by a defender. After observing the deals, I'm certain you will agree that it was virtually impossible to see through the deceit; and that if the deception had not been employed, the deceiver would have perished.

1.

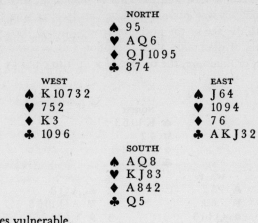

NORTH
♠ 9 5
♥ A Q 6
♦ Q J 10 9 5
♣ 8 7 4

WEST
♠ K 10 7 3 2
♥ 7 5 2
♦ K 3
♣ 10 9 6

EAST
♠ J 6 4
♥ 10 9 4
♦ 7 6
♣ A K J 3 2

SOUTH
♠ A Q 8
♥ K J 8 3
♦ A 8 4 2
♣ Q 5

Both sides vulnerable.

SOUTH	WEST	NORTH	EAST
1 NT	Pass	3 NT	Pass
Pass	Pass		

West opened the three of spades, and declarer surveyed his joint assets. He observed that if East held the king of diamonds, the contract would be easily makable. But if West held the diamond king, when he obtained the lead with that card he might well switch to the club suit, resulting in declarer's defeat.

So declarer captured East's jack of spades with the *ace,* not the queen! He then entered dummy via the heart ace, led the queen of diamonds and finessed, West's king winning.

Convinced that East held the queen of spades (after all, how many declarers win a jack with the ace when they could have won it with the queen?), West next played a small spade to East's "marked" queen. Declarer now romped in with ten tricks.

Suppose declarer had captured the opening spade lead with the queen. West, after winning his king of diamonds, would then undoubtedly have perceived the futility of continuing spades, since declarer would be known to still possess the spade ace. In view of dummy's established diamonds and dummy's heart strength, West would unquestionably then have made the "desperation" shift to a club—and declarer would have suffered a two-trick set.

To summarize, if East had the king of diamonds, then the three no-trump contract was guaranteed whether declarer won the opening lead with the ace or the queen of spades. But if West possessed the vital king of diamonds, then deception was necessary in order to eliminate, or minimize, the danger of a shift to clubs by West.

2.

```
                        NORTH
                     ♠ K 10 6 3
                     ♥ 4 2
                     ♦ A J 8 2
                     ♣ K 7 3
        WEST                            EAST
     ♠ 7 5 2                         ♠ A Q 8
     ♥ 7 6 3                         ♥ A Q 10 9 8
     ♦ Q 10 3                        ♦ 9 7 4
     ♣ 10 9 6 4                      ♣ J 5
                        SOUTH
                     ♠ J 9 4
                     ♥ K J 5
                     ♦ K 6 5
                     ♣ A Q 8 2
```

East-West vulnerable.

SOUTH	WEST	NORTH	EAST
1 ♣	Pass	1 ♦	1 ♥
Pass	Pass	1 ♠	Pass
1 NT	Pass	2 NT	Pass
3 NT	Pass	Pass	Pass

West opened a small heart, East won with the ace and returned a heart, declarer's jack winning. Declarer then led the jack of spades, West played low, as did dummy. East took this trick with his *ace!*

East now played back a heart, declarer winning the trick with his king. Actually East was a good player, and South knew that deception was a component part of East's equipment. South then cashed the king, ace, and queen of clubs, hoping that the adverse clubs would be divided 3-3, thereby promoting his fourth club into his ninth, and game-going, trick. When the clubs failed to break as hoped for, declarer now led the nine of spades, finessing West for the "marked" queen of spades (after all, how many defenders win a jack with the ace when they could have won it with the queen?). East then cashed his two remaining hearts, thereby defeating declarer's contract.

Suppose East had captured the spade jack with his queen instead of with the ace. Surely declarer would have credited East with possessing the spade ace, in view of East's vulnerable overcall. And what choice would declarer then have had but to attack the diamond suit and pray that West held the diamond queen and that the adverse diamonds were divided 3-3? But East's timely false-card lured declarer into staying with the spade suit, resulting in an unhappy declarer.

I'm sure you will agree that in each of the two above deals the deceived had nothing to be ashamed of. In each case, he took the natural and normal line of play. Yet, had the *deceiver* played naturally and normally, his victory would have been transformed into defeat, for the deceived would then have been forced to adopt the winning line of play.

Thus, situations will arise where technical efficiency is of no use and one's only hope is that the adversary will make an error. In such apparently hopeless situations, the only chance lies in making it easier for the adversary to err, by guiding him up the wrong path —and then trusting that nature will take care of him, and you.

And so we come to this conclusion: one should aim to get not only as many tricks as he is entitled to on the strict merit of the cards, but also as many more as he can get through the use of any deceptive tactics he can dream up. To sell an adversary a bill of goods that some condition exists that actually does not is considered, in the realm of bridgedom, "a thing of beauty, and a joy forever."

Without doubt, the most frequently occuring form of deception available to both declarer and the defenders is the technique of false-carding. It should be noted, as was mentioned earlier, that the declarer has a decided advantage over the defenders when it comes to the question of false-carding. He may false-card as he chooses without running the risk of misleading partner. But the defender who adopts such tactics often finds that the victim of his false-carding has turned out to be his partner, and not the declarer. In general, the defenders should proceed with caution in their employment of deceptive tactics because (1) it is usually more important to avoid deceiving partner than to deceive declarer; (2) an excess of false-carding fails to deceive as soon as declarer becomes aware of this habit of a player; and (3) the logic of the natural play is sacrificed. This warning to the defenders does not imply that declarer is exempt from heeding the warning, or that he has the right to false-card to his heart's content because his partner cannot become a victim. As a matter of fact, it is wrong to assume that since you have no partner to fool, no harm can come from false-carding as declarer; much harm can result, and quite often the opponents will be more deceived, or more uncertain as to your holding, if you tell the truth. Witness, for example, the following deal:

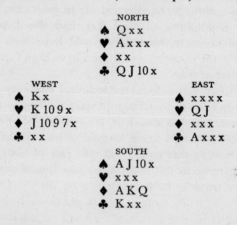

```
                        NORTH
                    ♠ Q x x
                    ♥ A x x x
                    ♦ x x
                    ♣ Q J 10 x
    WEST                                EAST
♠ K x                              ♠ x x x x
♥ K 10 9 x                         ♥ Q J
♦ J 10 9 7 x                       ♦ x x x
♣ x x                              ♣ A x x x
                        SOUTH
                    ♠ A J 10 x
                    ♥ x x x
                    ♦ A K Q
                    ♣ K x x
```

Both sides vulnerable.

SOUTH	WEST	NORTH	EAST
1 NT	Pass	2 NT	Pass
3 NT	Pass	Pass	Pass

West opened the jack of diamonds, which declarer captured with his *ace*. A club was then led, East's ace winning. East, although not unmindful of the tenet, "return partner's suit," nevertheless now shifted to the queen of hearts. Eventually declarer went down a trick. Had East, at trick three, played back diamonds—his partner's suit—declarer would easily have fulfilled his contract. How come East switched to a heart?

From East's point of view, West's opening lead of the diamond jack had denied the queen (had West held the Q-J, any number of times he would have led the queen). So East reflected on why declarer had won the jack with the ace, and not with the queen which he was known to possess. The only logical answer became apparent: declarer must have had the A K Q, in which case there was no waste in taking the trick with the ace. Therefore, the return of a diamond was a hopeless lead. Hence, the heart lead.

Had declarer won the opening lead normally, with the queen, East could not have known what the true state of affairs was in the diamond suit. West might well have held the A J 10 x x, and declarer the K Q x, in which case a diamond return by East would have defeated declarer at once; or, West might have held the K J 10 x x, and declarer the A Q x, in which case a diamond return by East would have established West's diamond suit. But, to the astute defender, when South captured the diamond jack with the ace (to be deceptive), declarer's hand became an open book.

The moral of the deal is, of course, that when nothing can be gained by deception, it is far better to play the cards honestly.

From the defenders' point of view, careless false-cards such as the above are too often employed to trick declarer—and they boomerang, with disastrous repercussions. The following is the most common variety of "cute" (and detrimental) defensive false-carding:

♥ A J 10 9

♥ 8 7 5   ♥ K Q 2

♥ 6 4 3

Declarer (South) leads the three of hearts, putting in the nine-spot from dummy—and the tricky East wins it with the *king,* his purpose being to deceive declarer into believing that the queen is in the West hand. Of what importance is it what declarer thinks? No matter how declarer subsequently plays the heart suit, *won't East always win another heart trick?* Why, then, mislead partner into believing that *South* possesses the queen of hearts? If East does deceive partner, then in the later play partner will refused to lead a heart, and East might desperately be wanting a heart lead to obtain a second trick in the suit. Why deceive partner, especially when declarer is immune to the deception? The deceit stands only to lose, and never to gain.

An apparently analogous situation, and yet completely different, is the following:

♠ A J 10 9 3

♠ K Q

Let us say that spades is the trump suit, although the same would apply if it were a side suit. Declarer leads the deuce of spades from the South hand, putting up the nine-spot from dummy. The normal false-card is to take the trick with the king, in the hope that by so doing declarer will be led to believe that West possesses the queen. The fear here is that declarer, left to his own resources, may next play the ace, catching your remaining unprotected honor. The capturing of the intital spade lead with the king *may* convince declarer that he should finesse West for the queen on the next lead of the suit, which would be proper if East's king were the normal and honest play. Bear in mind, however, that in the above situation you should not always win the trick with the king, for if you do you will mark yourself as a habitual falsecarder—and if you ever win the trick initially with the queen, declarer will know that you do not possess the king.

Before proceeding to the various strategems and tactical maneuvers available to both the defenders and the declarer, as will be observed in actual competition, a word of caution regarding your approach is in order. To attempt to memorize these deceptive plays, with the aim of putting them into a habitual pattern of behavior, will serve only to make a stereotyped player of you; and your opponents will get to know your style and profit thereby. For instance, a player who is known to always false-card is just as much of an open book as is the player who never false-cards. Therefore, in studying the deceptive tactics which will be presented, one's objective should be to *analyze and understand the motivation* that gave birth to them, rather than to memorize them in order to earmark them for immediate and future application.

CHAPTER 13

DECLARER'S DECEPTION IN ACTION

The thirty-two deals in this chapter illustrate the practical application of deceptive tactics by the declarer. These deals all arose in expert competition.

The first eleven deals (Section A) feature deception at trick one, and cover situations wherein declarer either false-carded, or by some other method of psychological strategy, created the illusion that a certain situation existed—a situation which, in reality, was a mirage. And as a result of declarer's deception, the defenders lost a battle that was theirs to win by brute force.

The remaining seventeen deals (Section B) cover cases in which declarer's deceit occurred subsequent to trick one, with the identical result being attained: the hypnosis of the defenders to such an extent that they never recovered until it was too late, resulting in declarer transforming imminent defeat into glorious victory; and proving thereby that deception is both a supplement and a complement to sheer power.

A.
DECEPTION AT TRICK ONE

1. This deal features a simple deceptive play by a declarer. Yet, to me it is one of the finest examples I have ever seen of convincing the opponents beyond a shadow of a doubt that a certain situation

existed—and too late they discovered that what had appeared to be reality was just a mirage.

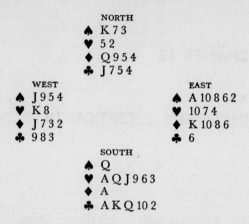

NORTH
♠ K 7 3
♥ 5 2
♦ Q 9 5 4
♣ J 7 5 4

WEST
♠ J 9 5 4
♥ K 8
♦ J 7 3 2
♣ 9 8 3

EAST
♠ A 10 8 6 2
♥ 10 7 4
♦ K 10 8 6
♣ 6

SOUTH
♠ Q
♥ A Q J 9 6 3
♦ A
♣ A K Q 10 2

South, Sam Fry, Jr., was playing a *six-club* contract. West opened the deuce of diamonds, declarer played the *queen* from dummy, East covered with the king, and declarer captured the trick with his singleton ace. South then led the ten of trumps, overtook it with dummy's jack, and tried the heart finesse, losing to West's king. West now triumphantly laid down the jack of diamonds, which declarer trumped and then waltzed in with his slam (by eventually trumping his queen of spades, after discarding dummy's spades on the established hearts).

At trick one, it was apparent to declarer that if the heart finesse lost, he was doomed to defeat—unless the opponents failed to switch to a spade. So, to take out insurance against West having the king of hearts, Sam put up the queen of diamonds from dummy at trick one, thereby creating the indelible impression that he held at least two diamonds. After all, who but an idiot (or an expert) would play the queen from dummy when he himself had only the singleton ace? Can you blame West for returning the jack of diamonds?

2. If deception is to accomplish its desired effect, it must be performed with spontaneity—not with hesitation. This point is illustrated on this deal:

NORTH
♠ 9 4 3
♥ J 6 5 3
♦ A 6 2
♣ 9 6 5

WEST
♠ 8 5 2
♥ 4
♦ 9 8 7 5 4 3
♣ 7 4 2

EAST
♠ 6
♥ A Q 10 9 8 7
♦ K Q J 10
♣ 8 3

SOUTH
♠ A K Q J 10 7
♥ K 2
♦ —
♣ A K Q J 10

Both sides vulnerable.

NORTH	EAST	SOUTH	WEST
Pass	1 ♥	6 ♠	Pass
Pass	Pass		

West opened with his four of hearts, on which dummy played the three, East took his ace—and South promptly dropped the king! After a few moments of deliberation, East returned the king of diamonds—and declarer was home.

Whether East's return was the logical one or not does not concern us here. What is of import is the motivation responsible for South's discard of the king of hearts.

From South's point of view, he *knew* that West had started with a singleton heart, for West, following accepted procedure, generally led the highest card in partner's suit. South observed the three-spot in dummy and the deuce in his own hand. The four-spot which was led figured to be West's only heart, since he had none higher and there were none lower. If, on the opening lead South had dropped the deuce, then East, observing the two, three, and four being played to the first trick, would also have known that West had originally started with a singleton heart—and a heart return would then have enabled West to ruff declarer's king for the setting trick.

So declarer, looking ahead, dropped the king on the opening lead—concealing the deuce—leading East to believe that declarer had started with the singleton king and that West had started with the four and deuce. And once East returned anything but a heart, the contract became assured, since dummy had come up with two lucky cards: the ace of diamonds, on which to discard the two of hearts, and the nine of trumps as an entry to dummy.

3.

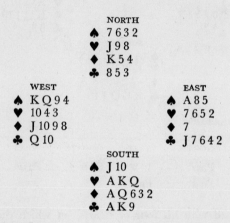

NORTH
♠ 7 6 3 2
♥ J 9 8
♦ K 5 4
♣ 8 5 3

WEST
♠ K Q 9 4
♥ 10 4 3
♦ J 10 9 8
♣ Q 10

EAST
♠ A 8 5
♥ 7 6 5 2
♦ 7
♣ J 7 6 4 2

SOUTH
♠ J 10
♥ A K Q
♦ A Q 6 3 2
♣ A K 9

Both sides vulnerable.

SOUTH	WEST	NORTH	EAST
2 NT	Pass	3 NT	Pass
Pass	Pass		

The jack of diamonds was led, dummy played the four, East played the seven, and declarer played the six. West automatically continued diamonds, reading East's seven-spot as a come-on. If declarer had won the opening lead, and continued diamonds to establish his fifth diamond, East's discards of the two of hearts and the two of clubs—denying interest in these suits—would have made the spade shift by West compulsory when West obtained the lead via the fourth diamond. A spade shift would then have defeated the contract.

4.

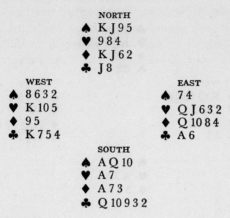

NORTH
♠ K J 9 5
♥ 9 8 4
♦ K J 6 2
♣ J 8

WEST
♠ 8 6 3 2
♥ K 10 5
♦ 9 5
♣ K 7 5 4

EAST
♠ 7 4
♥ Q J 6 3 2
♦ Q 10 8 4
♣ A 6

SOUTH
♠ A Q 10
♥ A 7
♦ A 7 3
♣ Q 10 9 3 2

Both sides vulnerable.

SOUTH	WEST	NORTH	EAST
1 NT	Pass	2 ♣ (1)	Pass
2 ♦	Pass	3 NT	Pass
Pass	Pass		

(1) The Stayman Convention.

West leads the club four, East's ace winning, South dropping the nine-spot—to convince East to continue clubs, East to reason that West has the 3 and 2, and therefore a 6-card suit. (As is apparent, a shift to hearts would defeat the contract.)

5.

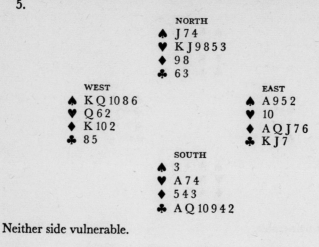

```
                        NORTH
                     ♠ J 7 4
                     ♥ K J 9 8 5 3
                     ♦ 9 8
                     ♣ 6 3
        WEST                              EAST
     ♠ K Q 10 8 6                      ♠ A 9 5 2
     ♥ Q 6 2                           ♥ 10
     ♦ K 10 2                          ♦ A Q J 7 6
     ♣ 8 5                             ♣ K J 7
                        SOUTH
                     ♠ 3
                     ♥ A 7 4
                     ♦ 5 4 3
                     ♣ A Q 10 9 4 2
```

Neither side vulnerable.

NORTH	EAST	SOUTH	WEST
Pass	1 ♦	2 ♣	2 ♠
Pass	4 ♠	Pass	Pass
Pass			

The opening lead was the six of clubs, king by East, ace by South. On this trick West dropped the eight-spot. South then cashed the ace of hearts, and followed by leading a *trump!* Why? Who knows? There is no rational explanation for the trump play. But South was convinced that West had no more clubs from his play of the eight-spot. Of course, had West played the five on the opening lead, he would be marked with the eight, since North would not have led the six from any 6-8 combination.

6.

NORTH
♠ J 10 7
♥ 10 5 2
♦ A J 5
♣ Q 9 8 6

WEST
♠ Q 8 5 3 2
♥ Q 7 4
♦ 7 6 3
♣ K 2

EAST
♠ 9 6
♥ A K 9 3
♦ 10 8 4
♣ 7 5 4 3

SOUTH
♠ A K 4
♥ J 8 6
♦ K Q 9 2
♣ A J 10

Both sides vulnerable.

SOUTH	WEST	NORTH	EAST
1 NT	Pass	2 NT	Pass
3 NT	Pass	Pass	Pass

The three of spades was led, the jack was played from dummy—and declarer won the trick with the king, thereby convincing West that declarer had started with the doubleton A K. Dummy was then entered via a diamond, and the club finesse taken, losing to West's king. West now continued spades, to establish his suit. Had declarer won the opening lead with the jack in dummy, West would have seen the futility of continuing spades—and a heart shift would have beaten declarer. Of course, if the club finesse had worked, declarer would have fulfilled his contract, and the "deliberate" loss of a spade trick—at trick 1—would not have mattered.

7.

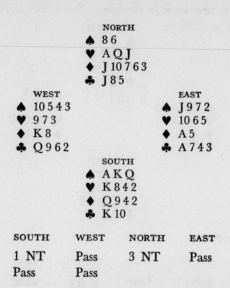

NORTH
♠ 8 6
♥ A Q J
♦ J 10 7 6 3
♣ J 8 5

WEST
♠ 10 5 4 3
♥ 9 7 3
♦ K 8
♣ Q 9 6 2

EAST
♠ J 9 7 2
♥ 10 6 5
♦ A 5
♣ A 7 4 3

SOUTH
♠ A K Q
♥ K 8 4 2
♦ Q 9 4 2
♣ K 10

SOUTH	WEST	NORTH	EAST
1 NT	Pass	3 NT	Pass
Pass	Pass		

The *deuce* of clubs is opened, East winning with the ace, and South drops the king! East knows that South has another club (since West's lead denoted a four-card suit). Will not East figure that South's remaining club is the queen, or else South would not have dropped the king? And so East may conclude that it is futile to continue clubs. A spade shift will then (probably) be made, won by declarer's king. Diamonds are then attacked—and if spades are continued, South makes his contract.

If a club is returned at trick 2, the contract is defeated automatically.

8. The next deal arose in the Open Pair Championships, held in Miami Beach in 1951.

NORTH
♠ Q 5
♥ A Q 6
♦ 8 6 5 4 2
♣ J 9 3

WEST
♠ 9 3
♥ 9 7 5 2
♦ 3
♣ K 10 7 6 5 4

EAST
♠ 7
♥ J 10 8 3
♦ A J 10 9
♣ A Q 8 2

SOUTH
♠ A K J 10 8 6 4 2
♥ K 4
♦ K Q 7
♣ —

North-South vulnerable.

SOUTH	WEST	NORTH	EAST
2 ♠	Pass	3 ♥	Pass
3 ♠	Pass	4 ♠	Pass
4 NT	Pass	5 ♦	Pass
6 ♠	Pass	Pass	Pass

The three of diamonds was opened—and South dropped the king on East's ace! The ace of clubs was then led, and trumped. That was that.

Had South dropped the seven of diamonds at trick 1, it would have been revealed that West had opened a singleton diamond (for no player would have led the three-spot from the K 3, the K Q 3, or the Q 3). A diamond would then have been returned for West to trump.

9. The following deal depicts deception as a counterattack to deception.

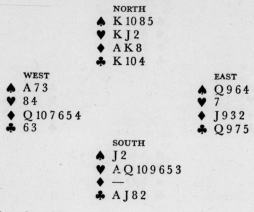

```
                         NORTH
                     ♠ K 10 8 5
                     ♥ K J 2
                     ♦ A K 8
                     ♣ K 10 4
     WEST                                    EAST
  ♠ A 7 3                                 ♠ Q 9 6 4
  ♥ 8 4                                   ♥ 7
  ♦ Q 10 7 6 5 4                          ♦ J 9 3 2
  ♣ 6 3                                   ♣ Q 9 7 5
                         SOUTH
                     ♠ J 2
                     ♥ A Q 10 9 6 5 3
                     ♦ —
                     ♣ A J 8 2
```

Neither side vulnerable.

NORTH	EAST	SOUTH	WEST
1 NT	Pass	6 ♥	Pass
Pass	Pass		

At one table in a team-of-four match, West made the deceptive opening of a small spade away from the ace, declarer played the five-spot from dummy, East put up the queen—and hurriedly returned a spade to West's ace, defeating the contract one trick.

At the other table, the same deceptive lead was made, but this declarer played the eight-spot from dummy. East assumed that declarer held the A x or A x x of spades, and put in the nine, rather than the queen. The contract was fulfilled with an overtrick (declarer later guessed the location of the club queen).

The play of the five gave the show away, for if declarer had held the A x or A x x, he would have played either the eight or ten from dummy (hoping that West had led away from the Q-J or from the Q-9 or J-9). But, at the second table, when dummy's eight-spot was played, East had a problem—and guessed wrong.

10.

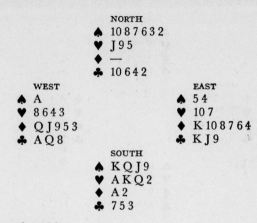

NORTH
♠ 10 8 7 6 3 2
♥ J 9 5
♦ —
♣ 10 6 4 2

WEST
♠ A
♥ 8 6 4 3
♦ Q J 9 5 3
♣ A Q 8

EAST
♠ 5 4
♥ 10 7
♦ K 10 8 7 6 4
♣ K J 9

SOUTH
♠ K Q J 9
♥ A K Q 2
♦ A 2
♣ 7 5 3

East-West vulnerable.

SOUTH	WEST	NORTH	EAST
1 ♠	Pass	4 ♠	Pass
Pass	Pass		

The queen of diamonds is led, and the five of hearts is discarded from dummy. This creates the impression of weakness in hearts. Declarer wins the trick with the ace, after which he leads the king of trumps. West wins and shifts to a heart. Trumps are drawn, after which two of dummy's clubs are discarded on declarer's hearts.

Had declarer discarded a club instead of a heart, West might well have shifted to a club, unappetizing as the lead was. But declarer certainly contributed in leading the West defender up the wrong path.

11.

NORTH
♠ Q 9
♥ 5 4 2
♦ A Q 8 7
♣ 10 8 3 2

WEST
♠ 10 3
♥ A Q 10 9
♦ 10 6 5 4 2
♣ 9 5

EAST
♠ A J 7 6 5 2
♥ K J 3
♦ J 9 3
♣ K

SOUTH
♠ K 8 4
♥ 8 7 6
♦ K
♣ A Q J 7 6 4

Both sides vulnerable.

EAST	SOUTH	WEST	NORTH
1 ♠	2 ♣	Pass	3 ♣
Pass	3 NT	Pass	Pass
Pass			

West opened the ten of spades, and declarer saw that he could get two spade tricks by putting up dummy's queen (with the ten of spades lead, East was marked with the A J of spades). But declarer knew that East would then surmise that South had two spade tricks, and that East would therefore probably shift to hearts.

Hoping to prevent the disastrous heart shift, South put up dummy's nine of spades on the opening lead. East, recognizing that he could now prevent declarer from winning two spade tricks, played the encouraging seven-spot, South's king winning.

Declarer then led the king of diamonds, overtook it with the ace, and led a club. Nine tricks were now there.

Shall we blame East for failing to diagnose the situation? If declarer were willing to throw away a spade trick, East was delighted to help him.

B.
DECEPTION SUBSEQUENT TO TRICK ONE

12.

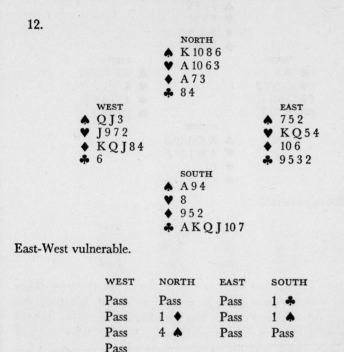

NORTH
♠ K 10 8 6
♥ A 10 6 3
♦ A 7 3
♣ 8 4

WEST
♠ Q J 3
♥ J 9 7 2
♦ K Q J 8 4
♣ 6

EAST
♠ 7 5 2
♥ K Q 5 4
♦ 10 6
♣ 9 5 3 2

SOUTH
♠ A 9 4
♥ 8
♦ 9 5 2
♣ A K Q J 10 7

East-West vulnerable.

WEST	NORTH	EAST	SOUTH
Pass	Pass	Pass	1 ♣
Pass	1 ♦	Pass	1 ♠
Pass	4 ♠	Pass	Pass
Pass			

The king of diamonds was led, with the ace winning. A club was then led to the ace, followed by the king of clubs, which West trumped. Declarer now made just four spades (this was a duplicate game).

But suppose that declarer had led the ten of clubs instead of the king at trick three. What West would trump this trick? If not, declarer could now lead another high club, and if West trumped, declarer would discard a diamond, and he would wind up making 11 tricks (which he needed to make a good score, since 10 tricks were guaranteed at three no-trump).

13.

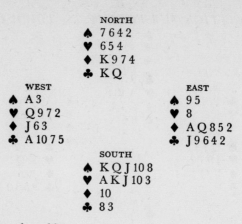

NORTH
♠ 7 6 4 2
♥ 6 5 4
♦ K 9 7 4
♣ K Q

WEST
♠ A 3
♥ Q 9 7 2
♦ J 6 3
♣ A 10 7 5

EAST
♠ 9 5
♥ 8
♦ A Q 8 5 2
♣ J 9 6 4 2

SOUTH
♠ K Q J 10 8
♥ A K J 10 3
♦ 10
♣ 8 3

North-South vulnerable.

SOUTH	WEST	NORTH	EAST
1 ♠	Pass	2 ♠	Pass
4 ♠	Pass	Pass	Pass

The two of hearts was led, taken by declarer's ten. Declarer didn't know for sure who was going to give whom a ruff, but from the lead of the deuce he was certain that the adverse hearts were divided 4-1 originally. He then led the *queen* of spades, and West declined to take it, figuring that his partner might have a singleton king. Another spade lead followed, and declarer was home. Had declarer led the king of spades originally, West would surely have taken it— and East could have ruffed a heart return.

14.

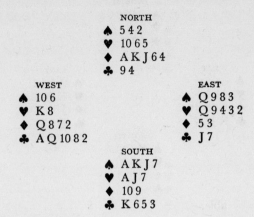

NORTH
♠ 5 4 2
♥ 10 6 5
♦ A K J 6 4
♣ 9 4

WEST
♠ 10 6
♥ K 8
♦ Q 8 7 2
♣ A Q 10 8 2

EAST
♠ Q 9 8 3
♥ Q 9 4 3 2
♦ 5 3
♣ J 7

SOUTH
♠ A K J 7
♥ A J 7
♦ 10 9
♣ K 6 5 3

Neither side vulnerable.

SOUTH	WEST	NORTH	EAST
1 ♣	Pass	1 ♦	Pass
1 ♠	Pass	2 ♦	Pass
3 NT	Pass	Pass	Pass

An overbid hand, which was made via deception by capitalizing on a standard psychological situation: nobody wants to waste anything.

A small club was opened, and East's jack taken by declarer's king. Then came the *nine* of diamonds, and West played low, the nine-spot winning the trick. Declarer now brought in the entire diamond suit via a finesse of the jack of diamonds. Had West covered the nine with the queen, declarer would have gone down—and, without a question, had declarer originally led the ten of diamonds, it would have been covered by the queen.

15. In this day and age, in all fields of competitive endeavor there are selected the "best —— of the year": best actor, best-dressed woman, best football team, etc. The following deal, featuring a play by declarer, was acclaimed by Albert H. Morehead, bridge editor of *The New York Times,* as the "best play by declarer for the year 1949." The hero of the deal was Howard Schenken.

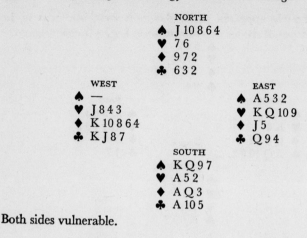

```
                          NORTH
                      ♠ J 10 8 6 4
                      ♥ 7 6
                      ♦ 9 7 2
                      ♣ 6 3 2
        WEST                              EAST
    ♠ —                               ♠ A 5 3 2
    ♥ J 8 4 3                         ♥ K Q 10 9
    ♦ K 10 8 6 4                      ♦ J 5
    ♣ K J 8 7                         ♣ Q 9 4
                          SOUTH
                      ♠ K Q 9 7
                      ♥ A 5 2
                      ♦ A Q 3
                      ♣ A 10 5
```

Both sides vulnerable.

EAST	SOUTH	WEST	NORTH
1 ♠	1 NT	2 ♦	Pass
Pass	2 NT	Pass	Pass
Pass			

West opened the six of diamonds, East played the jack, and Mr. Schenken captured the trick with his queen. It was obvious to South that it would be impossible for him to make the 4 spade tricks needed to fulfill his contract. East had opened the auction with a one-spade bid, and since there were but four spades outstanding, East had all of them. Therefore, since West would show out on the first round of spades, East would certainly hold up his spade ace until the fourth round, thereby effectively preventing Mr. Schenken from cashing dummy's fifth spade.

Mr. Schenken, without any hesitation, found the winning play. At trick 2 he returned a low diamond, which West captured, after which another diamond was led by West, clearing the suit. On this trick East discarded *the deuce of spades*, telling his partner not to lead spades. It now became a cinch for declarer, for there was no way that the defenders could prevent Howard from cashing 4 spades, 2 diamonds, the ace of clubs, and the ace of hearts.

Of course, it is apparent that if East had not discarded the two of spades, the contract could not have been fulfilled. But Mr. Schenken foresaw that East would discard—if given the opportunity

—what definitely appeared to be the most worthless card in his hand: the deuce of spades. And East did as hoped for by declarer.

16. The following deal may seem like some sort of fantasy, but it actually arose in real life and was played, trick for trick, as presented. The final contract by South was two no-trump. Let us look at all four hands as the play progresses:

NORTH
♠ 10 8 7 2
♥ A K 10 6 3
♦ J 6
♣ 8 6

WEST
♠ K J 9 4
♥ Q 8 2
♦ K 3
♣ K 5 4 3

EAST
♠ 3
♥ J 9 7 4
♦ A 10 8
♣ A Q 9 7 2

SOUTH
♠ A Q 6 5
♥ 5
♦ Q 9 7 5 4 2
♣ J 10

Against South's *two no-trump* contract, West opened the four of spades, dummy's seven of spades capturing the trick. I am certain that no declarer ever found himself in a more hopeless position, and our declarer was fully aware of it. It was futile to try to establish diamonds or hearts because of the lack of entries. Also, it seemed that the opponents would shift to clubs when they obtained the lead.

So declarer took the bull by the horns, and led a club from dummy. East played low, declarer put up his ten-spot—and it won the trick! Looking at all four hands, the reader may say that it was absurd for West not to have taken the king—and I'm sure that, in retrospect, West will be the first to agree with you. But West had what he thought was a valid reason for his declination: he did not have a good return to make, and he felt sure that he could always make his king later, since it appeared that declarer would continue to attack clubs.

Declarer then led a low diamond, and West hopped right up with his king. Seeing the diamond eight fall from the East hand, West decided that it was a come-on signal, so he continued the suit, East's ace capturing the trick. Convinced that declarer still had at least the K J of clubs remaining, East now made a "safe" exit with his remaining diamond, declarer's queen winning. Declarer now had nine tricks: 2 spades, 2 hearts, 4 diamonds, and a club. Unbelievable, perhaps, but "facts is facts."

17. It is an accepted psychological fact that the defenders will tend to shy away from leading a suit that declarer has attacked, figuring that if he is interested in developing a suit, they are not going to help him. By capitalizing on this principle, declarer fulfilled an "impossible" contract.

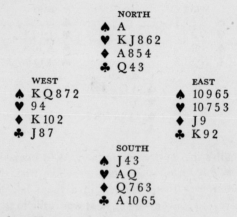

NORTH
♠ A
♥ K J 8 6 2
♦ A 8 5 4
♣ Q 4 3

WEST
♠ K Q 8 7 2
♥ 9 4
♦ K 10 2
♣ J 8 7

EAST
♠ 10 9 6 5
♥ 10 7 5 3
♦ J 9
♣ K 9 2

SOUTH
♠ J 4 3
♥ A Q
♦ Q 7 6 3
♣ A 10 6 5

Both sides vulnerable.

SOUTH	WEST	NORTH	EAST
1 ♦	Pass	1 ♥	Pass
1 NT	Pass	3 ♦	Pass
3 NT	Pass	Pass	Pass

This deal occurred in the Vanderbilt Championships of 1950. South was Lee Hazen.

West opened the seven of spades, dummy's ace capturing the trick. A count of the North-South hands revealed that there were only 8 tricks. It was apparent that the ninth trick could be made in only the club or diamond suit. Equally apparent was the fact that if the opponents were given the lead, they might cash four spade tricks.

At trick 2, Hazen cashed the ace of hearts, after which he took his queen of hearts. He then laid down the jack of spades!

Upon capturing the trick with the queen, West was convinced that declarer had started with the J 10 9 x of spades, and was trying to create a spade trick. West, therefore, discontinued playing spades and shifted to a club. Hazen played low from dummy—and whatever East played, South had created his ninth trick in clubs.

Had West cashed four spades, of course the contract would have been defeated. But Hazen's lead of the jack of spades talked West out of leading spades.

18. The next deal was played by P. Hal Sims in the early 1930's.[1]

In playing no-trump, it is relatively easy to snare the opponents into making misplays. Here is an example:

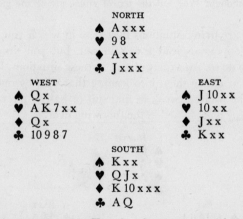

```
                    NORTH
                 ♠ A x x x
                 ♥ 9 8
                 ♦ A x x
                 ♣ J x x x
    WEST                          EAST
 ♠ Q x                         ♠ J 10 x x
 ♥ A K 7 x x                   ♥ 10 x x
 ♦ Q x                         ♦ J x x
 ♣ 10 9 8 7                    ♣ K x x
                    SOUTH
                 ♠ K x x
                 ♥ Q J x
                 ♦ K 10 x x x
                 ♣ A Q
```

Neither side was vulnerable. Knowing the opponents to be cautious players, partner and I bid the hand boldly:

SOUTH (Sims)	WEST	NORTH	EAST
1 NT	Pass	2 NT	Pass
3 NT	Pass	Pass	Pass

[1] Taken verbatim from *Money Contract* by P. Hal Sims (Simon and Schuster, N. Y., 1932)

West led the fourth best heart, and I at once took East's ten with my queen. I was aware that West was a good but not a great player, and I wanted him to remain in doubt as to the location of the jack.

I felt convinced that if I could keep him in doubt as to the position of this card, he would wait for the heart suit to be led to him instead of immediately clearing it himself.

Knowing that if East ever won the lead the jig would be up, I resolved to play the hand as dangerously as possible. I at once led a spade to the ace and played back a low diamond. On this I played the ten and West won with the queen. Now, as I had hoped, West reasoned thus:

1. That I would never have given him the lead unless I still held the J x x of hearts.

2. That in finessing the diamonds on the first round, I was attempting to force West to clear his heart suit, making my jack good for the ninth trick for the contract.

3. That his queen of spades would later give him another entry with which to clear the hearts.

After long thought West led the ten of clubs, giving me game.

19. There are many situations that arise in which you would like to have the opponents lead a certain suit, but you simply cannot force them to do so. An expert player, in these situations, has learned how to coax or entice them into leading that suit, by making them believe that he is either weak in that suit or has no interest in it. A play of this type is contained in the following deal:

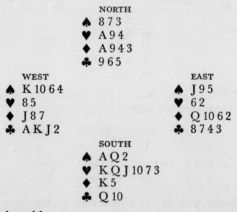

NORTH
♠ 8 7 3
♥ A 9 4
♦ A 9 4 3
♣ 9 6 5

WEST
♠ K 10 6 4
♥ 8 5
♦ J 8 7
♣ A K J 2

EAST
♠ J 9 5
♥ 6 2
♦ Q 10 6 2
♣ 8 7 4 3

SOUTH
♠ A Q 2
♥ K Q J 10 7 3
♦ K 5
♣ Q 10

East-West vulnerable.

SOUTH	WEST	NORTH	EAST
1 ♥	Pass	2 ♥	Pass
4 ♥	Pass	Pass	Pass

West opens the king of clubs, and follows with the ace of clubs. Then comes the jack of clubs, upon which declarer drops the deuce of spades. Looking at the dummy, West perceives that both the heart and diamond leads offer no hope; and that from declarer's discard of the deuce of spades, he seems to be disinterested in spades. So now West may shift to a spade. Whatever West ultimately does, certainly the discard of the deuce of spades has created a dangerous thought in West's mind: that declarer is weak in spades. In other words, the discard of the spade deuce was designed to entrap the gullible—and what did it cost?

20.

```
                    NORTH
                    ♠ A 8 6
                    ♥ A K J 3
                    ♦ A J 8 4
                    ♣ J 6
    WEST                            EAST
    ♠ K 7 4 2                       ♠ Q 10 9 3
    ♥ Q 10 9                        ♥ 8 5 4
    ♦ 7 5 2                         ♦ K Q 10
    ♣ A 8 4                         ♣ 10 5 3
                    SOUTH
                    ♠ J 5
                    ♥ 7 6 2
                    ♦ 9 6 3
                    ♣ K Q 9 7 2
```

Both sides vulnerable.

EAST	SOUTH	WEST	NORTH
Pass	Pass	Pass	1 ♦
Pass	1 NT	Pass	3 NT
Pass	Pass	Pass	

The South declarer was Adam Meredith, of England, who found himself in a hopeless contract. With a little luck and a big imagination, he proceeded to fulfill his contract—with an overtrick.

West opened a low spade, East's queen winning. The ten of spades was led, covered by the jack, king, and ace. Meredith now led the jack of clubs and *overtook it* with his king! Why West grabbed this trick is unknown. Possibly he thought declarer wanted to get to the South hand, and West just was not going to let him do it. A spade was now returned, East winning with the nine-spot. The king of diamonds was then laid down, taken by North's ace.

Meredith now calmly led the six of clubs and successfully finessed his nine-spot. He next took 3 more club tricks, followed by a successful finesse for the jack of hearts.

Had West not overtaken the jack of clubs with the king, West would not have captured the trick, and declarer would then have been unable to get to the South hand to take his club tricks.

21. Frequently it becomes readily apparent to declarer after the opening lead that his contract is impossible to fulfill if the opponents realize the full strength of their combined values. In such cases it is often possible for declarer to play in such a fashion that the opponents will fail to get together quickly enough; and as a consequence, declarer is enabled to sneak through a trick or two. Of such a type is the following deal, played at *three no-trump,* with South as declarer:

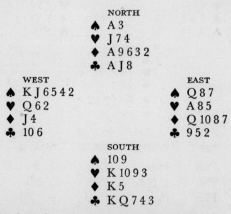

NORTH
♠ A 3
♥ J 7 4
♦ A 9 6 3 2
♣ A J 8

WEST
♠ K J 6 5 4 2
♥ Q 6 2
♦ J 4
♣ 10 6

EAST
♠ Q 8 7
♥ A 8 5
♦ Q 10 8 7
♣ 9 5 2

SOUTH
♠ 10 9
♥ K 10 9 3
♦ K 5
♣ K Q 7 4 3

West led the five of spades, and declarer quickly saw the hopelessness of his position; he had 8 tricks; and as soon as the opponents obtained the lead, they would cash at least 4 spade tricks. What to do? Should declarer take his 8 tricks and run? Or should he try to devise some strategem in an attempt to steal his ninth trick?

What our declarer actually did was to win the opening lead with dummy's ace of spades. He then led the jack of hearts, East followed with a low heart, declarer put up his king—and it won the trick!

When declarer led the jack of hearts, should East have taken the ace? Did East know who had the king of spades? (You and I know it, of course.) As far as declarer was concerned, if West had the ace of hearts, then declarer would lose two extra tricks. But he felt that the risk was warranted.

22.

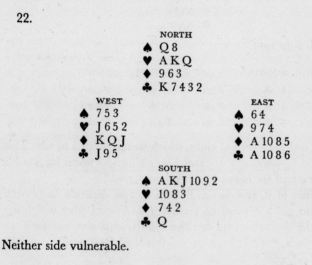

```
              NORTH
              ♠ Q 8
              ♥ A K Q
              ♦ 9 6 3
              ♣ K 7 4 3 2
  WEST                        EAST
  ♠ 7 5 3                     ♠ 6 4
  ♥ J 6 5 2                   ♥ 9 7 4
  ♦ K Q J                     ♦ A 10 8 5
  ♣ J 9 5                     ♣ A 10 8 6
              SOUTH
              ♠ A K J 10 9 2
              ♥ 10 8 3
              ♦ 7 4 2
              ♣ Q
```

Neither side vulnerable.

SOUTH	WEST	NORTH	EAST
2 ♠ (1)	Pass	4 ♠	Pass
Pass	Pass		

(1) The weak two bid.

One of the oldest deceptive plays known is the following. Three rounds of diamonds were cashed, followed by a heart shift. A small club was promptly played off dummy. Should East climb up with the ace? At any rate, he didn't; and South's queen won.

23.

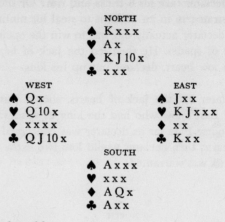

NORTH
♠ K x x x
♥ A x
♦ K J 10 x
♣ x x x

WEST
♠ Q x
♥ Q 10 x
♦ x x x x
♣ Q J 10 x

EAST
♠ J x x
♥ K J x x x
♦ x x
♣ K x x

SOUTH
♠ A x x x
♥ x x x
♦ A Q x
♣ A x x

Neither side vulnerable.

SOUTH	WEST	NORTH	EAST
1 ♣	Pass	1 ♦	Pass
1 ♠	Pass	3 ♠	Pass
4 ♠	Pass	Pass	Pass

West opened the queen of clubs, which was permitted to win. This was followed by another club, and East's king was taken by South's ace. The king and ace of spades were then played.

On the face of it, it seems as though success depends on playing diamonds, to get a discard of a club. This line of play will bring success if the defender who has the high trump also has three or more diamonds. As can be seen, on this deal East would ruff the third diamond, and declarer would now go down.

In all probability, by a deceptive play, declarer can bring home his contract. After drawing trumps, the ace of diamonds should be played, followed by a diamond to the king. Then the jack of diamonds (surely creating the impression that declarer held but a doubleton and is trying to coax East into covering with the queen). If East does not trump, declarer is home. He now leads a heart to the ace, and on the ten of diamonds discards his remaining club. Whether East trumps or not is now immaterial.

24. The following deal arose in the World's Team-of-Four Championships of 1947.

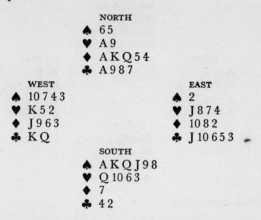

NORTH
♠ 6 5
♥ A 9
♦ A K Q 5 4
♣ A 9 8 7

WEST
♠ 10 7 4 3
♥ K 5 2
♦ J 9 6 3
♣ K Q

EAST
♠ 2
♥ J 8 7 4
♦ 10 8 2
♣ J 10 6 5 3

SOUTH
♠ A K Q J 9 8
♥ Q 10 6 3
♦ 7
♣ 4 2

The final contract was *seven spades,* obviously a gross overbid. South was Margaret Wagar, paired with John Crawford. The play was deceptively gorgeous.

West opened the king of clubs, which was taken by dummy's ace. Four rounds of trumps were then drawn. South now plunked down the queen of hearts—and West played small. Declarer then went about her business of establishing dummy's fifth diamond, to fulfill her contract.

West, in not covering, figured that South was trying to entice him into covering if he had the king. And if it were not covered South would go up with the ace (West reasoned) to attack the diamond suit for eventual discards—and West knew that the diamond suit was not going to break.

25.

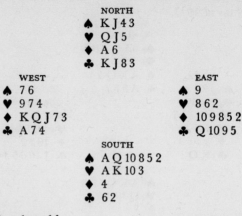

NORTH
♠ K J 4 3
♥ Q J 5
♦ A 6
♣ K J 8 3

WEST
♠ 7 6
♥ 9 7 4
♦ K Q J 7 3
♣ A 7 4

EAST
♠ 9
♥ 8 6 2
♦ 10 9 8 5 2
♣ Q 10 9 5

SOUTH
♠ A Q 10 8 5 2
♥ A K 10 3
♦ 4
♣ 6 2

North-South vulnerable.

NORTH	EAST	SOUTH	WEST
1 ♣	Pass	1 ♠	Pass
2 ♠	Pass	6 ♠	Pass
Pass	Pass		

This hand arose in a duplicate game where the overtrick was of vital importance. The king of diamonds was opened, taken by the ace. Trumps were then drawn, after which four rounds of hearts were played, a diamond being discarded from dummy on the fourth heart—to create the impression that South had started with two diamonds, and that he wanted to trump his second diamond in dummy. South then led a club—and West hopped right up with the ace (to make sure declarer wouldn't make an overtrick).

From West's point of view, South was known to have started with 6 trumps, 4 hearts, and presumably 2 diamonds—hence the club was a singleton. West, incidentally, was one of the world's greatest players.

26.

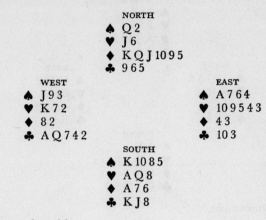

NORTH
♠ Q 2
♥ J 6
♦ K Q J 10 9 5
♣ 9 6 5

WEST
♠ J 9 3
♥ K 7 2
♦ 8 2
♣ A Q 7 4 2

EAST
♠ A 7 6 4
♥ 10 9 5 4 3
♦ 4 3
♣ 10 3

SOUTH
♠ K 10 8 5
♥ A Q 8
♦ A 7 6
♣ K J 8

East-West vulnerable.

NORTH	EAST	SOUTH	WEST
2 ♦ (1)	Pass	3 NT	Pass
Pass	Pass		

(1) The weak two bid.

The four of clubs was opened, and East's ten was captured by declarer's jack. The ace of diamonds was then laid down, followed by the king of spades.

This line of play created the impression that declarer had a singleton ace of diamonds, and that he wanted dummy's queen of spades as an entry. So East declined to take the ace of spades—and declarer had stolen his ninth trick. (Of course, East had no way of knowing what the actual setup was in clubs.)

27. The next deal serves as an illustration of the proverb: "Always look a gift horse in the mouth."

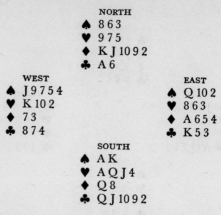

NORTH
♠ 8 6 3
♥ 9 7 5
♦ K J 10 9 2
♣ A 6

WEST
♠ J 9 7 5 4
♥ K 10 2
♦ 7 3
♣ 8 7 4

EAST
♠ Q 10 2
♥ 8 6 3
♦ A 6 5 4
♣ K 5 3

SOUTH
♠ A K
♥ A Q J 4
♦ Q 8
♣ Q J 10 9 2

Both sides vulnerable.

SOUTH	WEST	NORTH	EAST
1 ♣	Pass	1 ♦	Pass
2 ♥	Pass	3 ♦	Pass
3 NT	Pass	Pass	Pass

On the lead of the five of spades, East played the queen which South captured with the king. South then led the queen of diamonds, and followed with a small one from dummy. East held up the ace, figuring that possibly South had made a mistake by not overtaking. Declarer now shifted to clubs, playing the ace and another, to assure his contract.

East made a mistake. If South had been interested in establishing the diamonds, he surely would have overtaken the queen with the king. Of course, if East had won the queen with the ace, a return of partner's spade suit would have defeated the contract.

28.

NORTH
♠ A K 7 2
♥ 9 8 3 2
♦ 10 5
♣ 8 7 2

WEST	EAST
♠ Q J 10 9 8 6 4	♠ 5
♥ Q 10	♥ J 6 4
♦ 8 4	♦ 9 7 6 3 2
♣ 9 3	♣ 10 6 5 4

SOUTH
♠ 3
♥ A K 7 5
♦ A K Q J
♣ A K Q J

Neither side vulnerable.

SOUTH	WEST	NORTH	EAST
2 ♥	3 ♠	4 ♥	Pass
4 NT	Pass	5 ♦	Pass
7 ♥	Pass	Pass	Pass

If one were to look at all four hands, it would be apparent that it was impossible to fulfill the grand slam contract, since a trump trick must be lost. But South found the winning line of play—by employing deception at trick two.

The lead of the spade queen was captured by dummy's king. Although no discards were necessary, declarer's next play was the ace of spades from dummy—and East, as hoped for, ruffed with a small heart to prevent South from discarding. South, of course, overruffed. The ace and king of trumps now picked up all the adverse pieces, and that was that. How many players would have thought of the play of the ace of spades at trick two?

CHAPTER 14

STANDARD DECEPTIVE PLAYS
BY DECLARER

The various situations described in this chapter, although formerly considered very tricky, have by virtue of their repetitive occurrence become standardized and an integral part of the expert declarer's arsenal of psychological weapons.

It has been stated that, generally speaking, deceptive play is more effective (and less dangerous to employ) when it is wielded by declarer, for declarer's partner cannot be deceived. Yet this does not give declarer the license to be promiscuous; for if he is, much harm can come of it. However, the fact remains that during his term of office, declarer need suffer no inhibitions. One of his inalienable rights is to indulge in falsehoods, for only the enemy is there to believe them and to be led astray thereby. To capitalize on this liberty to tell lies, the astute declarer will do himself and partner a service by studying the art of lying, paying especial attention to standard deceiving situations, so that give-away thought will not be necessary at the table. In other words, insofar as possible, deceptive plays should be made at a normal nonchalant pace, without undue haste and without undue deliberation. It is to the understanding and mastery of lying with a straight face that this chapter is dedicated.

1. You are South, playing a *spade* contract, and West opens the king of hearts.

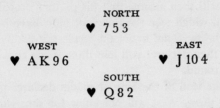

NORTH
♥ 7 5 3

WEST   EAST
♥ A K 9 6   ♥ J 10 4

SOUTH
♥ Q 8 2

On the lead of the king of hearts, the three is played from dummy, East plays the four—and you should play the *eight-spot* and not the deuce. You know, since you hold the deuce and the three and four are in evidence, that if you play the deuce, then West will know that his partner's four-spot was the lowest that he had, and West will therefore interpret it as a signal not to continue the suit. And if hearts are not continued, you will never make your queen of hearts. But if on the opening lead of the king of hearts, you play the eight-spot, then West might well assume that East has the deuce— and that therefore East's play of the four-spot was the beginning of a high-low signal to get West to continue the heart suit. And, if that is done, then you have just tricked West into giving you a heart trick. By playing the eight-spot at trick 1, you stand to gain a trick—and you have nothing to lose.

2. In many situations that appear to be comparable to the above, declarer often makes an untimely and incorrect false-card, thereby encouraging the leader to continue a suit that declarer was hoping would be discontinued. Such a situation is the following:

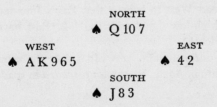

NORTH
♠ Q 10 7

WEST   EAST
♠ A K 9 6 5   ♠ 4 2

SOUTH
♠ J 8 3

Against South's *four-heart* contract, West opens the king of spades, East following with the four-spot (which, of course, *we* can see, but West cannot, is the beginning of a high-low signal to get West to continue the suit so he can trump the third round). If declarer now false-cards with the eight-spot (as is often done), West will undoubtedly notice the absence of *both* the two and three of spades—and will then assume that his partner probably has one of these cards, in which case the four-spot must have been the beginning of a high-low signal to get the spade suit continued. And if it is continued, then declarer will lose three spade tricks, East trumping the third round.

But if on the lead of the king of spades declarer plays normally, dropping the three, West will not know for sure where the deuce is: after all, South might easily have held just the 3 2 doubleton, with East holding the J 8 4. And if West does not continue spades, then declarer can always develop a spade trick after trumps are drawn. To false-card with the eight-spot is to invite disaster—and disaster will usually accept your invitation.

3. A situation virtually identical to that just presented in (1) and (2), above, is the following, in which the habit of false-carding automatically turns out to be a costly one. In this case the leader has *overcalled,* and is thus known to have a long suit. West has bid *spades,* and leads the king:

NORTH
♠ Q 8 3

WEST
♠ A K J 9 7

EAST
♠ 10 6 4

SOUTH
♠ 5 2

Quite naturally, and correctly, South should false-card with the five-spot, to lead West to believe that East's four-spot was the beginning of a high-low signal with the 4–2 (East having played the four-spot at trick 1).

But South, unfortunately, very often does the same thing in the following situation. Again, West has *overcalled* in spades:

NORTH
♠ Q 8 5 2

WEST
♠ A K J 9 7

EAST
♠ 4

SOUTH
♠ 10 6 3

On West's lead of the king, South mechanically—and incorrectly
—false cards with the six, East having played the four. West now
knows either (1) South still has the three-spot or (2) East has
initiated a high-low signal with the 4–3. In either case, it becomes
safe for West to lay down his ace, after which the truth becomes
known. Had South played the three-spot originally, West would not
know whether it was safe to lay down the ace at trick 2; for, in
this case, South's three might have been a singleton, with East holding the 10 6 4.

4. A situation that occurs most frequently is the following:

NORTH
♠ Q 7 3

SOUTH
♠ J 8

West opens the king of spades against South's *heart* contract, East
plays the deuce, and South drops the jack (assuming South doesn't
need a spade trick, and is trying to prevent West from cashing the
spade ace). This play is almost guaranteed to prevent West from
cashing the second spade; East's deuce was most discouraging, and
South's jack creates the impression that South has no more spades.
The opportunity for the use of this play can be observed in the
following deal:

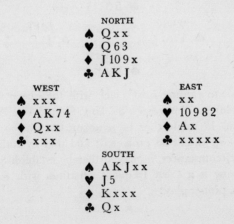

```
                       NORTH
                     ♠ Q x x
                     ♥ Q 6 3
                     ♦ J 10 9 x
                     ♣ A K J
        WEST                        EAST
      ♠ x x x                     ♠ x x
      ♥ A K 7 4                   ♥ 10 9 8 2
      ♦ Q x x                     ♦ A x
      ♣ x x x                     ♣ x x x x x
                       SOUTH
                     ♠ A K J x x
                     ♥ J 5
                     ♦ K x x x
                     ♣ Q x
```

Against South's *four-spade* contract, West opens the king of hearts, East plays the deuce, and South drops the jack, to "convince" West to abandon the suit. If West then shifts to a club or a spade, declarer, after drawing trumps, can get rid of his remaining heart on dummy's third club.

5. Against a *no-trump* contract, the following situation occurs quite often:

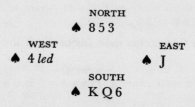

West leads the four-spot, and declarer captures East's jack with the queen. West now knows declarer still has the king; for if East had held the king, he would have played it. Declarer's proper play (normally) is to win the trick with the king, thereby concealing the whereabouts of the queen (since East, holding the Q–J, would have played the jack, as he actually did without possessing the queen).

However, if the situation were slightly different, the play of the queen could be the best "deceptive" play. Again, the contract is no-trump:

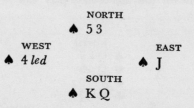

In this case, to capture East's jack with the queen would "tell" West that declarer still possessed the king. Should West subsequently obtain the lead, he might then be reluctant to cash the ace for fear that South's king might be protected; and that by cashing the ace in the latter circumstances, he would thereby establish South's king.

The following is a fairly frequent situation, with the deceptive play being the proper play:

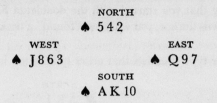

NORTH
♠ 5 4 2

WEST
♠ J 8 6 3

EAST
♠ Q 9 7

SOUTH
♠ A K 10

The false-card with the A K 10 or A K 10 x combination is most effective when third hand puts up the queen, which declarer wins with the ace. Each opponent may now credit his partner with the king.

6. The types of trick 1 situations that follow, although not too frequent in occurrence, have become recognized as standard, stock, deceptive plays:

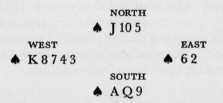

NORTH
♠ J 10 5

WEST
♠ K 8 7 4 3

EAST
♠ 6 2

SOUTH
♠ A Q 9

Against South's *no-trump* contract, West leads the four-spot, dummy's jack being played. If you don't particularly want the lead in the North hand, take your own jack with the queen, thereby creating the impression that you started with the doubleton A Q. Should West subsequently obtain the lead, he will probably play another spade to drop your ace—and you will now have three spade tricks.

7. An analogous situation is the following:

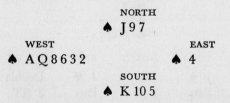

NORTH
♠ J 9 7

WEST
♠ A Q 8 6 3 2

EAST
♠ 4

SOUTH
♠ K 10 5

West leads the six of spades against your *no-trump* contract. Put up dummy's jack, and on it drop your ten-spot. West will then be led to believe that you started with the doubleton K 10—and if he later lays downs the ace, you will have "found" a trick.

8. Another type situation that arises quite often is the following:

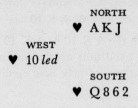

NORTH
♥ A K J

WEST
♥ 10 *led*

SOUTH
♥ Q 8 6 2

Against your *spade* contract, West opens the ten of hearts. Win it with dummy's ace or king—and whatever East plays, you play a higher one. That is, if East plays the five, play the 6; if East plays the 7, play your eight. West will then observe that there are outstanding lower hearts than are in evidence, and he may well conclude that East's card was the beginning of a come-on signal.

A neat trick 1 deceptive play occurred on the following deal, which was played in Great Britain some years ago:

NORTH
♠ x x
♥ J 10 x
♦ x x
♣ A 10 x x x x

WEST
♠ K Q J
♥ 9 x x
♦ A J 10 x x
♣ J x

EAST
♠ x x x x
♥ K Q 8 x x
♦ x x x
♣ x

SOUTH
♠ A 10 x x
♥ A x
♦ K Q x
♣ K Q x x

WEST	NORTH	EAST	SOUTH
1 ♦	Pass	1 ♥	Double
Pass	2 ♣	Pass	2 NT
Pass	3 NT	Pass	Pass
Pass			

West opened the nine of hearts, dummy's jack was put up, and East covered with the queen. Had declarer taken his ace, later on when West obtained the lead via the diamond ace (which he could be assumed to have by the bidding), the automatic heart continuation would have defeated the three no-trump contract.

So declarer permitted East's queen to capture the opening lead! East had no way of knowing whether declarer had started with the A x of hearts or the A x x of hearts (if the latter, then a heart continuation by East would give declarer another heart trick). East now took the normal action: he returned a diamond—his partner's suit —and in so doing created the ninth trick for declarer.

Let us now turn our attention to standard deceptive plays that are available to a declarer subsequent to trick 1. The recognition of these "type" situations will quite often enable a declarer to win a trick that he otherwise could not obtain.

9.

NORTH
♠ 8 7 5 3

WEST   EAST
♠ A 4   ♠ J 6 2

SOUTH
♠ K Q 10 9

Lead the three-spot from the dummy, and put up the king (not the queen), to get West to take his ace. Later on, you finesse against the jack.

If the queen is put up instead of the king, West is less likely to take his ace. Then, when you lead another spade from dummy, and East plays low, you will have a rough guess as to whether to finesse the nine-spot, or go up with the king to drop the jack. The situation might have been (instead of the above):

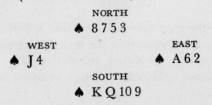

NORTH
♠ 8 7 5 3

WEST   EAST
♠ J 4   ♠ A 6 2

SOUTH
♠ K Q 10 9

Of course, in this latter situation, if you put up the king and it wins, you will still have to guess as to what to do when you lead a second spade, and East again plays low. But the point is that if you put up your king on the initial lead of the suit, and West has the ace, *he will take it.* Now the finesse for the jack is automatic. In other words, by going up with the king on the first spade lead, you put yourself in the position where you stand to gain, without standing to lose, through possibly eliminating a future guess.

10.

NORTH
♠ J 5

WEST   EAST
♠ 10 8 6 3   ♠ A 4

SOUTH
♠ K Q 9 7 2

Instead of leading a low spade from the South hand to dummy's jack (to be taken by the ace, resulting in the loss of two spade tricks), lead the jack from dummy first. East may well play the four-spot, figuring that you are going to finesse for the queen. When the jack wins, a second spade lead will drive out East's ace, and that will become the defenders' only spade winner. East's play of the low spade on the jack would have been correct had the holding been:

NORTH
♠ J 5

WEST   EAST
♠ Q 2   ♠ A 4

SOUTH
♠ K 10 9 8 7 6 3

11. Probably the most successful ruse that is perpetrated by the world of declarers is presented in the next illustration. The reason for its success is that the duped are victims of a slogan which was once a national shibboleth: "Always cover an honor with an honor."

NORTH
♠ K 8 4 3

SOUTH
♠ A J 10 9 2

You are in a *spade* contract and your West opponent has, for the last twenty years, been known always to cover an honor with an honor. So you lead the jack of spades—and if West has the queen, he will play it on your jack from force of habit. If, when you lead the jack, West does not cover, you will know that he does not possess the queen. You will now overtake your jack with dummy's king, and promptly finesse East for the queen.

Even if you do not know West's habits, the play of the jack is still the proper play, its purpose being to entice West into covering. If, however, West follows with a low spade, you are no better and no worse off than you were when you started. You will probably then play the king, followed by the ace, in the hope of dropping the queen. By leading the jack first, you *may* eliminate the necessity of guessing the whereabouts of the queen. It certainly costs you nothing to try it—and dividends may well accrue to you as a result.

Arising out of the above-described repetitive situation comes the following set play in which the declarer can often steal a trick:

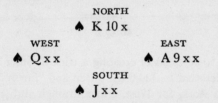

NORTH
♠ K 10 x

WEST
♠ Q x x

EAST
♠ A 9 x x

SOUTH
♠ J x x

Lead the jack out of the South hand. If West ducks, you will make two spade tricks by playing low from dummy. If, instead, you lead low to the ten-spot, you will make just one spade trick.

From West's point of view, when you lead the jack, he doesn't know whether you have the above holding, or whether you have the A J 9, in which case if he covered with the queen he would eliminate any guess that you would otherwise have to make. And, by covering, he would present you with three spade tricks. When you play the jack originally in the situation where you hold the J x x, West will

frequently play low from the Q x x holding simply because he doesn't
want to appear naïve (by covering) if you happen to hold the A J 9.

12.

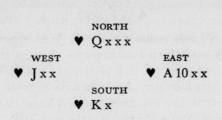

NORTH
♥ Q x x x

WEST   EAST
♥ J x x   ♥ A 10 x x

SOUTH
♥ K x

Lead a low heart from the North hand toward the king, which
wins. Then re-enter the North hand, and lead another low heart.
Having been caught in days gone by, East may think you started
with the K J doubleton, and he will (or may) then go up with the
ace, since he doesn't want to look silly again—for if you happen to
have the K J doubleton, and he doesn't take his ace, you will "steal"
the jack. In no other way can two heart tricks be made.

13.

NORTH
♠ A x

SOUTH
♠ Q x

If no other hope exists of creating a trick in other suits, desperation must be resorted to. Lead the queen and "finesse." On occasion
the fraud will work, for West, either through stubbornness or the
normal desire to preserve the king when he holds K x x or K x x x,
may refuse to cover the queen.

14. You are in a *heart* contract:

NORTH
♦ A Q 6 4

SOUTH
♦ J 2

If, from the bidding, East is known to be the possessor of the diamond king, correct deceptive play is to lead the deuce to the ace, and then lead the four of diamonds toward the concealed jack. If East fails to play the king, your jack of diamonds becomes a winner —and, more often than not, East, holding the K x x x, will not play the king, since he figures you will trump it (as you simultaneously establish North's queen).

15.

NORTH
♣ K 7 4

WEST   EAST
♣ J 3   ♣ A Q 2

SOUTH
♣ 10 9 8 6 5

Clubs is your trump suit. Lead to the king, which is taken by the ace; next time lead the four-spot from the North hand. East is quite likely to go up with the queen, figuring you for the jack.

Virtually identical to the above is the following:

NORTH
♠ x x

WEST   EAST
♠ Q x   ♠ A 10 x x

SOUTH
♠ K J x x x

Lead a low spade from the North hand, putting up the king. Next time lead the remaining spade from the North hand, hoping that East will assume you still have the queen (and had deceptively played the king at trick 1). If he goes up with his ace—dropping his partner's queen—you have just honestly stolen a trick.

16.

NORTH
♠ J 10 6 3

SOUTH
♠ A 7 2

The best play of this suit is to lead the deuce toward the jack, hoping that West will go up with the queen or king. If he does, next time lead the jack from dummy, and finesse East for the remaining honor. This play will lose whenever West started with the doubleton K Q, but it will gain whenever West has the Q x, the K x, the Q x x, the K x x (and goes up with his honor), which combinations are much more likely to exist than for West to have precisely the K Q doubleton. This situation is quite frequent in occurrence.

17.

NORTH
♥ 10 6

SOUTH
♥ A K Q 3

This is an infrequent situation. The best play to make four tricks is to promptly lead the three-spot toward the ten, hoping that West, with J x x x, J x x x x, etc. (or even J x x) will not go up with the jack, in which case the ten-spot will win a trick. The alternative play is to lead the ace to drop a singleton jack.

18. The subterfuge depicted in the following illustration is of a type frequently resorted to:

NORTH
♠ K 10 9 x
♥ A x x
♦ K J x
♣ x x x

SOUTH
♠ Q J x
♥ K Q x
♦ A Q x x x
♣ Q x

Against South's *three no-trump* contract, West opens a small heart, declarer's king winning. The *jack* of spades (not the queen) is then led, to tempt West not to take the ace (West assuming that East possesses the spade queen). If West doesn't take his ace, nine tricks are now there for the taking. If the queen of spades is led instead of the jack, the possessor of the spade ace will automatically grab it—and the distastrous club shift may then be made. Of course, if East happens to have the spade ace, you are doomed no matter which spade you lead.

19. Quite frequently when declarer doesn't want to break the trump suit, he can coax the opponents into doing it by getting them to believe that he wants to trump a loser or two in dummy. The deal that follows illustrates this psychological play:

NORTH
♠ K x
♥ x x x x x x
♦ x x x
♣ x x

SOUTH
♠ A J 10 9 x x
♥ A x
♦ A K x
♣ A x

Against South's *four-spade* contract, West opens the king of clubs. Declarer wins with the ace and returns his remaining club. Whichever defender wins this trick might assume that declarer is anxious to trump a club or two in dummy. The defense might now shift to a trump to prevent this—and if they do, they give declarer a free finesse for the queen.

20. As has been pointed out, if you are a habitual false-carder, the opponents will get to know you as such and will profit thereby. When you are the declarer, if you are observant, you can pick up many tricks against an opponent who is known to be an inveterate false-carder by counteracting his deception with knowledge. Although this particular point (of counteracting deception) should not properly be classified under the heading of "standard deceptive plays by declarer," it nevertheless is a standard psychological counterattack to deception; and as such belongs in this concluding sec-

tion on declarer's approach to deceptive tactics. Precisely how declarer can negate a specific type of false-carding by a habitual false-carder can be observed in the following repetitive situation:

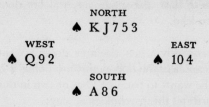

NORTH
♠ K J 7 5 3

WEST
♠ Q 9 2

EAST
♠ 10 4

SOUTH
♠ A 8 6

You lead the ace and, in the hope of talking you out of the finesse, East drops the ten. Unless East is a rank beginner, you probably finesse the jack anyway on the next round. But look at it this way:

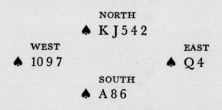

NORTH
♠ K J 5 4 2

WEST
♠ 10 9 7

EAST
♠ Q 4

SOUTH
♠ A 8 6

Again you lead the ace, and this time East, the same chronic and habitual false-carder, plays the four-spot. What do you deduce? Simply that East does not have a doubleton 10 4, 9 4, or 7 4, for with any of these combinations he would have dropped the higher one in order to "trick" you. Hence the conclusion that the finesse cannot be a winning play—so you play the king in desperation, with the hope of dropping the queen.

And, in conclusion, when playing against these habitual false-carders, if you don't explain why you had the "good luck" to catch the queen in situations comparable to the above, your same opponent will keep on false-carding in every possible situation—and you will find yourself in the position of always having an edge against him.

CHAPTER 15

THE DEFENDERS' DECEPTION
IN ACTION

The 36 deals in this chapter are devoted to a presentation of deceptive tactics by the defenders. All of these deals are reported as they occurred in expert competition.

The first 15 deals (Section A) feature deception at trick 1: a deceptive opening lead, a false-card by the partner of the opening leader, or a combination of both.

The remaining 21 deals (Section B) cover deceptive plays that occurred subsequent to trick 1.

A. *Deception at Trick 1*

1. One of the neatest swindles ever perpetrated on an unsuspecting declarer is the following:

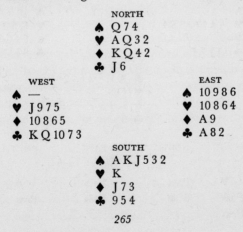

```
                    NORTH
                    ♠ Q 7 4
                    ♥ A Q 3 2
                    ♦ K Q 4 2
                    ♣ J 6
     WEST                                EAST
     ♠ —                                 ♠ 10 9 8 6
     ♥ J 9 7 5                           ♥ 10 8 6 4
     ♦ 10 8 6 5                          ♦ A 9
     ♣ K Q 10 7 3                        ♣ A 8 2
                    SOUTH
                    ♠ A K J 5 3 2
                    ♥ K
                    ♦ J 7 3
                    ♣ 9 5 4
```

NORTH	EAST	SOUTH	WEST
1 ♥	Pass	1 ♠	Pass
1 NT	Pass	3 ♠	Pass
4 ♠	Pass	Pass	Pass

West opened the club king, East overtook with the ace, and returned the eight-spot, West's queen winning. Everybody at the table was convinced that East had started with the doubleton A 8, and when West returned the ten of clubs, declarer naturally ruffed the trick with the queen of trumps. Eventually declarer then had to lose a spade and a diamond, for a 1-trick set.

Although it turned out to be a losing play, South did the right thing, for the only distribution that could beat him (assuming East had started with just two clubs) was for either of the opponents to have started with all of the four missing trumps. As fate would have it, that's just what was, and East's deception had paid off.

2.

Masters Pairs: 1955

```
                    NORTH
                ♠ Q 7 5
                ♥ 8
                ♦ A Q 10 9 7
                ♣ A K 10 6
    WEST                            EAST
♠ J                             ♠ 10 6
♥ A J 10 9 7 6 4                ♥ K 5 2
♦ 6                             ♦ 8 4 3 2
♣ Q J 9 4                       ♣ 8 7 5 2
                    SOUTH
                ♠ A K 9 8 4 3 2
                ♥ Q 3
                ♦ K J 5
                ♣ 3
```

WEST	NORTH	EAST	SOUTH
		(J. Ehrlenbach)	
4 ♥	Pass	Pass	4 ♠
Pass	6 ♠	Pass	Pass
Pass			

A look at the above four hands will indicate that there is no way of defeating declarer's six-spade contract. Nevertheless, by virtue of a brilliant defensive false-card, the East defender succeeded in creating a trend of thought in declarer's mind which led to declarer's defeat.

West opened the ace of hearts, upon which Ehrlenbach, East, dropped the king! West, of course, continued with another heart, which was ruffed by dummy's queen (to prevent the "obvious" overruff). When East followed to the second round of hearts, South was certain that the only plausible excuse for East's false-card was that East possessed the J–10–6 of spades. So the seven of spades was led from dummy, and finessed! West's singleton jack took the setting trick.

Before you criticize declarer, remember one thing: East would also have made the false-card if he *had* had the J–10–6 of trumps— and declarer would then have become a temporary genius instead of a gullible victim.

3.

NORTH
♠ J 9 8
♥ A Q
♦ A K J 8 2
♣ J 7 6

WEST
♠ 7 6 4 3
♥ K 9 7 5 2
♦ 7 4
♣ 5 3

EAST
♠ K Q 10
♥ 8 6 3
♦ 6 5 3
♣ 10 9 8 4

SOUTH
♠ A 5 2
♥ J 10 4
♦ Q 10 9
♣ A K Q 2

Both sides vulnerable.

SOUTH	WEST	NORTH	EAST
1 NT	Pass	6 NT	Pass
Pass	Pass		

West opened the three of spades, dummy's eight was put up— and East played the queen! When declarer took this with his ace,

268 Psychological Strategy in Contract Bridge

there was no doubt in his mind but that West had the spade ten, for what sane East, holding the Q–10, would have played the queen instead of the ten?

South immediately returned a spade—and he was down at trick three.

Had East played "normally"—by putting up his spade ten at trick 1—declarer would have had no option but to resort to the heart finesse for his twelfth trick, and it would have worked. East's deception had accomplished its intended result.

4.

Men's Team Championship: 1949

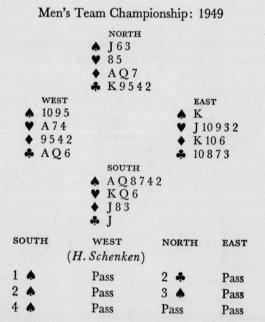

```
                      NORTH
                   ♠ J 6 3
                   ♥ 8 5
                   ♦ A Q 7
                   ♣ K 9 5 4 2
        WEST                        EAST
     ♠ 10 9 5                    ♠ K
     ♥ A 7 4                     ♥ J 10 9 3 2
     ♦ 9 5 4 2                   ♦ K 10 6
     ♣ A Q 6                     ♣ 10 8 7 3
                      SOUTH
                   ♠ A Q 8 7 4 2
                   ♥ K Q 6
                   ♦ J 8 3
                   ♣ J
```

SOUTH	WEST	NORTH	EAST
	(*H. Schenken*)		
1 ♠	Pass	2 ♣	Pass
2 ♠	Pass	3 ♠	Pass
4 ♠	Pass	Pass	Pass

Schenken opened the nine of spades—and declarer had something to think about!

Later, declarer said that he had been skeptical about a player of Schenken's ability leading a singleton trump, but on the bidding it was by no means impossible. So declarer decided to believe the lead. That, of course, placed East with the K 10 5, and to run the suit without loss, dummy's jack had to be used as a cover, so that East's ten-spot could later be finessed. Curtains for declarer!

5.

Men's Pair Championship: 1956

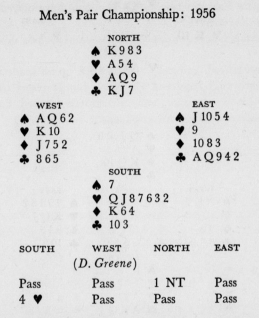

NORTH
♠ K 9 8 3
♥ A 5 4
♦ A Q 9
♣ K J 7

WEST
♠ A Q 6 2
♥ K 10
♦ J 7 5 2
♣ 8 6 5

EAST
♠ J 10 5 4
♥ 9
♦ 10 8 3
♣ A Q 9 4 2

SOUTH
♠ 7
♥ Q J 8 7 6 3 2
♦ K 6 4
♣ 10 3

SOUTH	WEST	NORTH	EAST
	(D. Greene)		
Pass	Pass	1 NT	Pass
4 ♥	Pass	Pass	Pass

Against the *four-heart* contract, Dick Greene opened the ten of trumps, away from the K 10 doubleton. Declarer couldn't believe that West had led away from the king, and assumed that, in all probability, the lead had been from the 10–9 doubleton. So (probably giving silent thanks to Greene for "revealing" the trump situation and saving him from a losing finesse), South played the trump ace—and went down one.

Greene's reasoning in making his lead was this: South's jump to four hearts denoted a long heart suit, and North, for his one no-trump opening bid, figured to have the heart ace. Thus Greene could smell the successful heart finesse against himself if declarer were left to his own resources—and his lead talked declarer out of the finesse.

Note that if by some chance South held a long heart suit like A Q J x x x, and North happened to hold x x x, Greene would still make his king of hearts, since South could not be expected to diagnose the true situation, and would subsequently take another heart finesse against East. That is:

NORTH
♥ x x x

WEST   EAST
♥ K 10   ♥ x x

SOUTH
♥ A Q J x x x

6.

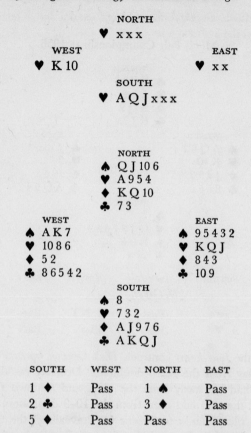

NORTH
♠ Q J 10 6
♥ A 9 5 4
♦ K Q 10
♣ 7 3

WEST   EAST
♠ A K 7   ♠ 9 5 4 3 2
♥ 10 8 6   ♥ K Q J
♦ 5 2   ♦ 8 4 3
♣ 8 6 5 4 2   ♣ 10 9

SOUTH
♠ 8
♥ 7 3 2
♦ A J 9 7 6
♣ A K Q J

SOUTH	WEST	NORTH	EAST
1 ♦	Pass	1 ♠	Pass
2 ♣	Pass	3 ♦	Pass
5 ♦	Pass	Pass	Pass

That three no-trump was an ironclad contract is immaterial. West, Gloria Turner, deceptively opened the ace of spades against the five-diamond contract (the king is the normal lead from an A K x combination). She then shifted to a low heart which was captured by dummy's ace.

If you were declarer, would you not assume that East held the spade king? Our declarer did. After cashing the king and queen of trumps, he then laid down dummy's queen of spades, discarding a heart when East followed with a low spade. West, of course, won this trick, and led a heart to defeat the contract.

Had the king of spades been opened, declarer would undoubtedly have established one of dummy's high spades for a heart discard by ruffing out the ace of spades.

7.

NORTH
- ♠ K 10 4
- ♥ J 9 8
- ♦ Q J 9
- ♣ Q J 10 4

WEST
- ♠ 8 3
- ♥ 6 5 2
- ♦ A K 7 5 3
- ♣ 8 6 2

EAST
- ♠ Q J 6
- ♥ A 4
- ♦ 10 8 6 4
- ♣ K 9 5 3

SOUTH
- ♠ A 9 7 5 2
- ♥ K Q 10 7 3
- ♦ 2
- ♣ A 7

SOUTH	WEST	NORTH	EAST
1 ♠	Pass	1 NT	Pass
2 ♥	Pass	2 NT	Pass
3 ♥	Pass	3 ♠	Pass
4 ♠	Pass	Pass	Pass

Expecting dummy to show up with minor suit strength, West opened the *ace* of diamonds. He then shifted to a heart, which East won, after which a heart was returned, declarer taking it in his own hand. Then followed the ace and king of trumps, leaving the queen outstanding. Declarer now had to avoid the loss of a club trick in order to fulfill his contract.

Under normal circumstances, he would have taken the club finesse. But declarer assumed—from the opening lead—that East held the diamond king. So he led the queen of diamonds, and discarded his club. As is apparent, West's diamond king captured this trick.

Very simply, declarer didn't know the location of the club king. But he "knew" that East held the diamond king, for with the A K x of diamonds, West was supposed to open the king and not the ace.

8. One final illustration of the deceptive opening lead by a defender, the hero of this deal being your author:

Thursday, April 22, 1948
The San Francisco Chronicle

Contract Contacts: Brilliant
Opening Lead by Karpin

by
Maureen Bailey

Charles Solomon, one of the top-ranking life masters of the country and a widely read bridge author and columnist, told us about the following hand which stars a brilliant opening lead by Fred Karpin, another luminary of the contract world. . . . The bidding went:

NORTH	EAST	SOUTH	WEST
1 ♥	Pass	3 ♣	Pass
3 ♦	Pass	4 NT	Pass
5 ♥	Pass	7 NT	Pass
Pass	Pass		

The five-heart call was the Blackwood response to show two aces. Now you are West on opening lead with the following:

♠ J 10 9 7
♥ 6 2
♦ K 9 8
♣ J 7 5 3

What do you lead?

Well, here was Mr. Karpin's reasoning before he made that choice, as Mr. Solomon related it to us:

"South's three-club bid, followed by his subsequent jump to seven no-trump seems to indicate that he holds a very good club suit. The fact that South, after finding that North held two aces, plunged right into the 7 NT contract without inquiring about kings, seems to substantiate my suspicion that South's club suit is pretty solid. In fact, I'm just about sure that South expects to make that grand slam on the basis of bringing home his clubs. But—South doesn't know, as I do, that the club suit is not going to break. I could, of course, make the perfectly safe opening of the jack of spades. However, if I do that, declarer may be forced to take the diamond finesse after finding out about the club situation and that diamond finesse may be all he needs to make his contract. So . . .

"I'll lead a diamond on the reasonably sound assumption that declarer will surely not risk a finesse on the very first trick unless no better play is available. Here goes with the nine of diamonds.

"And as you will see by looking the entire hand over, this is the only opening which will defeat the contract.

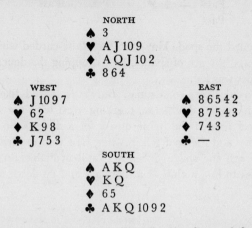

NORTH
♠ 3
♥ A J 10 9
♦ A Q J 10 2
♣ 8 6 4

WEST
♠ J 10 9 7
♥ 6 2
♦ K 9 8
♣ J 7 5 3

EAST
♠ 8 6 5 4 2
♥ 8 7 5 4 3
♦ 7 4 3
♣ —

SOUTH
♠ A K Q
♥ K Q
♦ 6 5
♣ A K Q 10 9 2

"No declarer in his right mind will take that diamond finesse on the opening lead with what looks like six sure club tricks, four sure heart tricks, three sure spade tricks, and the ace of diamonds for frosting. Whereas, if West makes any other opening, declarer will try out his club suit, find it doesn't break and be forced to finesse the diamonds whether he likes to or not."

9.

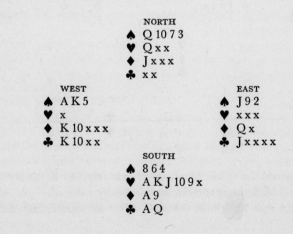

NORTH
♠ Q 10 7 3
♥ Q x x
♦ J x x x
♣ x x

WEST
♠ A K 5
♥ x
♦ K 10 x x x
♣ K 10 x x

EAST
♠ J 9 2
♥ x x x
♦ Q x
♣ J x x x x

SOUTH
♠ 8 6 4
♥ A K J 10 9 x
♦ A 9
♣ A Q

WEST	NORTH	EAST	SOUTH
1 ♦	Pass	Pass	Double
Pass	1 ♠	Pass	3 ♥
Pass	4 ♥	Pass	Pass
Pass			

West opened the spade king, and East false-carded with the nine. Then followed the ace of spades, East dropping the deuce. Now the five of spades was led.

What was declarer to assume? Surely it looked like East had started with the 9 2 doubleton, marking West with the spade jack. And declarer needed the spade queen for a discard. So he put up the ten-spot—and the roof fell in when East won the trick with the jack. Although the spade queen was still available for a discard, declarer had to lose a club or a diamond and go down a trick.

10.

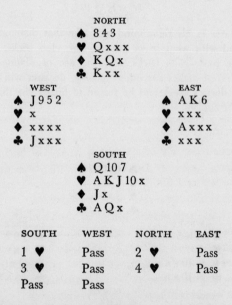

NORTH
♠ 8 4 3
♥ Q x x x
♦ K Q x
♣ K x x

WEST
♠ J 9 5 2
♥ x
♦ x x x x
♣ J x x x

EAST
♠ A K 6
♥ x x x
♦ A x x x
♣ x x x

SOUTH
♠ Q 10 7
♥ A K J 10 x
♦ J x
♣ A Q x

SOUTH	WEST	NORTH	EAST
1 ♥	Pass	2 ♥	Pass
3 ♥	Pass	4 ♥	Pass
Pass	Pass		

West opened the spade deuce, which was taken by East's ace. East then played back the spade six, and declarer "naturally" put up the ten, hoping that East held the jack. After all, surely East did not have the king so what hope was there except to rely on Lady Luck having given East the jack. When West captured this trick with the jack, declarer became a doomed man.

11.

```
                    NORTH
                 ♠ A 6 2
                 ♥ K Q 5
                 ♦ 10 8
                 ♣ A Q 10 5 3
     WEST                            EAST
  ♠ 9 7 5                         ♠ J 8 4 3
  ♥ J 8 2                         ♥ 10 9 6 4
  ♦ J 9 7 6 3                     ♦ A Q 2
  ♣ 8 7                           ♣ K 6
                    SOUTH
                 ♠ K Q 10
                 ♥ A 7 3
                 ♦ K 5 4
                 ♣ J 9 4 2
```

NORTH	EAST	SOUTH	WEST
1 ♣	Pass	2 NT	Pass
3 NT	Pass	Pass	Pass

Many years ago, the play which is the theme of this deal was deemed to be a beautifully deceptive play. Through repetitive usage, it has now become accepted as a standard play.

West opened the six of diamonds and East put up the queen which declarer took with the king. When the club finesse lost, East returned the ace and then the deuce of diamonds, after which West ran his diamonds to hand declarer a one-trick set.

Suppose East had played normally and had gone up with the ace of diamonds at trick 1. When he would next return the diamond queen, declarer would decline to take his king, and would take the third lead of diamonds. Then, when East subsequently obtained the lead via the king of clubs, he would be unable to return a diamond —and West would never get to cash his diamonds.

Of course, if declarer had been clairvoyant, he would have declined to win the diamond queen at trick 1. But how could he possibly have known that West didn't have, for example, the A J 9 6 3, and East the Q 7 2, in which case if declarer didn't take the diamond king, the defense would immediately take 5 diamond tricks. Consequently, declarer had to win the diamond queen, and stake everything on the club finesse.

12.

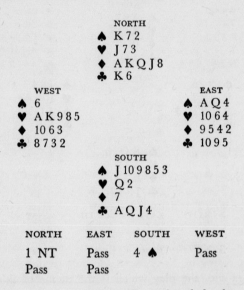

```
                        NORTH
                     ♠ K 7 2
                     ♥ J 7 3
                     ♦ A K Q J 8
                     ♣ K 6
        WEST                          EAST
     ♠ 6                           ♠ A Q 4
     ♥ A K 9 8 5                   ♥ 10 6 4
     ♦ 10 6 3                      ♦ 9 5 4 2
     ♣ 8 7 3 2                     ♣ 10 9 5
                        SOUTH
                     ♠ J 10 9 8 5 3
                     ♥ Q 2
                     ♦ 7
                     ♣ A Q J 4
```

NORTH	EAST	SOUTH	WEST
1 NT	Pass	4 ♠	Pass
Pass	Pass		

West opened the king of hearts, East played the four, and South dropped the queen. The idea was to panic West into a search for fast defensive tricks in clubs. Now if West believes that South is really out of hearts, he will shift to a club. If West continues with the ace of hearts, declarer will go down, since he eventually will lose two trump tricks.

What can West do about it? He should attempt to reconstruct the entire suit. If South's queen is really a singleton, how come East played the four-spot from the 10 6 4 2? The answer is he didn't——ergo, South's queen cannot be a singleton. So West refuses to panic and cashes the ace of hearts.

From declarer's point of view, the false-card is proper. If he fails to drop the queen, West will automatically continue hearts. But if he drops the queen, West must pause for reflection—and South has time to pray that West will come up with the wrong answer.

13.

NORTH
♠ Q 5
♥ A Q 6
♦ 8 6 5 4 2
♣ J 9 3

WEST
♠ 9 3
♥ 9 7 5 2
♦ 3
♣ K 10 7 6 5 4

EAST
♠ 7
♥ J 10 8 3
♦ A J 10 9
♣ A Q 8 2

SOUTH
♠ A K J 10 8 6 4 2
♥ K 4
♦ K Q 7
♣ —

SOUTH	WEST	NORTH	EAST
2 ♠	Pass	3 ♥	Pass
3 ♠	Pass	4 ♠	Pass
4 NT	Pass	5 ♦	Pass
6 ♠	Pass	Pass	Pass

This deal was presented earlier in this text (p. 229) as an example of a deceptive false-card by declarer. On the opening diamond lead, South dropped the king, thereby leading East to believe that West had led from Q x x originally. And, of course, when East then laid down the club ace, declarer romped in with his contract, later discarding his losing diamond on dummy's queen of hearts.

East should not have been fooled by South's deceptive false-card. South had employed the Blackwood Convention, and with the full knowledge that North-South were missing two aces, he had barged right into the slam. Surely South figured to be void of clubs. The best chance of defeating the contract, therefore, must be a diamond return.

If there is any theme to this deal, it is that reliance on the bidding is quite often the key to overcoming a declarer's chicanery.

14.

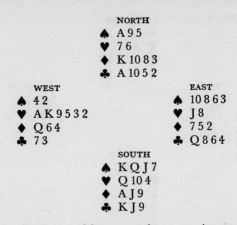

NORTH
♠ A 9 5
♥ 7 6
♦ K 10 8 3
♣ A 10 5 2

WEST
♠ 4 2
♥ A K 9 5 3 2
♦ Q 6 4
♣ 7 3

EAST
♠ 10 8 6 3
♥ J 8
♦ 7 5 2
♣ Q 8 6 4

SOUTH
♠ K Q J 7
♥ Q 10 4
♦ A J 9
♣ K J 9

West opens the deuce of hearts against your *four no-trump* contract (your *partner* bid badly) and East's jack is captured by your queen. Being accustomed to playing with "honest" players, you naturally assume that the 8 adverse hearts are divided 4–4, since the lead of the deuce, as the fourth-highest, shows a 4-card suit.

So you cash 4 spade tricks and then play back a heart. After the defenders take 3 heart tricks, they must return either a club or a diamond, thereby giving you a free finesse for the queen, and your tenth trick. But, as becomes evident as the hearts start pouring forth from West's hand, West has led the deuce from a 6-card suit!

15. The deliberate misleading of partner by a false-card is the only proper play in certain situations:

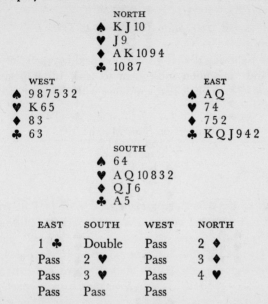

NORTH
♠ K J 10
♥ J 9
♦ A K 10 9 4
♣ 10 8 7

WEST
♠ 9 8 7 5 3 2
♥ K 6 5
♦ 8 3
♣ 6 3

EAST
♠ A Q
♥ 7 4
♦ 7 5 2
♣ K Q J 9 4 2

SOUTH
♠ 6 4
♥ A Q 10 8 3 2
♦ Q J 6
♣ A 5

EAST	SOUTH	WEST	NORTH
1 ♣	Double	Pass	2 ♦
Pass	2 ♥	Pass	3 ♦
Pass	3 ♥	Pass	4 ♥
Pass	Pass	Pass	

West opened the six of clubs, dummy's seven was put up—and East covered with the *king,* thereby creating the impression that he did not possess the queen; for if the latter card had been held, it would have been played conventionally instead of the king (the bottom card of equals. Actually, on the seven-spot, the nine would have been the technically correct card to play). East's reason was obvious: he was anxious to have partner lead spades, and not clubs.

Declarer, after capturing the opening lead with the club ace, entered dummy via the king of diamonds and led the jack of hearts, West's king winning. Since West "knew" that partner did not have the queen of clubs (from partner's original play of the king), West had no alternative but to make a spade lead. Declarer now went down.

Had West continued clubs after winning the heart king, declarer would have walked in with his contract; for he would have been able to discard his spades on dummy's diamonds. Admittedly, even if East had not false-carded at trick one, West might still have shifted to spades; but East properly wanted to guarantee the spade shift if West ever obtained the lead. The deception assured it.

B. *Deception Subsequent to Trick 1*

16. The following deal is a transition deal between "deception at trick 1" and "deception subsequent to trick 1." It begins with a deceptive lead at trick 1, and continues with the same deception at trick 3.

Culbertson-Sims Match: 1933

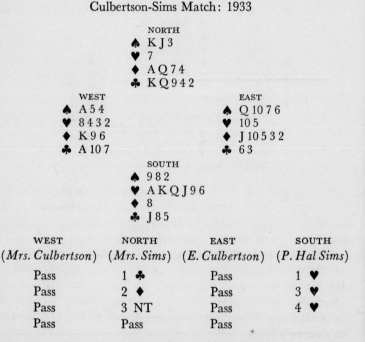

NORTH
♠ K J 3
♥ 7
♦ A Q 7 4
♣ K Q 9 4 2

WEST
♠ A 5 4
♥ 8 4 3 2
♦ K 9 6
♣ A 10 7

EAST
♠ Q 10 7 6
♥ 10 5
♦ J 10 5 3 2
♣ 6 3

SOUTH
♠ 9 8 2
♥ A K Q J 9 6
♦ 8
♣ J 8 5

WEST	NORTH	EAST	SOUTH
(*Mrs. Culbertson*)	(*Mrs. Sims*)	(*E. Culbertson*)	(*P. Hal Sims*)
Pass	1 ♣	Pass	1 ♥
Pass	2 ♦	Pass	3 ♥
Pass	3 NT	Pass	4 ♥
Pass	Pass	Pass	

Deciding from the bidding that a spade lead seemed to be indicated, Mrs. Culbertson opened the four of spades. After some thought, Hal Sims played low from dummy, and East's ten-spot captured the trick. A club was then returned, West's ace winning. Now Mrs. Culbertson returned the five of spades.

As is rather apparent, if Sims had put up dummy's king, he would have taken the remainder of the tricks. But he could not bring

himself to believe that Mrs. Culbertson would have underled the
ace of spades twice in a row, so he played the jack from dummy.
East, of course, won with the queen, and returned a spade to
West's ace for the setting trick.

17.

National Team of Four Championships: 1946

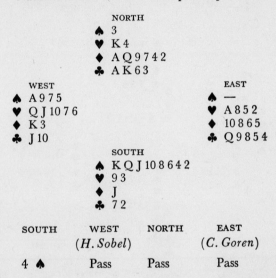

NORTH
♠ 3
♥ K 4
♦ A Q 9 7 4 2
♣ A K 6 3

WEST
♠ A 9 7 5
♥ Q J 10 7 6
♦ K 3
♣ J 10

EAST
♠ —
♥ A 8 5 2
♦ 10 8 6 5
♣ Q 9 8 5 4

SOUTH
♠ K Q J 10 8 6 4 2
♥ 9 3
♦ J
♣ 7 2

SOUTH	WEST (*H. Sobel*)	NORTH	EAST (*C. Goren*)
4 ♠	Pass	Pass	Pass

The queen of hearts was opened, covered with the king, and taken
by the ace. A heart was then returned, won by West's ten. Now
the jack of clubs was played and captured by dummy's ace, after
which dummy's singleton spade was led, and South's king was taken
by West's ace. West then played the ten of clubs, which was won
by dummy's king.

Declarer's only problem now was how to get back to his hand to
draw Mrs. Sobel's remaining trumps. He led the ace of diamonds—
and on it Mrs. Sobel dropped the king! After study, declarer decided to ruff a club. This was overruffed by Mrs. Sobel—and declarer was down one.

Declarer had a 50–50 guess. After all, the diamond king might
well have been a singleton. But if a small diamond had been played

by West instead of the king, declarer might well have elected to
re-enter his hand via a diamond.

From West's point of view, the deception could lose nothing. After
East had failed to follow on the first round of spades, Helen knew
that declarer had nothing left in his hand but spades.

18.

National Mixed Pair Championships: 1939

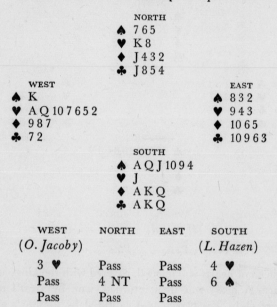

```
                         NORTH
                      ♠ 7 6 5
                      ♥ K 8
                      ♦ J 4 3 2
                      ♣ J 8 5 4
        WEST                              EAST
     ♠ K                                ♠ 8 3 2
     ♥ A Q 10 7 6 5 2                   ♥ 9 4 3
     ♦ 9 8 7                            ♦ 10 6 5
     ♣ 7 2                              ♣ 10 9 6 3
                         SOUTH
                      ♠ A Q J 10 9 4
                      ♥ J
                      ♦ A K Q
                      ♣ A K Q
```

WEST	NORTH	EAST	SOUTH
(*O. Jacoby*)			(*L. Hazen*)
3 ♥	Pass	Pass	4 ♥
Pass	4 NT	Pass	6 ♠
Pass	Pass	Pass	

The ace of hearts was opened, followed by another heart,
dummy's king winning. As declarer was about to finesse for the king
of trumps, a thought suddenly struck him: why was Jacoby leading
a second heart when he knew full well that Hazen figured to be
out of hearts and that he couldn't get to dummy except via a heart?
Obviously, the answer was that he wanted to put declarer in dummy
to take the spade finesse. So Hazen spurned the finesse, and went up
with his ace of spades, to catch Jacoby's singleton king.

Jacoby's lead at trick 2 was beautifully deceptive—with any other
lead, declarer would have had no choice but to lay down his trump

ace in the hope of matching the king. Unfortunately for Jacoby, Hazen recognized his plot and didn't fall for it.

19. The following situation occurs quite frequently:

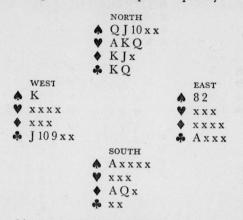

NORTH
♠ Q J 10 x x
♥ A K Q
♦ K J x
♣ K Q

WEST
♠ K
♥ x x x x
♦ x x x
♣ J 10 9 x x

EAST
♠ 8 2
♥ x x x
♦ x x x x
♣ A x x x

SOUTH
♠ A x x x x
♥ x x x
♦ A Q x
♣ x x

Against South's *six-spade* contract, West opened the jack of clubs, taken by East's ace; and a club was returned. Declarer then laid down dummy's queen of spades, East following with the eight-spot. The finesse was now taken, losing to West's singleton king.

In all probability, even if East had not false-carded with the eight, declarer would have taken the finesse, since it was the percentage play. Yet if we look at the situation through declarer's eyes, if the eight were an "honest" play, then it was impossible for West to have a singleton king, since the deuce was outstanding (but East could have held the doubleton K 8).

If, instead, East had played the deuce, there would have existed the theoretical possibility that East held the 8 2 (as he did) and that therefore West's king was unguarded.

The false-card of the eight stood to gain everything and to lose nothing.

20.

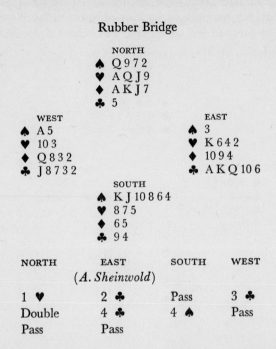

Rubber Bridge

NORTH
♠ Q 9 7 2
♥ A Q J 9
♦ A K J 7
♣ 5

WEST
♠ A 5
♥ 10 3
♦ Q 8 3 2
♣ J 8 7 3 2

EAST
♠ 3
♥ K 6 4 2
♦ 10 9 4
♣ A K Q 10 6

SOUTH
♠ K J 10 8 6 4
♥ 8 7 5
♦ 6 5
♣ 9 4

NORTH	EAST	SOUTH	WEST
	(*A. Sheinwold*)		
1 ♥	2 ♣	Pass	3 ♣
Double	4 ♣	4 ♠	Pass
Pass	Pass		

The theme of this deal is the "convincing" of a declarer that a
certain situation existed, thereby "compelling" him to adopt a losing
line of play. Without the defensive chicanery, declarer would easily
have fulfilled his contract.

West opened the three of clubs, which was captured by East's
queen. East, Alfred Sheinwold, did not like his team's prospects as
he gazed at the dummy, and he concluded that the hope of the defenders collecting four tricks in "honest" fashion was not good. So
he resorted to deception.

At trick 2 he led the six of hearts, West's ten-spot being captured
by dummy's jack. In declarer's mind, the "fact" was born that
Sheinwold had led a singleton. A trump lead was then made, West's
ace winning, after which West returned the three of hearts. Convinced that West held the king, declarer finessed dummy's queen.
Sheinwold took this trick with his king, returned a heart, and West
ruffed for the setting trick.

Is there a declarer who, when Sheinwold led the six of hearts at trick 2, would not have placed the king of hearts in the West hand? And once he came to this conclusion, was he not a doomed man?

21.

```
                        NORTH
                      ♠ A K J
                      ♥ Q 9 5 3 2
                      ♦ 9 6 2
                      ♣ A 3
        WEST                              EAST
      ♠ 9 6                             ♠ Q 10 8 5
      ♥ K J 10                          ♥ 8 7 4
      ♦ J 4                             ♦ Q 10 7 5
      ♣ Q 10 9 8 6 2                    ♣ J 7
                        SOUTH
                      ♠ 7 4 3 2
                      ♥ A 6
                      ♦ A K 8 3
                      ♣ K 5 4
```

SOUTH	WEST	NORTH	EAST
1 ♦	Pass	1 ♥	Pass
1 NT	Pass	3 NT	Pass
Pass	Pass		

West opened the ten of clubs, dummy's ace winning. To develop the heart suit seemed proper, so declarer led a heart to his ace, intending next to lead a heart toward dummy's queen. But on the ace of hearts, West dropped the king! And, of course, declarer promptly abandoned the heart suit, being 100 percent certain that the king was a singleton, and that the adverse hearts were divided 5–1. Having 8 tricks now, he hopefully attacked the spade suit, playing for either the queen to be in the West hand or for the spades to be divided 3–3. When neither of these prospects materialized, his contract was defeated.

What accounted for West's brilliant false-card? From his point of view, he knew that declarer's normal next play would be a small heart toward dummy, thereby establishing the suit. Hence, the "sacrifice" of the king.

On this matter of sacrifice, the reader will note that this play would not have resulted in the loss of a trick even if declarer had been sufficiently clairvoyant to have diagnosed the situation. Is it not true that if declarer had the ace and another heart, then all West would ever make would be 1 heart trick? Even with the king being tossed on the pyre, did not West still have the J 10 (against dummy's queen), a sure winner if hearts were continued? At worst, West's false-card of the king merely postponed the development of a heart trick for him. At best—exactly what did happen: the seduction of declarer.

22. There is a type of deceptive play that, on superficial examination, appears to be dangerous. In the hands of the novice it is, admittedly, a dangerous play to make. In the hands of the expert, however, it has been rendered nondangerous, for he has learned to wield it with *no visible hesitation:*

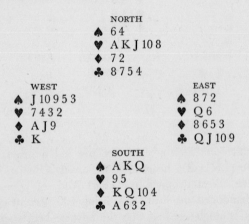

```
                    NORTH
                 ♠ 6 4
                 ♥ A K J 10 8
                 ♦ 7 2
                 ♣ 8 7 5 4
    WEST                          EAST
 ♠ J 10 9 5 3                  ♠ 8 7 2
 ♥ 7 4 3 2                     ♥ Q 6
 ♦ A J 9                       ♦ 8 6 5 3
 ♣ K                           ♣ Q J 10 9
                    SOUTH
                 ♠ A K Q
                 ♥ 9 5
                 ♦ K Q 10 4
                 ♣ A 6 3 2
```

West led the jack of spades against South's *three no-trump* contract, declarer's queen winning. Declarer then played the nine of hearts, letting it ride. East nonchalantly followed with the six-spot!

Honestly, now, would you not finesse again for the queen, being certain that West held her? Our declarer did, and went down 2 tricks.

From East's point of view, he might well have been sacrificing the queen. But he properly felt that it was a worthwhile risk; for if

he won with the queen, all of dummy's hearts would be good. So
he took his calculated risk—and it paid off.

As a final word on East's "abnormal" hold-up play, let me state
that if you have the urge to live dangerously—as East did—make
your play without hesitation. If, on declarer's lead of the nine of
hearts East had deliberated for a while prior to declining to take
his queen, declarer would not have taken the second heart finesse.

23. A deal almost identical to the preceding one is the following,
the defenders being Waldemar von Zedtwitz, East, and Harry
Harkavy, West.

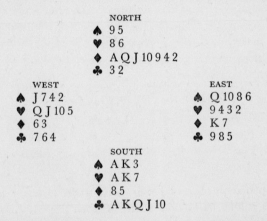

```
                    NORTH
                 ♠ 9 5
                 ♥ 8 6
                 ♦ A Q J 10 9 4 2
                 ♣ 3 2
    WEST                          EAST
 ♠ J 7 4 2                     ♠ Q 10 8 6
 ♥ Q J 10 5                    ♥ 9 4 3 2
 ♦ 6 3                         ♦ K 7
 ♣ 7 6 4                       ♣ 9 8 5
                    SOUTH
                 ♠ A K 3
                 ♥ A K 7
                 ♦ 8 5
                 ♣ A K Q J 10
```

Although six diamonds was a guaranteed contract, North-South
arrived at *six no-trump,* against which West opened the queen of
hearts. This was taken by declarer's king, after which declarer led
the eight of diamonds, and took the finesse. The eight-spot won the
trick when von Zedtwitz followed with the seven-spot.

South then cashed 5 club tricks, West discarding two spades while
East discarded two hearts. West, incidentally, was very careful to
hold on to the "insignificant" six of diamonds, since he knew that his
partner must have the diamond king (if declarer had this card,
then everybody was wasting a lot of time playing out the deal).

If you were declarer, and had not seen all four hands, would you
take the diamond finesse again? Probably. And then you too would
go down 2 tricks.

24.

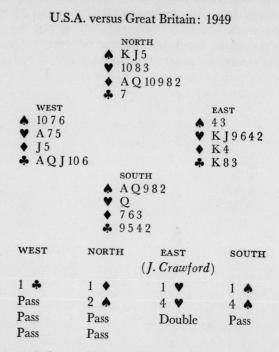

U.S.A. versus Great Britain: 1949

NORTH
♠ K J 5
♥ 10 8 3
♦ A Q 10 9 8 2
♣ 7

WEST
♠ 10 7 6
♥ A 7 5
♦ J 5
♣ A Q J 10 6

EAST
♠ 4 3
♥ K J 9 6 4 2
♦ K 4
♣ K 8 3

SOUTH
♠ A Q 9 8 2
♥ Q
♦ 7 6 3
♣ 9 5 4 2

WEST	NORTH	EAST	SOUTH
		(J. Crawford)	
1 ♣	1 ♦	1 ♥	1 ♠
Pass	2 ♠	4 ♥	4 ♠
Pass	Pass	Double	Pass
Pass	Pass		

West opened the ace of hearts, after which another heart was led, South ruffing. A low diamond was then played, dummy's ten-spot being put up. With no telltale hesitation, John Crawford followed with the four-spot.

Declarer then drew 3 rounds of trumps, after which he led another low diamond, covered by West's jack, dummy's queen—and East's king. The defenders then took 4 club tricks, inflicting a 3-trick set on declarer.

Dangerous deception, the reader might say? Well, it might have cost East a trick, but a doubled contract was at stake—and Crawford felt that if he took his king, thereby establishing dummy's diamond suit, there would be no hope of beating declarer. As can be observed, he was right.

25. The following type of play is a standard deceptive play, and the opportunity for its use arises frequently enough to warrant examining it closely. On the following deal, which arose in a tournament, only the matter of an overtrick was involved; but our West defender did not know this when he made his deceptive play:

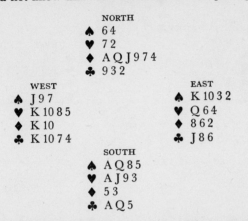

NORTH
♠ 6 4
♥ 7 2
♦ A Q J 9 7 4
♣ 9 3 2

WEST
♠ J 9 7
♥ K 10 8 5
♦ K 10
♣ K 10 7 4

EAST
♠ K 10 3 2
♥ Q 6 4
♦ 8 6 2
♣ J 8 6

SOUTH
♠ A Q 8 5
♥ A J 9 3
♦ 5 3
♣ A Q 5

Against South's *three no-trump* contract, West opened the four of clubs, East's jack being taken by declarer's queen. The three of diamonds was then led and West put up the king! Looking at all four hands, you would, of course, take the king with the ace, and bring in the entire diamond suit. But what if East's king were a singleton, as it appeared to be to declarer? In this case, East would have started with the 10 x x x of diamonds—and to take the king with the ace would prevent declarer from cashing more than three diamond tricks. So, to guarantee the making of five diamond tricks —and his contract—declarer permitted West's king to win the trick. I wonder how many defenders would have "earned" their king of diamonds had they been sitting in the West seat?

26.

Masters Team of Four Championships: 1955

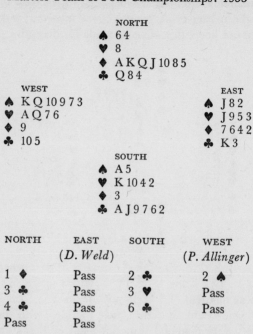

NORTH
♠ 6 4
♥ 8
♦ A K Q J 10 8 5
♣ Q 8 4

WEST
♠ K Q 10 9 7 3
♥ A Q 7 6
♦ 9
♣ 10 5

EAST
♠ J 8 2
♥ J 9 5 3
♦ 7 6 4 2
♣ K 3

SOUTH
♠ A 5
♥ K 10 4 2
♦ 3
♣ A J 9 7 6 2

NORTH	EAST (*D. Weld*)	SOUTH	WEST (*P. Allinger*)
1 ♦	Pass	2 ♣	2 ♠
3 ♣	Pass	3 ♥	Pass
4 ♣	Pass	6 ♣	Pass
Pass	Pass		

This deal serves as a splendid example of steering declarer away from the proper way of playing a hand.

West opened the king of spades, which was captured by declarer's ace. Declarer now surveyed the possibilities. First, East had to have the king of trumps, for otherwise the contract was doomed to defeat. So declarer promptly led his singleton diamond to dummy's ace, after which he led the queen of trumps. The defenders now co-operated beautifully: East played low and West dropped the *ten-spot!* This play "convinced" declarer that West had no more trumps, and that East had started with the K–5–3 of trumps. Hoping to "coup" East, declarer then prepared to cash as many diamonds as he could—but West ruined declarer by trumping the king of diamonds (upon which declarer discarded his losing spade), and cashed the ace of hearts for the setting trick.

Of course, had declarer been clairvoyant, he could have made his contract by drawing trumps. But how could declarer have diagnosed the true situation? Could not West's ten-spot have been a singleton?

27.

A Tournament in 1952

```
                        NORTH
                    ♠ 10 9 7 5
                    ♥ A 5 4
                    ♦ Q J 7 6
                    ♣ 6 5
      WEST                              EAST
  ♠ 2                                ♠ K J 4 3
  ♥ 10 6                             ♥ 9 8 7 3
  ♦ A K 10 9                         ♦ 8 5 3
  ♣ Q J 10 9 8 3                     ♣ 4 2
                        SOUTH
                    ♠ A Q 8 6
                    ♥ K Q J 2
                    ♦ 4 2
                    ♣ A K 7
```

Neither side vulnerable.

SOUTH	WEST	NORTH	EAST
1 ♣	Pass	1 ♦	Pass
1 ♠	Pass	2 ♠	Pass
3 NT	Pass	4 ♠	Pass
Pass	Pass		

The opening lead of the queen of clubs was captured by declarer's ace, after which he played the king of clubs, and then he ruffed a club. East overruffed this trick with his *king!*

This play firmly established in declarer's mind the fact that West held the jack of trumps, for surely East would have otherwise over-ruffed with the jack instead of with the king.

East returned a diamond, West cashing his king and ace of that suit. He then played another diamond, dummy winning. "Know-ing" that West possessed the jack of trumps, declarer then took his ace and queen of trumps, hoping to drop West's (hypothetical) jack.

When West showed out on the lead of the queen, declarer belatedly realized that he had been duped.

Had East overruffed with the jack of spades instead of with the king, declarer would have subsequently made the normal play of finessing East for the king of spades.

28.

```
                        NORTH
                        ♠ A 10 9 6
                        ♥ J 5
                        ♦ A J 7 2
                        ♣ K 9 4
        WEST                                EAST
        ♠ Q 8 4 2                           ♠ —
        ♥ Q 8 3 2                           ♥ 10 9 7 6 4
        ♦ 10 4 3                            ♦ 9 8 6 5
        ♣ J 6                               ♣ A Q 10 3
                        SOUTH
                        ♠ K J 7 5 3
                        ♥ A K
                        ♦ K Q
                        ♣ 8 7 5 2
```

Both sides vulnerable.

SOUTH	WEST	NORTH	EAST
1 ♠	Pass	3 ♠	Pass
4 ♠	Pass	Pass	Pass

West made an inspired opening of the jack of clubs, which was covered by dummy's king and East's ace. Then came the queen of clubs which won the trick, followed by the ten of clubs. West trumped this trick (although the ten-spot was high), and shifted to a small heart, declarer's king winning.

From declarer's point of view, West's voluntary trumping of East's high ten of clubs seemed to denote a lack of interest in spades —and presumably he would not have trumped if he were concerned with the protection of the spade queen. Hence it looked like West had no interest in spades.

And so, when declarer captured West's heart return with the ace, he led a spade to dummy's ace—and West now had another trump trick.

Of course, South might still have gone down if left to his own resources. Nevertheless, an assist must be given to West for creating the impression that his trump holding was worthless, thereby leading South to conclude that East possessed the queen of spades.

29.

National Men's Pair Championship: 1955

```
                    NORTH
                    ♠ 9 3
                    ♥ A Q
                    ♦ A Q 10 7 6 4
                    ♣ 10 9 8

    WEST                            EAST
    ♠ 10 4 2                        ♠ A K 8 6 5
    ♥ J 10 8 5 3 2                  ♥ 7 4
    ♦ J 3                           ♦ 9 5
    ♣ A 5                           ♣ K J 7 4

                    SOUTH
                    ♠ Q J 7
                    ♥ K 9 6
                    ♦ K 8 2
                    ♣ Q 6 3 2
```

NORTH	EAST	SOUTH	WEST
	(*E. Kaplan*)		(*I. Erdos*)
1 ♦	1 ♠	1 NT	2 ♥
3 ♦	Pass	3 NT	Pass
Pass	Pass		

This deal depicts some razzle-dazzle defense which had declarer coming and going—and he finally went the way of all flesh.

Ivan Erdos, West, opened the deuce of spades which Edgar Kaplan, East, captured with the *ace* (not the king). He then led the *king* of clubs and continued with the four of clubs.

Our poor declarer was now in a quandary: it certainly looked as though Kaplan had the ace of clubs, judging by his lead of the king. So South put up his queen of clubs which was taken by West's ace. West now played another spade, East won with the king, and cashed the jack and seven of clubs, to inflict a 2-trick set on declarer.

What motivated Kaplan to defend as he did? On the bidding,

South was marked with the king of hearts (South had bid three no-trump without knowing that North had the A Q of hearts). So Kaplan assumed (hoped) that Erdos had the ace of clubs for his "free" two-heart bid. Hence the play of the king of clubs at trick 2, which "convinced" declarer that East held the ace of clubs.

30.

NORTH
♠ 8 2
♥ 9 5
♦ K Q 10 8 5
♣ A K J 3

WEST
♠ 5
♥ 8 6 4 3 2
♦ J 9 3 2
♣ Q 10 9

EAST
♠ Q J 6 4
♥ A K 7
♦ 7 6 4
♣ 7 5 2

SOUTH
♠ A K 10 9 7 3
♥ Q J 10
♦ A
♣ 8 6 4

SOUTH	WEST	NORTH	EAST
1 ♠	Pass	2 ♦	Pass
2 ♠	Pass	3 ♣	Pass
3 ♠	Pass	4 ♠	Pass
Pass	Pass		

West's lead of the heart three was captured by East's king, after which East cashed his heart ace. He now led the seven of clubs, hoping to persuade South that this card was a singleton.

Upon winning this trick in dummy, declarer led a trump and put up his ace. To attempt to take a safety-play by leading another club to dummy seemed to declarer to be rather naïve, for East figured to trump this trick. So declarer laid down his king of spades—and his contract flew out of the window.

Suppose East had returned a heart or a diamond at trick 3 (instead of a club)? Declarer's plays would then have become automatic: the cashing of the trump ace, followed by a club to dummy's ace, after which the eight of trumps would be led and finessed, as a safety-play against East having started with the Q J x x of trumps. But East's deceptive play made declarer feel that he couldn't afford this safety-play.

31.

```
                    NORTH
                 ♠ J 9 5
                 ♥ A K 4
                 ♦ K 10 6 3
                 ♣ K 6 2
     WEST                            EAST
  ♠ 7 6 3                         ♠ K 10
  ♥ Q 8 5 3                       ♥ 10 9 7 6 2
  ♦ 9 7                           ♦ J 8 5
  ♣ Q J 9 4                       ♣ A 10 5
                    SOUTH
                 ♠ A Q 8 4 2
                 ♥ J
                 ♦ A Q 4 2
                 ♣ 8 7 3
```

NORTH	EAST	SOUTH	WEST
1 ♦	Pass	1 ♠	Pass
1 NT	Pass	3 ♦	Pass
3 ♠	Pass	4 ♠	Pass
Pass	Pass		

After East had won the third club trick with his ace (West having opened the queen of clubs), he shifted to the ten of hearts, dummy's king taking West's queen. Declarer now led the five of trumps—and East nonchalantly put up the king! When declarer took this with his ace, it was quite "obvious" that East had started with the singleton king, and that West had started with 10 7 6 3. So declarer now led a low spade, finessed dummy's nine—and lost his game when East took the trick with the ten.

Had East played "normally," by putting up the spade ten on the initial spade lead, declarer would also have played normally, finessing his queen and subsequently catching East's king.

South really cannot be criticized for going wrong. East made a good play—and it might well have been that he had only a singleton king, in which case winning play would have necessitated finessing West for the ten-spot.

32.

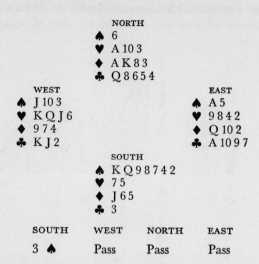

NORTH
♠ 6
♥ A 10 3
♦ A K 8 3
♣ Q 8 6 5 4

WEST
♠ J 10 3
♥ K Q J 6
♦ 9 7 4
♣ K J 2

EAST
♠ A 5
♥ 9 8 4 2
♦ Q 10 2
♣ A 10 9 7

SOUTH
♠ K Q 9 8 7 4 2
♥ 7 5
♦ J 6 5
♣ 3

SOUTH	WEST	NORTH	EAST
3 ♠	Pass	Pass	Pass

West's opening lead of the king of hearts was taken by dummy's ace. The singleton spade was led, East put up the five, and declarer's king captured the trick, West following with the three-spot. Declarer then led a low spade, East's ace falling. Later, declarer's queen of spades was led, felling East's jack. Declarer lost a trick in each suit, to fulfill his contract.

It looks like a routine hand, but suppose West had dropped the ten (or the jack) of spades on the first spade lead. Might not declarer have been led to believe that West had started with the doubleton J 10, in which case, the second spade lead of the *queen* would fell West's jack and East's ace, thereby resulting in the loss of just one spade trick? But when West played the three-spot, he gave declarer no chance to go wrong, for with the ace, jack, and ten still outstanding, declarer's only chance to avoid the loss of more than one spade trick was for East to have the singleton ace remaining.

33. The deceptive opening lead of the ace from an A K x combination has been illustrated earlier in this chapter. But on the next deal, after the deceptive opening lead of the ace from an A K x x, an even more deceptive lead was made at trick 2, and it talked declarer out of the winning line of play. The hero of the deal, which

has become a classic illustration of deceptive leads, was Albert Morehead.

NORTH
- ♠ Q J 9 4
- ♥ J 8 3
- ♦ Q 6 5
- ♣ 10 8 2

WEST
- ♠ A K 5 2
- ♥ 10 9 7
- ♦ 10 9 3
- ♣ A 7 3

EAST
- ♠ 10 8 6 3
- ♥ 5 4
- ♦ K 4
- ♣ Q J 9 6 4

SOUTH
- ♠ 7
- ♥ A K Q 6 2
- ♦ A J 8 7 2
- ♣ K 5

SOUTH	WEST	NORTH	EAST
1 ♥	Pass	1 NT	Pass
2 ♦	Pass	2 ♥	Pass
4 ♥	Pass	Pass	Pass

West opened the ace of spades—and shifted to the *nine* of diamonds at trick 2. Declarer logically assumed that the nine was either a singleton or part of a 9 x doubleton; and that therefore East had some combination of the king and ten. So he put up dummy's queen, East covered with the king, and declarer's ace won. Trumps were then drawn, ending in dummy, after which the six of diamonds was led, and the finesse taken against East's "marked" ten-spot. West, of course, won with the ten-spot, and led the ace of spades, declarer trumping. Eventually, declarer had to concede two club tricks, and suffered a one-trick set.

If declarer had been left to his own devices (if West had made the neutral lead of the heart ten at trick 2), he probably would have fulfilled his contract. After drawing trumps, he would have led a small diamond off dummy, and finessed his jack. The ace would then have dropped East's king, and dummy's queen would have picked up West's ten-spot, thereby avoiding the loss of a diamond trick. But, unfortunately for declarer, he was steered away from the winning line of play.

34.

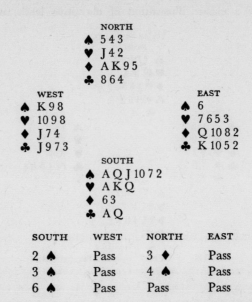

| NORTH |
| ♠ 5 4 3 |
| ♥ J 4 2 |
| ♦ A K 9 5 |
| ♣ 8 6 4 |

WEST	EAST
♠ K 9 8	♠ 6
♥ 10 9 8	♥ 7 6 5 3
♦ J 7 4	♦ Q 10 8 2
♣ J 9 7 3	♣ K 10 5 2

| SOUTH |
| ♠ A Q J 10 7 2 |
| ♥ A K Q |
| ♦ 6 3 |
| ♣ A Q |

SOUTH	WEST	NORTH	EAST
2 ♠	Pass	3 ♦	Pass
3 ♠	Pass	4 ♠	Pass
6 ♠	Pass	Pass	Pass

The ten of hearts was opened, South winning with the king. A diamond was then led to the ace, and declarer took the finesse in spades—and West followed with the nine-spot. Convinced that the spade king was favorably located, declarer then re-entered dummy via the diamond king, to take another spade finesse. When East showed out, declarer was doomed, for he couldn't get to dummy to take the club finesse.

Had West taken the first trump lead with his king, declarer would have been able to return to dummy later to take the successful club finesse (instead of finessing again for the spade king). But West convinced declarer that the spade suit was the suit to stay with—and thus killed dummy's entry for a club finesse.

35.

False Security

NORTH
- ♠ A Q J 2
- ♥ A 10 6 4
- ♦ A Q 4
- ♣ A 3

WEST
- ♠ 8 6 3
- ♥ 9 7 3
- ♦ 7 6 5
- ♣ K J 7 4

EAST
- ♠ K 7 5
- ♥ 8 5 2
- ♦ K 9 3 2
- ♣ Q 10 2

SOUTH
- ♠ 10 9 4
- ♥ K Q J
- ♦ J 10 8
- ♣ 9 8 6 5

Against South's *three no-trump* contract, West opened the club four, which was captured by East's queen when dummy played low. The ten of clubs was returned and won by dummy's ace.

Declarer came to his hand via the heart king, after which he tried the spade finesse, losing to East's king. From his partner's lead of the four-spot, East knew that West had started with just four clubs (the three-spot was in dummy and the deuce in East's hand). Prospects for defeating three no-trump seemed rather slim. So East did not return his deuce of clubs, his purpose being to give declarer the impression that East was out of clubs, and to get declarer to attempt the diamond finesse. East therefore played back a low spade, a "safe" return. Declarer fell for the bait, reasoning that since East did not return a club, he had no more clubs. Declarer won the trick with dummy's jack, re-entered his own hand via the heart queen, and tried the diamond finesse, East's king winning. East's club return then enabled West to cash two club tricks to defeat declarer. Of course, declarer had nine tricks all along, but he was led to believe that the try for the overtricks involved no risk.

36.

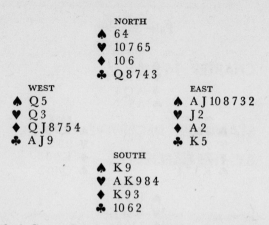

NORTH
♠ 6 4
♥ 10 7 6 5
♦ 10 6
♣ Q 8 7 4 3

WEST
♠ Q 5
♥ Q 3
♦ Q J 8 7 5 4
♣ A J 9

EAST
♠ A J 10 8 7 3 2
♥ J 2
♦ A 2
♣ K 5

SOUTH
♠ K 9
♥ A K 9 8 4
♦ K 9 3
♣ 10 6 2

In this deal, Goren, South, was partnered by Helen Sobel. Against
East's *four-spade* contract, Goren cashed the ace and king of hearts.
Right at this point he was end-played; whether he returned a heart,
a diamond, a club, or a spade, declarer would gain a trick.

But Goren found the way out. He led the nine of spades! Declarer
won with dummy's queen, and who could blame him for assuming
that North had the spade king? He then led another spade, finessing
his ten-spot. Goren won with his now-singleton king, played another
heart, and declarer eventually lost a diamond trick, to suffer a 1-
trick set.

CHAPTER 16

STANDARD DECEPTIVE PLAYS
BY THE DEFENDERS

From an academic standpoint, it should be noted that in most situations, the art of deception, or false-carding, should not become a habitual or automatic maneuver. Each new deal, no matter how much similarity in pattern or detail it seems to bear to its predecessors, invariably has some point of dissimilarity; and, in most cases, it may have only a superficial resemblance to apparently similar situations which have been encountered previously. In theory, almost all false-carding situations require some forethought, like any other play, and should, if possible, be worked out a move or two ahead.

However, when circumstances demand an immediate and unhesitating decision in order to reap the benefit of any chicanery, one cannot take a time-out at the table to determine whether the particular situation at hand requires a false-card or not. Such studied analysis would negate the utility of any false-card, for it would expose the intended deceit. Deception, to accomplish its objective, must be spontaneous, and must be performed with neither undue haste nor undue deliberation. In other words, it must be effected as though it were the perfectly normal and natural play. It is to the accomplishment of this objective of spontaneous reaction that this chapter is dedicated: to make the reader familiar with all the types of deceptive situations that have arisen in the past, so that when he is confronted by comparable situations, he will be in the learned position of devoting *as little time as possible* to working out the answers at the table.

As has been evidenced throughout the preceding chapters, deceptive tactics by the defenders must be handled with care. The reason for this is, of course, that in most cases the defenders must cooperate to the maximum extent in order to defeat declarer. And, when a deceptive play is apt to either mislead or confuse partner, the defense will probably collapse. But there are certain standard situations wherein a defender can deceive declarer to good effect, with the deception having no detrimental result so far as partner is concerned. Some of these deceptive plays are quite frequent in occurrence, and have become set plays; others, although arising much less often, nevertheless come up frequently enough to warrant studying and earmarking for future reference and employment.

1. Probably the oldest defensive chestnut is the following:

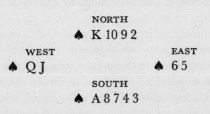

NORTH
♠ K 10 9 2

WEST   EAST
♠ Q J   ♠ 6 5

SOUTH
♠ A 8 7 4 3

Declarer is in a *spade* contract, and he leads the three of spades. It is accepted psychological strategy for you, sitting West, to put up the queen, thereby hoping to induce declarer into believing that your queen is a singleton. The desired effect of the play is to get declarer to now finesse your partner for the jack. Of course, this play will not work all or even most of the time, since it has become a standard play known to all players. The expert player, in this falsecarding situation, has learned to mix them up: sometimes he plays the jack and sometimes the queen. In the long run, by playing the queen, you will possibly win a trick with the jack more often than you will win a trick with the queen if you put up the jack on the first spade lead. From declarer's point of view, when he sees the queen put up, he knows that about half the time you were dealt a blank queen, and that you had no choice when you played that card. And in the remaining half the time—when you were dealt the doubleton Q–J—about half of *that* time you play the queen, and in the other half you play the jack. So when the queen is played to the first trick, mathematically it figures to be a singleton about 75 percent of the time.

The same deceptive play (with the Q–J) is also available to you —and applicable to the same extent—when you are on lead. Suppose that in the above situation South had opened the bidding with one spade, been raised by North to two spades, and finally contracted for game at *four spades*. In this case, holding the doubleton Q J of spades, you would be reasonably sure that the declarer and dummy had the outstanding high spades. The opening lead of the *jack* of spades might well lead declarer into thinking that your partner possessed the queen, since if you had that card, your normal lead would have been the queen. But, if you have acquired a reputation for always leading the jack from a doubleton Q J, declarer will correctly diagnose the situation and catch your queen. If, however, you are known to mix them up, declarer may well accept the lead of the jack at face value and be misled, fatally.

If you think you do not want any part of this psychological warfare, permit me to point out that if West avoids leading spades altogether, declarer, left to his own resources, will probably cash the ace and king of spades, playing for the 4 adverse spades to be divided 2–2. And even if you do not agree, surely you will concur in the following: if a spade is not led originally, then declarer, as soon as he leads trumps, 50 percent of the time will lay down the ace first, thereby automatically avoiding the loss of a spade trick no matter which honor you drop, since your other honor must fall on his next lead of the suit. And, even if he had led the king from dummy on his first spade lead, dropping your queen or jack, he would still have a 50–50 chance of guessing whether your honor was a singleton or part of the Q-J doubleton. By leading the jack (or queen) yourself, you deprive declarer of the opportunity of laying down his ace first—and in so doing, you create for yourself a greater possibility of winning a trick.

2. The opportunity to employ this standard deceptive play arises often:

NORTH

♠ K Q 10 2

EAST

♠ A 4 3

Let us say that South is playing a *no-trump* contract, and he leads a low spade out of the South hand, putting up the king. Your only correct play is to let him win it *without any hesitation* on your part. If you capture the king with the ace, then on the next lead of the suit by declarer, he is a cinch to successfully finesse your partner for the jack. But if you decline to take your ace on the first lead of the suit, then declarer may well be led to believe that West possesses the spade ace. And, if he needs just two spade tricks, then on the second lead of the suit from the South hand, he will probably put up North's queen; and when you win this trick with the ace (to declarer's surprise), you will have established partner's jack. Either of the following might be the situation:

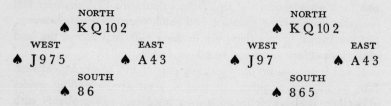

On the subject of playing low, without any hesitation, on the first spade lead: when the king is played from dummy, do not go into a profound study as to whether to take your ace or not. If you do, you might just as well show declarer your ace, for he will know you have it. Make up your mind not to take the ace even before declarer gets around to leading the suit. Then declarer will have a pure guess as to the location of the ace.

A blood relative of the above play is this situation:

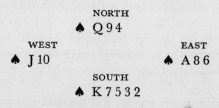

Spades is the trump suit. Declarer leads the deuce and puts up dummy's queen after your partner follows with the ten (or the jack). Play the six-spot, *not the ace*. When declarer then leads another spade out of the North hand, play the eight-spot. Declarer will now automatically play low from the South hand, and your partner's remaining honor will capture the trick 100 times out of 100.

If you take the queen with the ace, declarer *may* cash the king on the next round of the suit, hoping that West started with the J 10 doubleton. As is apparent, by not taking the ace—leading declarer to believe that you don't have it—you will put your team in the position of having everything to gain and nothing to lose.

3. The next frequently occurring situation has already been illustrated, and is now presented merely to include it in this section on standard deceptive plays:

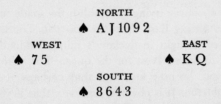

Declarer leads a low spade, putting up North's jack. Win it with the king, deceptively, so that on the next lead of the suit declarer will tend (you hope) to finesse your partner for the queen, rather than playing North's ace to drop your queen. But do not make this false-card all the time; for if you do, whenever you win the trick with the queen, declarer will know that you don't have the king.

As was also pointed out, many bridge players apply this false-card promiscuously whether they hold the doubleton K Q or the K Q x, and in so doing mislead partner:

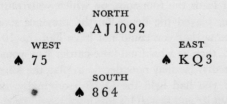

In this case, who cares about influencing declarer? When declarer leads low from the South hand, and puts up the spade jack on the first lead, *always win it with the queen.* Partner will then know you still have the king; whereas if you win the first trick with the king, partner will give declarer credit for the queen.

4. A standard deceptive play available to the defenders is the following:

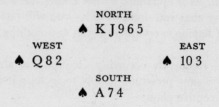

NORTH
♠ K J 9 6 5

WEST
♠ Q 8 2

EAST
♠ 10 3

SOUTH
♠ A 7 4

Declarer is obviously trying to establish the spade suit, and he lays down the ace. Sitting East, *drop the ten-spot*. The ten is bound to start a train of thought in declarer's mind. Undoubtedly declarer had intended to finesse West for the queen. But, with the ten being dropped by you, he may now feel that perhaps you started with the Q 10 doubleton. It is obvious, however, that if you always play the ten-spot in situations similar to the above, the opponents will fail to take you seriously. That is:

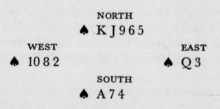

NORTH
♠ K J 9 6 5

WEST
♠ 10 8 2

EAST
♠ Q 3

SOUTH
♠ A 7 4

If, on declarer's lead of the ace, you drop the three, then when declarer next leads the four-spot, on which your partner plays the eight (having played the deuce on the previous spade lead), declarer will know that you could not have had the 10 3 doubleton; for if you did, then as a habitual false-carder you would have played the ten originally. He may now decide to play the king to drop your queen, for if you had held the Q 10 3 originally, he couldn't do anything about it; and hence, his sole hope would be that you started with the doubleton Q 3.

In situations analogous to the above, West can help out tremendously by false-carding:

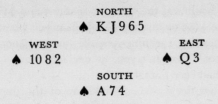

NORTH
♠ K J 9 6 5

WEST   EAST
♠ 10 8 2   ♠ Q 3

SOUTH
♠ A 7 4

On the lead of the ace, West should drop the eight-spot. Then on the lead of the four from the South hand, West should play the ten. Declarer will now be confronted with an out-and-out guess, since, from his viewpoint, the situation might well be:

NORTH
♠ K J 9 6 5

WEST   EAST
♠ Q 10 8   ♠ 3 2

SOUTH
♠ A 7 4

From the defensive viewpoint, when declarer leads the ace (the dummy being the K J 9 6 5), the defender who does not have the queen knows that his partner has it; and the defender's slogan should now become "protect our queen." (Of course, if declarer also has the queen, in addition to the ace, the defenders cannot alter their predestination.)

Familiarity with the above type of false-card enabled Mike Michaels, one of the nation's top players, to create a spur-of-the moment variation of the play. The deal arose in a National Championship:

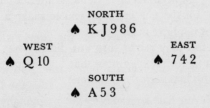

NORTH
♠ K J 9 8 6

WEST   EAST
♠ Q 10   ♠ 7 4 2

SOUTH
♠ A 5 3

The remainder of the cards are unimportant. At one stage of the bidding, however, South had raised North's spade bid, pretty much marking the ace of spades as being in the South hand. The final contract was *six no-trump*, with the North hand being the dummy.

At trick two, South led the three of spades—and Mike played the queen into the jaws of dummy's K–J. Can you blame declarer for subsequently leading the nine-spot off dummy and finessing East for the ten-spot? Wouldn't you, as declarer, have concluded that West's queen had been a singleton?

As to whether declarer's original play of the three-spot, rather than the ace, was correct, is immaterial. It is quite apparent that if he had played the ace first, he would have brought in the entire suit without loss. But, then, declarers have been known to make mistakes (even as you and I), and the defense should remain alert to capitalize on them.

5. A variation of this type of situation is the following:

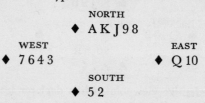

NORTH
♦ A K J 9 8

WEST
♦ 7 6 4 3

EAST
♦ Q 10

SOUTH
♦ 5 2

Let us assume that the contract is *no-trump,* and the declarer is attacking the diamond suit. He leads the ace from the North hand— and on it you drop the queen. Will not declarer be led to believe that the ten-spot is in the West hand, and will he then not enter the South hand in order to lead a low diamond and finesse your partner for the ten-spot? Of course, it is true that, in the above illustration, the declarer might have finessed for the queen if East had made the normal play of the ten-spot originally. However, the initial play of the queen makes it (almost) an absolute certainty that he will finesse for the ten, enabling you to make a trick which you might or might not have made otherwise.

Of course, this play might turn out disastrously, as is frequently the end result of a deceptive play that boomeranged. For instance, suppose that this had been the situation:

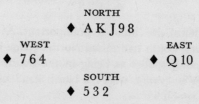

NORTH
♦ A K J 9 8

WEST
♦ 7 6 4

EAST
♦ Q 10

SOUTH
♦ 5 3 2

On the play of the ace, if you drop your queen, declarer will then cash the king (prior to finessing for the ten-spot). And with your ten-spot falling, declarer will now have five diamond tricks. If, in this illustration, you had played normally by following with the ten-spot, then you would have stood a respectable chance of winning a trick with your queen via declarer's subsequent unsuccessful diamond finesse.

Nevertheless, if you had diagnosed the situation, and had come to the conclusion that declarer had started with only two diamonds (instead of three), then your play of the queen on the first lead of the suit would have tended to gain you a trick.

6. A recurring false-carding situation is the following, in which the false-carder has everything to gain and nothing to lose:

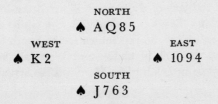

NORTH
♠ A Q 8 5

WEST
♠ K 2

EAST
♠ 10 9 4

SOUTH
♠ J 7 6 3

South leads the three of spades and finesses the queen. East should drop the *nine,* thereby tending to influence South into believing that the following distribution exists:

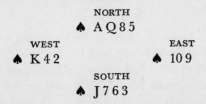

NORTH
♠ A Q 8 5

WEST
♠ K 4 2

EAST
♠ 10 9

SOUTH
♠ J 7 6 3

South will probably now return to his hand to lead the jack, hoping to drop East's ten-spot while finessing West's king. If he does, then East's ten-spot (in the first illustration, with 10 9 4) will become a winner. If, in the first illustration, East does not false-card, South will have no choice but to lay down the ace to catch the king, since if West had started with either the K 10 2 or the K 9 2, South would have to lose a spade trick no matter how he subsequently played the suit.

A beautiful spur-of-the-moment variation of the above type of false-card was employed in a National Championship event by Dick Freeman, of Washington, D. C.

Let's put you in the South seat, as declarer at *six no-trump:*

NORTH

♣ A Q 6

SOUTH

♣ J 9 7 3 2

You lead the deuce of clubs, West puts up the four-spot, dummy's queen is played and it wins, East dropping the eight-spot. Would you not assume that East had either the singleton eight—in which case you would have to lose 1 club trick—or that he had been dealt the doubleton 10 8, in which case if you now get back to the South hand and lead the jack of clubs, you will avoid the loss of any club tricks by catching East's now-singleton ten while simultaneously smothering West's king? So you return to the South hand via some other suit, lead the jack of clubs—and West fails to follow suit! You must now lose two club tricks. Here was the actual distribution:

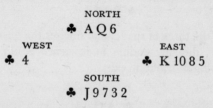

NORTH

♣ A Q 6

WEST

♣ 4

EAST

♣ K 10 8 5

SOUTH

♣ J 9 7 3 2

There are two angles involved in Dick's refusal to take his king on the first lead of the club suit, and his simultaneous false-card of the eight-spot. First, if he had taken the king, then declarer's next lead would automatically have been a club to the ace, revealing the fact that West was now void—and East's ten-spot would then be finessed, resulting in East making just one club trick. Second, if in refusing to take the king on the first lead, he had played the five-spot, then declarer might well have decided to play West for the K x originally, and would then have laid down the ace. And, again, when West would show out, East's ten-spot would be finessed successfully. But the play of the eight-spot on the first club lead led declarer to realize that if the eight were East's normal play, then the king was possessed by West; and that East might well have held the doubleton 10 8 at the outset. Of course, this was precisely the impression and the trend of thought East hoped to induce in declarer's mind by his deceptive play—and East's triumph was well deserved.

In each of the eight situations that follow, a defender knows that he is doomed unless he takes the initiative in leading declarer astray. Each of these plays has, in experience, been demonstrated as having the ability to create a trick that would be lost if deception were not resorted to:

7.

NORTH
♠ J 9 2

WEST   EAST
♠ 7 4 3   ♠ K 10

SOUTH
♠ A Q 8 6 5

Spades is the trump suit (although it could be a side suit). Declarer leads the deuce of spades from the dummy, and East should play the *king*. When declarer takes it with the ace, he will automatically then lead a low spade and finesse dummy's nine. East will now make his ten-spot. It would take a clairvoyant South to diagnose the true situation—and, frankly, if South were that good, you do not belong in the same league with him. As is apparent, if East mechanically plays the ten-spot on the initial spade lead, South will finesse the queen and avoid the loss of a spade trick no matter how he subsequently plays the spade suit.

8. Comparable to the above is the next situation, in which the North hand has no other entry. The contract is *no-trump:*

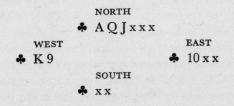

NORTH
♣ A Q J x x x

WEST   EAST
♣ K 9   ♣ 10 x x

SOUTH
♣ x x

South leads a low club, with the obvious intention of finessing (who would be willing to settle for just one club trick with that lovely club suit?). If West plays normally, by putting up the nine, declarer will win six club tricks via a successful finesse. But if West deceptively puts up the king, declarer will (in all probability) let him hold the trick, for if the king is a singleton—as it appears to be —then East will be holding the 10 x x x, in which case declarer will make only 3 club tricks if he takes the king with the ace.

A similar situation is the following:

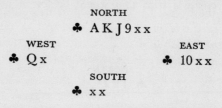

NORTH
♣ A K J 9 x x

WEST
♣ Q x

EAST
♣ 10 x x

SOUTH
♣ x x

The contract is again *no-trump*, and the North hand has no other entry. When South leads a low club, put up the *queen*. If declarer assumes it to be a singleton (and why shouldn't he?), he might well let you win the trick, since if it is a singleton, then your partner must possess the 10 x x x. And, if declarer takes your "singleton" queen, he will then be unable to win more than 3 club tricks; whereas, if he permits your queen to win, he has guaranteed himself 5 club tricks.

The expert application of this type of play can be observed in the following deal:

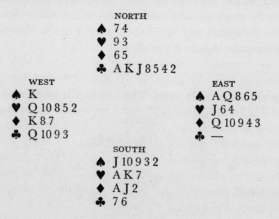

NORTH
♠ 7 4
♥ 9 3
♦ 6 5
♣ A K J 8 5 4 2

WEST
♠ K
♥ Q 10 8 5 2
♦ K 8 7
♣ Q 10 9 3

EAST
♠ A Q 8 6 5
♥ J 6 4
♦ Q 10 9 4 3
♣ —

SOUTH
♠ J 10 9 3 2
♥ A K 7
♦ A J 2
♣ 7 6

Against South's *three no-trump* contract, West opened his fourth-best heart, which was taken by declarer's king. It was declarer's intention to then lead a club and play low from dummy if West followed with a club. This would guarantee the making of 6 club tricks no matter how the adverse clubs were divided. And if, on the low club lead (the six-spot), West had played his three-spot, declarer would actually have made all 7 club tricks, since the six-spot would have been a winner.

But when declarer led the six of clubs at trick 2, West nonchalantly put up the queen. Declarer grabbed this with the king, for who could resist the urge when the queen had all the earmarks of being a singleton? The lure of a "sure" overtrick was simply too much for declarer—and it cost him his contract.

9.

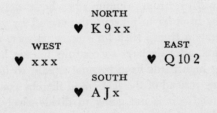

```
                    NORTH
                ♥ K 9 x x
   WEST                      EAST
♥ x x x                      ♥ Q 10 2
                    SOUTH
                ♥ A J x
```

A small heart is led from the North hand, East follows with the deuce, and South puts up the jack, which wins. It is now obvious to East that South possesses the heart ace. When South next cashes the ace of hearts, East must drop *the queen!* (at no cost, actually, since the queen and ten have become equals). In all probability, South will assume that East started with the Q 2 doubleton, and will then finesse dummy's nine spot, which will be captured by East's ten.

If East plays "honestly," and drops the ten of hearts on declarer's lead of the heart ace, East will still be marked with the queen. Declarer will now have no option but to play the king of hearts, felling the queen, and thereby making 4 heart tricks.

The principle involved in East's deceptive false-card is this: if you can spare it, always play a card you are known to possess. The occasions for the employment of this principle of deception arise quite frequently. For example:

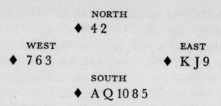

NORTH
♦ 4 2

WEST
♦ 7 6 3

EAST
♦ K J 9

SOUTH
♦ A Q 10 8 5

Let's say that South is playing a *heart* contract; and before touching trumps, he leads the deuce of diamonds. When you (as East) play the nine, he successfully finesses his queen. He next leads the ace of diamonds, with the obvious intent of ruffing a diamond (or two) shortly. On the ace, drop your *king*. Surely declarer cannot know the true state of affairs, and he will naturally tend to assume that you started with the K 9 doubleton. He may become frightened at this point, and abandon his original plan of ruffing a diamond, and may decide to draw most of dummy's trumps (fearing that you will overtrump dummy); or he may ruff a diamond high in dummy in order to prevent an overruff by you—and in so doing may create a trump trick for you or partner. As in the previous illustration, after declarer successfully finesses his queen, your two remaining high cards have become equals, so it costs nothing to drop the king instead of the jack—and thereby convince declarer that the diamond suit is not going to divide nicely, whereas you know full well that it is; and, if you play the jack on the lead of South's ace, he will know that you still possess the king (the successful finesse of the king having demonstrated that you possess the king).

10.

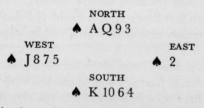

NORTH
♠ A Q 9 3

WEST
♠ J 8 7 5

EAST
♠ 2

SOUTH
♠ K 10 6 4

South leads the four of spades. Sitting West, play the *eight*. Presuming your honesty, when the trick is captured by North's ace, South will "know" that you originally held either the singleton eight or a doubleton J–8. Undoubtedly, he will now lay down

North's queen, to guard against East having started with the J 7 5 2 originally. You have just "stolen" a trick.

If on the first spade lead, you "economically" follow with the five-spot, when declarer captures the trick with the ace, he will have no idea as to which of the defenders might have four spades—and he *might* then lead a small spade from the North hand. When East shows out, it will then be revealed that you started with the J 8 7 5 —and you will be finessed out of your jack. Declarer will then have himself 4 spade tricks.

Admittedly, by putting up the eight-spot on the first spade lead, there is no guarantee that declarer will go wrong. But I'll wager that 49 times out of 50, he *will* go wrong; if, instead, you play the five-spot, declarer will go wrong only about half the time: 25 times out of 50. Aren't these good odds, especiallly when they are "on the house?"

11.

NORTH

♠ A J 9

SOUTH

♠ 4 3 2

Before introducing the defensive deceptive play involved in the above setup, let us take a quick look at it from the declarer's point of view. Suppose you are South, playing the above combination. The percentage play is to lead low from the South hand, and to finesse the nine-spot. This will enable you to win two spade tricks whenever West possesses any combination of the Q 10 or K 10 (Q 10 x, Q 10 x x, K 10 x, K 10 x x, etc.). The play of the nine will not gain a trick whenever West holds the K Q x, the K Q x x x, etc. Mathematically, the odds that West possesses some combination of the K 10 *or* Q 10 are much better than that he possesses some combination of the K Q. According to our experts, the original play of the nine (third hand) will win about twice as often as will the third-hand play of the jack. Since this is the case, if you are sitting West, gazing upon the A J 9 in dummy, you know that when declarer leads a low one from his own hand, it is his intention to put up the nine-spot from dummy:

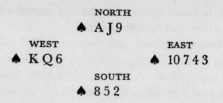

NORTH
♠ A J 9

WEST   EAST
♠ K Q 6   ♠ 10 7 4 3

SOUTH
♠ 8 5 2

Hence, when he leads the deuce, *play low*—the six-spot in the above situation. Your partner's ten will now win the trick.

As of this moment, then, the above second-hand play of a low card should become a standard deceptive play, with the odds in your favor. Much more often than not, declarer will finesse against the ten-spot and dummy's nine will be captured by your partner's ten (if declarer happens to have the ten, then he can always make two tricks in this suit, whether you split your honors or not).

Directly related to the above is the following:

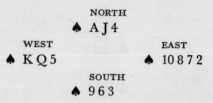

NORTH
♠ A J 4

WEST   EAST
♠ K Q 5   ♠ 10 8 7 2

SOUTH
♠ 9 6 3

Let us say that the contract is *hearts,* and you, West, win a trick early in the play. No lead by you seems attractive, except spades. Lead the *five* of spades. In almost every case declarer will play the four-spot from the North hand, hoping that you led away from some combination of the Q 10 or K 10, in which case East's other honor will capture the trick, but later declarer will be able to finesse against your remaining honor. Again, if declarer happens to have the ten (instead of the nine), he will always make two tricks no matter whether or not you lead the suit. More significant, however, is the fact that if you don't lead this suit, and declarer is left to his own resources, out of desperation he will have no choice but to ultimately finesse the jack, to make two spade tricks.

12. Before presenting the next defensive bit of deception (which is analogous to that just presented), let me again transpose you to declarer's seat to handle a standard combination:

NORTH
♣ Q 10 2

SOUTH
♣ 9 8 4

You lead the nine of clubs, and West plays the five-spot. Would you not play low from dummy, finessing West for the jack? Mathematically, this is the percentage play. If you put up the queen and East happens to have *either* the ace or king, you will never win a club trick. But if you play small, and East does *not* have the jack (a 50–50 proposition), then you will always win a club trick.

And so, we come to this:

NORTH
♣ Q 10 2

WEST   EAST
♣ A K 5   ♣ J 7 6 3

SOUTH
♣ 9 8 4

South leads the nine of clubs. Play the *five-spot,* not the king. South will let the nine ride, and your partner's jack will capture the trick.

Another possibility inherent in this situation is, of course, to take the nine with the king. The next time declarer leads the suit (say the eight-spot), play the five. Declarer will now have to guess as to whether to put up the queen or not. The better play, however, is to play low on the first lead of the suit, in which case the declarer is almost a cinch to misguess the true situation.

13. The contract is *no-trump,* and North has bid spades.

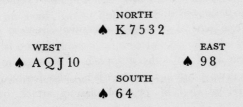

NORTH
♠ K 7 5 3 2

WEST   EAST
♠ A Q J 10   ♠ 9 8

SOUTH
♠ 6 4

You elect to open the queen of spades, and dummy plays low, your queen winning. Follow through with the jack; declarer will almost surely give your partner credit for the ace, and will play low from dummy. When your jack wins, lay down the ten, which will also win a trick for you.

The logic behind this continuing deceptive defense is this: everytime you lead a high spade, declarer is afraid to put up the king for fear that if he does your partner may run the entire suit against him by taking the king with the ace. Hence the refusal to cover with the king, to prevent what may otherwise turn out to be immediate defeat.

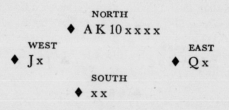

The contract is *diamonds.* Declarer leads low from the South hand. Put up the *jack,* which North's king will win. Declarer may now conclude that you started with the Q J x; and, upon returning to the South hand, he will lead another diamond, upon which you play low (naturally). Declarer *might* now finesse dummy's ten. How else could your side ever make a diamond trick?

Thus we conclude our discussion and presentation of the major defensive deceptive plays which the ingenuity of man has devised. Obviously there are other shenanigans that bridge players have perpetrated on their fellow men. And additional ones will be created with the passage of time.

There is one general strategical deceptive situation that should be presented—for the sake of completeness, if for no better reason. This concerns itself with the approach of attempting to deceive declarer whenever possible, if partner is not also deceived, to thereby cause declarer to alter his original plan of attack, or to simply

confuse him so that his operations will be based on a misconception.
For example:

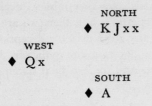

NORTH
♦ K J x x

WEST
♦ Q x

SOUTH
♦ A

Diamonds are trumps. South, the declarer, leads the ace of diamonds, obviously intending to draw trumps. *Drop your queen*—just
to muddle the issue! You know your queen will be captured by the
king on the next round anyway. In dropping the queen, you will
tend to implant in declarer's mind the concept that the queen is a
singleton. Declarer will then give your partner credit for the remaining diamonds. Who knows what declarer might now do in desperation, or in panic, if he figures that the trumps are divided badly.
And all along the situation might have been:

NORTH
♦ K J x x

WEST   EAST
♦ Q x   ♦ 10 9 x

SOUTH
♦ A x x x

With the queen falling on the first round, declarer will now assume that he must lose a diamond trick, since the queen is "obviously" a singleton:

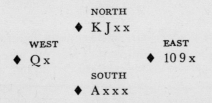

NORTH
♦ K J x x

WEST   EAST
♦ Q   ♦ 10 9 x x

SOUTH
♦ A x x x

Of course, your partner may *also* trust his eyesight and assume
that your queen was a singleton. He will then give declarer credit
for the remaining diamonds (including the one you still possess),

and partner may then be led astray in his subsequent defense. However, in experience, stratagems such as the above are worthwhile risks (on a risk versus gain basis), for they mislead declarer much more often than they mislead partner. But, then, we are discussing a long-run situation—and on any given deal the deception may adversely affect partner, with declarer profiting thereby because of his immunity to the deception. And so, as a final statement on defensive deception: *Handle with Care.*

ADDENDUM TO CHAPTER 16

Here is an article entitled "Rare Deception," by Terence Reese.[1]

There is a group of plays which, so far as I know, has escaped analysis. It centers around the play of the jack from J 9 combinations. I first thought about such play when I was South and a suit was distributed thus:

(a)

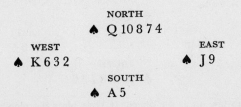

South lays down the ace and East, we will assume, follows with the nine. Now what is South to do on the next round? If he finesses the seven it will not avail him to find that East had the K 9 to begin with, for another trick will still be lost to West's J x x x. Therefore, South will go up with the queen, his only chance for four tricks being to find East with J 9.

Suppose, however, that East drops the jack on the first lead. Now it will look to South as though East might have K J; he will surely finesse the eight and lose two tricks.

Alter the high cards slightly and situations will arise which are similar but not the same:

[1] This article has been taken in its entirety from *The Bridge World,* April, 1957. Permission to reprint has been granted by A. Moyse, Jr., publisher of *The Bridge World* and by Terence Reese, author of *Master Play, Reese on Play,* and many other works which have become classics in the field of contract bridge play.

(b)

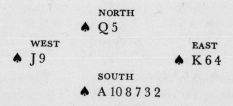

NORTH
♠ A 10 8 6 3

WEST   EAST
♠ Q 5 4 2   ♠ J 9

SOUTH
♠ K 7

If the king drops the nine on the first round, South will go up with the ace on the second round, playing East for Q 9 or J 9. But if East drops the jack on the first round, South will finesse on the second round; he will work out that if East has Q J alone, one trick must be lost in any event to West's 9 x x x; if East's jack is single, however, the hand will be under better control if the finesse is taken.

In the next example, we put the long suit in declarer's hand:

(c)

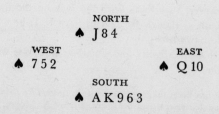

NORTH
♠ Q 5

WEST   EAST
♠ J 9   ♠ K 6 4

SOUTH
♠ A 10 8 7 3 2

South leads low up to the queen. If West plays the nine and the queen is headed by the king, South may play for the drop of the jack on the next round. But if West plays the jack on the first round, South will surely finesse the eight on the way back.

The play of the queen from Q 10 alone, when the cards are as follows, appears in every chapter on deceptive play:

(d)

NORTH
♠ J 8 4

WEST   EAST
♠ 7 5 2   ♠ Q 10

SOUTH
♠ A K 9 6 3

The effectiveness of the jack from J 9 in similar situations has been overlooked. For example:

(e)

NORTH
♠ 10 8 4

WEST
♠ K 7 5

EAST
♠ J 9

SOUTH
♠ A Q 6 3 2

If East plays the jack on the first round, South will finesse the eight on the way back and a trick will be stolen by the defense. [On the first lead, the four-spot is led from the North hand, South finessing his queen. FLK] This play is equally effective when South holds K Q x x x.

Transfer one of the high honors to dummy and the play still works:

(f)

NORTH
♠ K 8 7

WEST
♠ A 6 3

EAST
♠ J 9

SOUTH
♠ Q 10 5 4 2

When a small card is led from the table [the North hand. FLK] the play of the jack by East can hardly lose; for if West holds the ten, the jack and nine are equals, and if South holds the ten he will be led astray. It is easy to see what will happen in the present diagram: after the jack has fetched the queen and ace, South will finesse the eight on the next round, playing West for A 9 x x.

Perhaps the most interesting feature of this group of plays is its effectiveness when the J 9 are accompanied by a higher honor:

(g)

NORTH
♠ Q 8 4

WEST
♠ 7 5 3

EAST
♠ K J 9

SOUTH
♠ A 10 6 2

Declarer plays the four from table; and if East plays the nine, the ten will surely be finessed. But try the jack from East; now South will put on the ace and finesse the eight on the way back, playing West for 9 7 5 3.

The combination A J 9 offers still more opportunities:

(h)

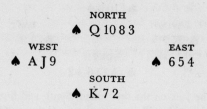

NORTH
♠ Q 10 8 3

WEST
♠ A J 9

EAST
♠ 6 5 4

SOUTH
♠ K 7 2

A familiar situation in which normal play will result in declarer's winning three tricks. But try the play of the jack by West, second-hand. The queen wins in dummy, and on the way back South will surely finesse the seven, playing West for A J alone.

Here is another funny one:

(i)

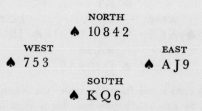

NORTH
♠ 10 8 4 2

WEST
♠ 7 5 3

EAST
♠ A J 9

SOUTH
♠ K Q 6

Once again, with normal play, and assuming sufficient entries, declarer will win three tricks. Now try the play of the jack by East on the first round. South will win with the queen and, as likely as not, will play the king from hand, intending, if this loses to the ace, to finesse the eight later. It is true that, with sufficient entries, South can escape this pitfall by leading from dummy on the second round and not "unblocking"; but he may well omit to do that, having convinced himself that the nine is with West.

Make it a long suit over the A J 9 and once more the jack may gain.

(j)

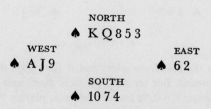

NORTH
♠ K Q 8 5 3

WEST
♠ A J 9

EAST
♠ 6 2

SOUTH
♠ 10 7 4

South leads the four, and West's jack is headed by the queen. Declarer may finesse the seven on the way back.

The more you look at these A J 9 situations, the more it will strike you that the play of the jack can hardly lose and may gain in surprising ways. The field is full of interest, and readers who experiment around it will come across many other opportunities for a defensive coup.

10.50
(½)